THEY CALL ME GABRIEL

Anar Nanji

THEY CALL ME GABRIEL

NOTE FROM THE AUTHOR

The word "spirituality" is defined in various ways. Some emphasise its religious nature, while others focus on aspects of the inner self. At its essence is the belief that there is something more to our existence than what we physically observe.

This story is a fictional biography of Angel Gabriel, through which various spiritual concepts are explained. The book should not be attributed to any one belief system. What is important is to extract the lessons that may be drawn from it, and my wish is that you find the book helpful, and that it eases your way through life. At the very least, I hope it opens up the possibility that we are more than what we experience in this world.

ACKNOWLEDGEMENT

To all those who have helped me along the way – thank you.
I am grateful that our paths have crossed.

1 LIGHT

In the beginning there was light, and in the end, there was darkness. Its shadow penetrated everywhere — in man's hearts, in his thoughts, and in his actions. Darkness begat darkness, and as the shadow spread, it cast a grey haze throughout. Very little thought was given to the light. Man was about the body — the vessel that encapsulated the light — about how to display it, clothe it, satisfy its urges, and re-create it in man's image. Man was about the life of privilege he could live, accumulating wealth, and finding ways to spend that wealth, all in the misguided attempt to distinguish himself from his brother, to elevate himself high above his fellow man. Materialism was the new god. The sun shone brightly and illuminated the world, but there was darkness everywhere: prejudice, greed, corruption, poverty, slavery, violence.

How many times would God send me to bring a message to man to move towards light? And why, during every intercession, did they get it so wrong? Could humanity not understand that there were fundamental principles and values by which they were to live on Earth? That there were eternal laws established by God? Why could humanity not comprehend that man's relationship to his fellow man was predicated on light and love, and that the quest for peace and enlightenment was applicable to all and not just a few? Why did humankind not understand that there were no chosen people, nor a specific, chosen path? Every being was part of this energy and force that many called God, and every being not only had the right to live in light, but was obliged to strive to achieve this enlightenment.

I am known by humanity as Angel Gabriel (in what is today the Jewish and Christian traditions) and Angel Jibrael (in what is today the Muslim tradition), although throughout my existence and depending on how and where I interceded, I have been accorded various names. Some have even addressed me as Archangel, although I do not know what the difference between an angel and an Archangel is, and for that matter, the difference between human and angel. We are the same, for we have come into being from the same light. You are my brother, my sister, my mother, my father, my child, my friend. The only difference between us is that you have chosen to place your light in a vessel; in other words, you have chosen to be born a human being. Throughout history, I also have chosen to cover my light and be born a human being, but these occasions have been rare, as I much prefer to remain unhindered, in my purest state of existence.

This is my life story, my autobiography, from my "birth" millions of years ago (although I was not born, but rather "came into being"), to my "death" (although I will never die, but merge into the Universal Force many call God). Let me explain this in more detail. I came into being during the event a number label as the Big Bang, when God ignited His energy and you and I burst forth. I began as light, twinkling and sparkling in the universe. You also began as light, twinkling and sparkling throughout the universe. We mingled as light, basking in the glory of our creator, who has come to be known by numerous names: God, Allah, Yahweh, Brahma, Bhagvan, the Father, the Mother, the Elohim, the Almighty, the Creator, Mother Nature, the Alpha, the Omega, the Great Spirit, Brahman, the Beginning, the End, the Everything, the Nothing, the Universe, the Force, the Energy, and many other similar designations. I consider all these names to be synonymous, and refer to them interchangeably, one for the other, for they are the same, the One.

In the beginning there was light, and in the beginning you were light – a beautiful light that shone brightly with love, compassion, warmth, and wonder. There were billions of us, and we all existed in perfect harmony in a place referred to as the heavens, loving and caring for one another through our individual existence, content in the knowledge that we originated from a single source and were one and the same.

Then a time arose when God decided to create the Earth and all the beauty within it. He formed the vast waters, both sweet and salty; composed the soils and enriched them to grow grasses, trees, plants, and flowers; and He generated various creatures, from the microscopic to the colossal. And then God created the most complex organism of all – out of clay and water,

He shaped the body of man and woman — a vessel to contain your light. God gave you the choice to fill this container with your light in order to experience His creation. And you did. Through the reproductive process, you produced more vessels, which in turn provided the opportunity for more of you to encapsulate your light, and thus, you began to populate the Earth.

As the population increased in various regions, you began to look upon one another as the "other", for the containers looked different. They were coated with a range of hues and colours, moulded into two separate genders, of varying heights, weights, and configurations; some were symmetrical, and others asymmetrical, but all embodied the same light that twinkled and sparkled throughout the universe. But you did not see, because as time went on, you forgot who you were. You did not recognise your own light in yourselves and in each other. So the darkness began. And the more you could not and would not see, the darker it became. And this is where the story begins....

As I flitted throughout the heavens, twinkling and sparkling, and basking with you in the glory of our light, I realised that those of you who chose to be born on Earth were forgetting who you were. You imagined that the whole of your being was the dust and water of your shell. You began to believe that you were the container, and not the light within. In fact, some of you actually believed that there was no such thing as the Light.

You see, many millions of years ago (in the way time is measured on Earth), as you populated the planet, you began to be blinded by the beauty around you. As the Universe created more and more life in the world to reflect its splendour, you became hypnotised by this beauty. At first this attraction was the same that we experienced as sparkling lights mingling in the heavens — you recognised the light in all the life around you: in the air, water, earth and fire; in the plants, trees and flowers; in the stones, rocks and mountains; in the insects, fish and animals; and in each other. Some of you began to be mesmerised by the magnificence, and you entered a hypnotic state. You believed that this physical loveliness was your home, and where you belonged. But it was only a reflection of your home — it was an illusion. Nonetheless, you deemed this illusion to be reality, and furthermore, you thought that it could be possessed...and that is when the trouble began.

So I sat watching as you were blinded by outer beauty, disappointed in the choices you were making, but steadfast in the belief that this was just a temporary indulgence. I had no doubt that you would return to lightness. And many of you did. But some of you did not.

As time evolved on Earth, you populated it with more beings, with many more of you choosing to indulge in darkness. I began to worry, and could not comprehend why you would choose such immediate gratification and be less than you were. Then came a moment when you began to inflict pain and suffering on your fellow man, and I stood up to take a closer look. I could not believe what I observed, and my thoughts ran rampant: What was happening to the twinkling and sparkling lights with whom I rejoiced throughout the universe? Why were you hurting each other? Why were you damaging one another's physical bodies? Why were you trying to take a life and extinguish the light within? Did you not realise that the light was eternal and inextinguishable? Could you not see your own light in each other?

I remained standing and watched as you began to destroy one another with hatred, jealousy, and violence. I watched for a few thousand years, and then I could no longer endure it. I flitted around from human to human, trying to spark your memory, willing you to remember that you were beings of light, and to not be intoxicated by the physical materiality surrounding you. I beseeched you to refrain from being weighed down by that which you could only see with your physical eye. Why were you choosing to be less than you were? Why could you not remember that you were spirit, just like me, beings of light created by the Almighty? I cried out in frustration.

Suddenly, a surge of warmth enveloped me, and I realised that God had seen my distress. With a wholesome, reassuring voice, God called out to me, "My child, My shimmering light of love. Come closer to Me." I sank deeper within the glowing, tender warmth. God continued, "You are full of power and strength, yet you seem disturbed. Why are you in such a state?"

"I am worried for my fellow beings, for they are sinking into darkness," I replied, "and they are a part of You and me." A wave of love and affection further engulfed me.

God said, "My child, you have remained as pure and light as

9

the moment you first burst forth. Do not be disappointed. Humanity will remember who they really are and will return to lightness. For those who need a nudge, I will send them signs and reminders to help guide them."

While I wholeheartedly accepted God's response, there was still something bothering me deep within. God seemed to wait patiently while I built up the courage to ask. "But why did You create the Earth to begin with and make it possible for us to be tempted by the darkness lurking within? I cannot help thinking that if Earth had not been created in the first place, we would not have this problem."

God smiled benevolently. "There is darkness and lightness within all forms of life including within My children, and all is a part of Me. I created the Earth as a gift to My children, and by bestowing free will, have given them free reign to appreciate that which comes from within Me. It is for each of My children who choose to enter physical life on Earth to make further choices on how each wishes to behave. Will each choose lightness over darkness in every instance?"

I reflected upon this for a while. It was difficult for me to comprehend that darkness existed within all, including within me. Or more accurately, it was difficult to accept that darkness also existed within me. I had only ever experienced light; it had never even occurred to me to admit I had baser instincts, never mind to give in to them. And then to couple these with a physical life on Earth was unimaginable to me; it was irrational to choose momentary pleasure over unending joy, and especially when that pleasure was at the cost of others. Why would any being choose a short, fleeting life over eternal existence and peace? Yet, this was the predicament of my fellow beings on Earth. I could not just stand here in heaven and watch humanity destroy itself, for not only were they destroying each other, they were also damaging the light within: their true selves. I had to do something to help.

"How do I help my fellow beings? It distresses me to see them inflicting such pain on one another, for each is only hurting himself."

God said, "Will you be part of the signs, reminders, and guidance that I send to your siblings to steer them away from their darkness?"

"Yes!" I replied enthusiastically, "Yes, I will be part of Your work to help my siblings!" I sparkled with joy, ready for the effort that lay ahead.

Little did I know that this promise would test me to the core of my being. The challenges that I would have to face, the choices that I would have to make, and the depths of depravity to which humanity would sink, would bring me to my knees in utter desperation before God.

This will become clearer as my story unfolds, however, before we proceed, I wish to describe how my interaction with God takes place.

You see that I have couched my communication with God as a conversation between two separate beings, both anthropomorphised, one superior to the other, so that you may comprehend the interaction. However, this is not how it actually happened. The interface with God was non-verbal and without a separation into distinct beings. I was, and still am, part of God, a fraction of the whole, and our communication was simply a "knowing"; it was understood. For example, many of you know what a loved one is thinking or feeling, without needing to communicate verbally or sign with any body language – you just know. That is how my communication with God took place, and still does today. Some of you may recognise this as the stillness within; the inner voice; your instinct.

From this point forward, I relate my story in the third person in order to distance myself from the subject, for there are parts of this narrative that are too emotional for me to bear. They dig up memories of great happiness and profound sadness, and in order to maintain my equilibrium and be firmly centred in God, I must detach myself from the persona of Angel Gabriel.

2 GABRIEL

Gabriel was overwhelmed by his commitment to God. He felt elated at being given this opportunity, but there was much work to do. He turned to God for guidance, and in particular, on how to deliver the signs and messages to humanity.

"My child," said God, "you must continue to intervene with each individual, to bring each human being out of his and her slumber. Show them who they are and ignite their light within. Give them the message that each is a part of the Whole; each is a part of Me. Scale up your intervention to be able to reach vast swathes of humanity. Request help from others to manifest the signs. Unfold the message by rolling it out step-by-step, so that humanity is able to walk towards the truth and find its way home."

So Gabriel began his search for beings who would help bring the message of God to humankind.

He scoured the heavens, traversing through the space/time continuum. He came across billions of sparkling lights who existed throughout the universe, and asked as many as he could if they would help him with his task. As he explained his story of how all this came about, quite a few thought he was making too big a deal of the dalliances of human beings on Earth.

"Really, very few of us take on human form. Earth is a minute speck in the universe and it is hardly populated. Why overreact like this?" asked one.

"All will sort itself out," said another, reassuringly. However, others were sympathetic to Gabriel's concerns.

"If God requested you to address the problems developing on Earth, then we would love to help," said one. Regardless of viewpoints, every single encounter elicited the inevitable question: what was it like to meet God?

"It is powerful and overwhelming, yet it feels so natural," said Gabriel, "It is like coming home. You simultaneously feel energised and calm."

"But what is it about you? Why would God speak to you?" Gabriel was asked during one of his conversations.

"I do not know." Gabriel had wondered this himself, given that of the billions of sparkling lights he came across, not one had indicated that they, too, had spoken with God. "In any case, I need to get on with the job. There is so much work to do."

He gathered all those who chose to help and counted about a million sparkling lights willing to make this commitment, a pledge really, to guide humankind.

Each of these sparkling lights followed Gabriel's example and began to intervene with humanity on a one-to-one basis, manifesting signs to ignite the light within each person. As time went on, a few succeeded, and human beings were jolted awake from their hypnotic state. They began to realise that there was more to their existence than just the physical world, and indeed, their origins were esoteric. Many were sufficiently awakened to perceive the sparkling lights who had helped them.

"You are beautiful and pure!" exclaimed these human beings, "How we long to revel with you in light and grace!" Humanity began to refer to the sparkling lights as "angels" – messengers from the celestial sphere. But human beings did not realise that they, too, were sparkling lights and originated from "above".

The "angels" continued to intercede with humanity as Gabriel monitored their progress: the heavens were abuzz with all the activity. There were some quick successes with many reaching a number of human beings to awaken their consciousness, however most of the angels failed to connect. The vast majority of humanity still existed in the illusion that everything around them on Earth was real and absolute. They were sinking further into darkness.

"What shall we do?" the angels queried, "We have only managed to awaken a few. Even then, those who recognise us believe us to be different from them. They believe that we are composed of light, and that they are not. They actually believe that they are their body, the outer shell that contains the light! They do not see that we are the same, and that they just chose to inhabit a body for a short period of time. And on top of all this, they are calling us "angels"! Do they not see that we are all the same beings?"

Despite the lack of significant progress, Gabriel was pleased that they had achieved some success, for it meant they were on the right track. He addressed the gathering. "Do not be concerned about being called angels. If we are being labelled as such, then they, too, are angels, for we all burst forth from the same light and are therefore siblings. The important thing is that we have begun to rouse humanity. With every triumph, we can begin to develop each human being so that he and she recognises the light within to its fullest form. Humankind will then understand that they are no different from us, and are indeed, our siblings-in-light."

However, the angels needed to refine their approach. It was extremely difficult to dart haphazardly from one human to the other, trying to appeal to each individual's consciousness. They needed to recruit even more angels, to team up and concentrate their efforts on helping groups of humans.

Gabriel continued, "Of the billions of sparkling lights, or "angels" as we are now called, go and seek more of those who are amenable to help, and ask them to join us in awakening our brothers and sisters." The angels responded and flew hither and thither throughout the heavens, returning to Gabriel with many more who were excited to contribute to this great effort.

"How wonderful! This is more than I expected!" exclaimed Gabriel, "This puts us in a position to assign an angel to each human being, to provide signs and reminders to ignite the light within. The angels can watch over and guide each man and woman to recognise who and what they really are. We can now impact the whole of humanity!" So the angels began their work in earnest to help their fellow beings remember their origins.

As time on Earth moved on, and the Creative Force continued to evolve all life forms, both plant and animal alike, the angels persisted in their efforts to awaken their charges. Gabriel watched and reacted where necessary. He fluttered around monitoring the teams as they carried out their duties; he advised angels who found it difficult to get through to their charges; and he intervened directly in the most challenging and gruelling cases, especially where violence was concerned. He sparkled with joy when a human being awoke, and regardless of their degree of awakening, celebrated with his fellow angels. But he also observed that a great many beings remained unenlightened. Something more had to be done. He gathered the millions of angels who were helping, and shared his plans with them.

"We are making progress, but much of humanity remains in darkness," said Gabriel, "We must broaden our strategy. We need to find other ways of jolting humanity awake. The deeper they fall into obscurity, the more difficult it is to reach them. We must understand how and why humanity is mesmerised by the physicality of Earth." Murmurings of agreement reverberated throughout the crowd. "I have therefore decided to visit Earth in physical form. I will wait for an appropriate human body to be created, and will enter Earth as a newborn human being." The angels gasped.

"Are you sure you want to do that?" asked one angel, "Is it not too drastic a step?"

"It will enable me to understand why our brothers and sisters get so attracted to the physical, three-dimensional beauty around them," said Gabriel, "They become so riveted. I really need to understand how and why they forget their true selves."

"It would certainly help us with our work," responded another angel.

Gabriel continued, "I must find a suitable set of parents who will be able to nurture my physical being. They need to teach me about life from a corporeal perspective. Once I am independent, my plan is to try to influence and teach my fellow beings about who they really are. Perhaps by this direct physical approach, we will achieve more. In any case, by me entering Earth in this way, we may learn new ways of successfully awakening humanity."

One angel spoke up, "We will support you and continue our work from here. But while you are limited by your existence in the three-dimensional world, it would be a good idea to leave someone in-charge here."

"Yes, that would be prudent. Who would like to fulfil this function?" asked Gabriel. The angels stirred uncomfortably and looked at one another. Gabriel was surprised that no one jumped at this opportunity. Suddenly, the crowd began to part.

"I will make this commitment," came a strong, booming voice from within. All turned towards the sound and saw a towering, glorious figure rising from their midst. His light glowed self-assuredly, throwing out rays of great luminosity. His energy drew in all those around him.

"I am called Michael," he asserted with quiet authority. Gabriel gazed at him admiringly.

"Thank you, Michael," said Gabriel, "Lead the angels, and monitor Earth and all life forms within. If you require it, call upon me, for I will not break my bond with the light – I will not forget who I am."

"Very well," responded Michael with a bow of his head. The angels noticed the respect that Michael accorded Gabriel and wondered whether Michael knew something they did not. Had they taken Gabriel's presence for granted?

"And Michael," said Gabriel, "When I need help while in human form, I will call upon you to assist me."

"I will be there for you," Michael replied reverently.

Gabriel left the group and scanned the world searching for parents who would enable him to live a life full of worldly experience. He needed guardians who would be able to teach him about the world and all it had to offer, so that he could obtain a good grounding in what it was that made human beings forget who they actually were. He identified a couple who wanted to have a baby as a testament of their love for one another. Gabriel chose these parents, and asked God to ensure that he was born male: it would give him greater exposure to the world and its intoxicating nature given the dominant role of the male in society at this time.

Once the couple conceived, Gabriel withdrew into himself and remained secluded in preparation for the journey. He revelled in the tranquillity of silence and was loath to leave such a peaceful state. However, when the time finally came, he reluctantly slipped into the body of the infant male.

Gabriel immediately felt oppressed. The weight of the human body suffocated him. He tried to reposition himself but realised he now required his appendages for movement: he did not know how to control them. He was so used to sparkling and twinkling all over the universe, flitting from one place to another.

"I am literally trapped inside this physical body," thought Gabriel. He tried to compose himself.

"It will be okay," thought Gabriel, repeating this over and over to himself.

When the birthing process began, he felt the pressure bearing down on him, carrying him through the passage.

"This is excruciating!" thought Gabriel, as he was squeezed from all sides. Finally, he pushed through only to be struck by a piercing brightness and bitterly cold air. Gabriel was shocked into silence: he was freed from his constraining environment, but felt completely helpless and imprisoned in a human body. He began to panic; he had to leave.

"God!" Gabriel cried out, "I cannot stand this heavy, stifling body! I am returning home!" His eyes rolled back in his head, and his breath slowed to a shallow wheeze.

God spoke to Gabriel in a serene and soothing voice, "My pure and beautiful child of light, I will welcome you home with open arms. Calm yourself and look within, and then let me know your decision." Gabriel turned his gaze inward and saw God smiling in all His glory, and also saw Michael and other angels radiating light, projecting all their love and warmth towards him.

"For less than a second, I forgot where to find You," said Gabriel, as he sighed with relief. "I forgot that You are with me, and within me, and we are never apart. God, I will continue with my task, and I accept that my light will be shrouded by this shell of clay and water. I accept this gift of a strong and healthy body, and will look after it and treat it with respect." And with the decision made, Gabriel howled at the top of his lungs and opened his eyes to see several human beings leaning over him with tears streaming down their faces, relieved that the newborn boy was alive.

My parents named me Gabriel, and in deference to the very first time I was born on Earth, I have kept this name to this day, regardless of whether in subsequent births on Earth (of which you will learn) I have been called other names, or whether I manifested as a boy or girl. In fact, I have been born female more often than male. You may not know this (or more accurately, you may not remember this), but angels have no gender. They are androgynous – they have both masculine and feminine characteristics. This means that your true self, the whole of your being, is both masculine and feminine. The male/female divide is only a physical, three-dimensional, Earth concept. I have, however, chosen to refer to myself as "he" throughout this story, as it makes for easier reading and acceptability for the majority of humankind as it exists today, a predominantly patriarchal society. But rest assured that the "he" also means the "she", for I am both masculine and feminine, and neither facet is superior to the other; they are equal.

Similarly, I have chosen to refer to God as "He", but could easily call God "She" or "It", for God encapsulates both the masculine and feminine, as well as neutral qualities.

Gabriel lived a relatively long and fulfilling life. He remained on Earth as a physical being for just enough time to enable him to experience all of life's attractions and teach his fellow man, at least those who would listen, about their true nature. When he was considered to be old by society's standards, he shed his body and passed into his original essence, and became his shimmering and glowing self again. The angels received him with love and warmth, and welcomed him with song.

"How relieved I am to be back home!" exclaimed Gabriel, "I am overjoyed to rid myself of the illusions of Earth and come back to reality!"

"What did you learn?" asked a few angels.

"I learnt how difficult it is to remain strong in the belief that I am light and power itself," said Gabriel, "As I grew older, I became more and more earth-bound, struggling with daily life, and grappling with elders who did not believe that I was an angel, let alone that they, too, were great beings of light. They did not believe that I could and was conversing with angels. Michael, whenever we had our discussions, my parents would ask me with whom I was speaking. When I told them it was Michael, my friend and brother, at first they thought this was sweet. As I grew into my adolescent years, they became concerned about my sanity! Some relatives believed that a malevolent force was influencing me. It worried my parents so much, that I stopped conversing with you and only connected with you in quieter moments."

Gabriel turned to address everyone, "It is very difficult for human beings to believe that something exists when they cannot physically observe it. And for those who do believe, most have a skewed view of their origins, and it is challenging to convince them otherwise. So we must speak to our fellow angels who wish to be born on Earth and prepare them for their sojourn in the world – they must be forewarned to refrain from becoming earth-bound when they enter their physical body. We must establish a system to prime angels about their Earth experience. They must remember that they are spiritual beings and not physical beings, and that when they are born, they must maintain their link with the light." Everyone nodded in agreement.

Gabriel continued, "I also observed that many more humans were being born, and in fact, the birth rate was increasing. This means that more of us are choosing to experience Earth and the physical life within it. However, once in human form, very rarely can one of us angels get through to our siblings from this realm. I believe we will make better progress if some of us also go into human form to directly teach humankind and awaken them to their true selves." Whisperings and murmurings rose from the crowd as they shifted uncomfortably.

"Now, I must rest for a while and centre myself in God," said Gabriel, as he turned away. "Michael, please would you continue filling in for me a while longer?" Michael bowed his head in acceptance, but was disappointed not to be able to have an in-depth, more meaningful discussion with Gabriel, as he knew that there was much more to Gabriel's experience than was discussed with the wider group. Michael also needed more help in managing and protecting all life forms, given that during the years of Gabriel's life on Earth, many more angels had chosen to visit Earth to experience physical life at the same time. They hoped that Gabriel's presence would keep them steadfast in the knowledge that they were beings of light.

Gabriel sensed Michael's unease. "Is there something troubling you, Michael?"

Michael did not want to probe Gabriel and simply responded, "I need more help to protect the life forms on Earth."

"I understand," said Gabriel, "Let us ask another of our siblings to help you." Gabriel faced the crowd. "Would anyone like to help Michael with this responsibility?" There was an awkward silence.

After a few moments, a gentle and soothing voice said, "I am known as Raphael." When he came forth, Gabriel saw a pristine light shimmering so brightly that it brought tears of joy to observe such pure love.

Gabriel said, "Hello, Raphael. Will you help Michael with his task?"

"Yes, I will. I pledge my commitment," said Raphael, bowing his head reverently. Again, the angels noticed the respect accorded to Gabriel, and they whispered amongst themselves.

"Thank you, Raphael," said Gabriel, "you will be of great help to us."

"Please let us know if we can support you further," said Michael, as he reached out to Gabriel.

"Thank you, Michael," said Gabriel, "Keep watch over everything until my return."

With matters now in hand, Gabriel ascended the dimensions and withdrew into God to rest, but more importantly, to discuss with God that which he had not shared with his fellow angels: not only did human beings not remember who they actually were, but the hearts of men and women were darkening. And this darkening meant that there was an absence of love, the true essence of God.

3 FREE WILL

Gabriel submerged into God and wept for days. He was greatly affected by his experience as a human being. It was one thing when angels forgot who they were when they took human form, but it was quite another to embrace darkness. How could they steal from one another? How could they hurt and maim each other? How could they kill their fellow beings?

Gabriel questioned God, "Did You know that they were letting each other starve? Did You know that they were enslaving each other into forced servitude? Did You know that the coupling of men and women was now not just for procreation, but was, for the most part, to satisfy the body's urges? Did You know that the bodies of vulnerable men, women and children were utilised to satisfy the physical, sexual urges of the more dominant? Can You imagine! Using the bodies of children, the time during which humans are most connected to the light, and are in their purest, most innocent form! Did You know that wealth, power, and possession were replacing You as the new god?"

Gabriel was grief-stricken and remonstrated God. "How could You let all this happen? Why have You not intervened to stop my brothers and sisters from darkening themselves so? How could You not protect the weak and vulnerable, and let injustice prevail? Why have You let Earth grow so dark? You created us, the universe, and everything in it. Why have You forsaken us?"

Gabriel continued his lamentation and implored God for answers. A loving energy gradually enveloped him and Gabriel sheltered within God for quite some time, for his light had become dull with sadness.

When he felt strong enough, and his being shone brightly again, Gabriel raised his head and invoked, "In the name of God, the most Beneficent, the most Merciful".

"Do you feel better?" asked God.

"Yes, my Lord," answered Gabriel, lowering his gaze.

"Good, because now you are ready to receive My response," said God, "If I had answered your questions as you were asking them, you would not have heard Me, nor would you have understood My words. What you wanted was an immediate response from Me – and accountability." Gabriel realised his mistake and was embarrassed by his behaviour. How could he have let his emotions get the better of him? "But what you needed was silence from Me, and a place to lay down your head," continued God.

"My Lord, please forgive me," wept Gabriel, as he knelt down.

God drew him closer and smiled compassionately. "Of course, Gabriel, of course! My child, I provide you with what you need, not what you want. I respond to your needs, not your desires. And sometimes what you require is silence from Me in order for you to learn that which you do not know, and to experience that which is incomprehensible to you. It is the only way that you will understand, evolve, and grow closer to Me."

"Yes, my Lord," said Gabriel.

"Gabriel, I am always with you and all My other children. And when you choose to inhabit Earth as a human being, I am still with each and every one of you. To all My children, those who choose to enter Earth and those who remain in their angelic form, convey these words: Whether you view Me as a force of energy permeating time and space, or whether you personify Me into form and figure, know that I am Ever-Present. I have never forsaken you, nor will I ever do so. I am with you through your joys and happiness, as well as through your trials and tribulations. I am with you when you make good choices and when you take bad decisions. I carry you forward through your struggles and difficulties. I shelter you, and blanket you with My love and grace. I am Brahma, the most powerful, who can right your wrongs, and change your destiny with a flick of my fingers, or a look from my eyes, or by a mere thought. But I will not do that, for it would take away that most powerful quality I bestowed upon you when you first burst forth: Free Will."

"I have seen all the death and destruction you are carrying out, destroying both yourselves and the Earth. I know your thoughts, and your intentions, for I am the Elohim, the All-Knowing. I see what you are doing to each other, and to the other life forms I created. I feel the pain and suffering you inflict on yourselves and on others, for I am Allah, the Compassionate, and it hurts Me. Do you not realise that what you do unto the least of you, you do unto Me, for I am the Father and the Mother?"

A wave of realisation overcame Gabriel. God was so intrinsic to our being, that whatever we experienced in our individual existence, so did He. To whatever we subjected ourselves or others, we also subjected Him.

"When you hurt each other, whether physically, mentally or emotionally, you are only hurting yourselves, as well as Me, for not only are we all connected through the same essence, but you are a part of Me. You all burst forth from Me and will return to Me, for I am the Alpha, the Omega, the Beginning and the End." Gabriel listened intently to God's words.

"It is not in your nature to possess that which has been created by and through My Spirit, for it belongs to no one. The Earth and its land is not yours to own, or to possess; you are only the custodians and must protect and preserve. The natural resources made available to sustain all life forms do not belong to you, nor to any one life form, but are to be shared and abundantly imbued with your energy, the life force within you, in order to replenish that which you take. You may care for another organism, but you may not possess it, be it mineral, plant, animal, or human.

24

Everything just is, and all life forms must just be."

"That which you create through your minds and your bodies are not your creations; it is My Creative Force working through you, which is a part of all of us. It is part of Me, you, him and her. The creations are ours. No <u>one</u> can possess or own."

"Gabriel," continued God, "Now that you have regained your strength, we have much work to do. Go and convey these words, My message, to the angels in the heavens and to humanity on Earth. Tell My angels that we must work hard to awaken the souls of men and women, and jolt humankind from its state of delusion. We must bring them back to reality. Choose from amongst you the purest angels who agree to be born on Earth, and I will send missives through them to guide humankind to the Truth. Gabriel, you must prepare these angels for their mission before they enter Earth, and guide them throughout their Earthly lives. They must learn from your experience, and where they make mistakes, you must try to rectify these. Do you agree to take on this duty, Gabriel?"

"Yes, My Lord," pledged Gabriel, "I will undertake this responsibility. I just ask that Michael and Raphael be permitted to help me."

"Yes, My child," said God, "as long as they freely agree. Now be on your way, for My children on Earth are suffering. And remember, My child, that I am always with you; I never leave you. My blessings are continuously on you, especially for strength and courage to help My children, and guide them home to Me."

Gabriel bowed his head and said, "Thy Will be done on Earth as it is in Heaven." And with those words, Gabriel burst forth from within, and began his descent through the heavens. He heard whispers, light sighs of air all around, as he glided down.

"There he is, that is Gabriel," said one angel, pointing.

"He has returned from above!" said another.

"He is not just an angel, you know. He is an Archangel," said a third.

"Oh, I did not know! And here I was going to treat him just like us, a normal angel!" came a reply.

"What is an Archangel?" thought Gabriel, "First we are being distinguished as angels, different from humankind, which is just not true. And now the angels are being further divided into Archangels and angels. What is happening to us?"

Gabriel sought out Michael and Raphael. He saw them busy at work, helping both angels and humans alike. Before he could approach them, they sensed his presence and turned towards him.

"Welcome back, Archangel Gabriel," said Michael.

"Thank you, Michael," said Gabriel, "but please call me Gabriel. I do not know where this title of Archangel comes from."

Raphael inquired, "Were you able to rest and recover from your visit to Earth?"

"Yes, very much so," said Gabriel, "However, there is a lot of work ahead and I want to speak to both of you privately." A crowd had begun to congregate around them – Gabriel steered them to a quiet corner, and they spoke at length.

He conveyed God's message and also explained that he was undertaking responsibility to guide angels who agreed to be born on Earth and receive messages to transmit to humanity. Gabriel wanted their help but God emphasised that the decision to undertake this extra duty had to be theirs.

"But, of course!" said Michael, "I will definitely help for as long as you will have me. I give you my commitment."

"It is an honour to be part of this work," said Raphael, "You have my unreserved commitment."

"Excellent!" said Gabriel. He was delighted to have such reliable partners to share the workload. Over time, it would prove to be the best tripartite team ever created, based on love, integrity, and generosity of spirit; and each would come to rely heavily on the other two, for unbeknownst to them, times of great hardship lay ahead.

"Now, let us gather everyone so that I can convey God's message to them," said Gabriel.

He called out to the angels, who came at once and settled themselves. As Gabriel addressed them, he seemed to have a renewed enthusiasm, and everyone delighted in how passionately he spoke. And then came the words that set in motion a series of events that Gabriel would come to regret: "Who would like to be born on Earth through whom God will send missives to guide humankind to the Truth?" Over one hundred thousand angels volunteered for the assignment.

"Are you the purest and lightest, and will you be able to remain strong and steadfast in your mission?" asked Gabriel, "Will you be able to prevent your egos from manifesting and taking over your true selves?"

They all replied, "Yes, we are and we will!"

"Will you be able to overcome all the adversity that will come your way, and still remain faithful and loyal to God?" asked Gabriel.

"Yes, we will!" the angels replied in chorus. And with that promise, Gabriel took them at their word, and began his work in earnest to prepare them for their purpose.

However, not all the angels who had volunteered were the purest. Many had already visited Earth in human form and had experienced the intoxication of the physical world. They were tainted by darkness, and were being pulled deeper into its shadow: their egos had begun to form.

When I reflect upon this scenario today, I cannot believe how trusting I was. I spent many thousands of years regretting that I did not see the troublemakers; that I did not notice the arrogance and pride that had begun to creep into the persona of many angels. I just took everyone at their word, believing that beings of light would never intentionally and willingly choose to move away from their essence. It was beyond my comprehension, and still is today, that any being, whether in angel or human form, would turn their back on God, on Pure Love, for the sake of immediate gratification, knowing full well that these experiences on Earth were temporary. I have, however, finally come to terms with my naivety and accepted that beings, whether in spirit or human form, are at different stages of maturity and development. And that some are not really whom they appear to be.

4 DIMENSIONS

The over one hundred thousand angels who agreed to take on this work for God convened at the appointed place and time. With Michael and Raphael at his side, Gabriel began to teach.

"Dear angels, we are all beings of light, who burst forth from God, the origin of everything. In a sense, He "gave birth" to us, so we could be considered His children. We emanate from Him and are made of the same matter as He: powerful energy and light."

"God created the universe and all that lies within it. He formed the galaxies, the stars, and the planetary systems, including Earth. Within this three-dimensional structure, He provided the opportunity for us to experience all His creation. On Earth, this encounter is through the human body, an object made out of clay and water, in both masculine and feminine form. God gave us the choice, the free will, to decide whether or not to be born on Earth, and further, the option of being born male or female, and many of us have chosen to enter the earthly existence. However, instead of honouring God's glory through our thoughts and actions, we have forgotten who we really are, what our purpose in life is, and the reasons why we chose to be born on Earth in the first place."

"Let me expand on this concept of existence: of where, how, and why we all exist. Within the Universe, in the great "I AM THAT I AM", there are seven dimensions of existence. These dimensions are actually our levels of consciousness; our awareness and enlightenment. Each level is a reflection of the state of our being. The higher the dimension, the higher our consciousness, or put more accurately, the greater our awareness and the more enlightened we are, the higher the dimension in which we exist."

Gabriel gave the angels some time to absorb this information, as he noticed that most had not realised that there were several levels of existence. He continued, "We exist as light and energy. We have no particular physical form, but are composed of minuscule particles that vibrate at various rates. The greater our enlightenment, the faster our energy vibrates. The lower our awareness, the slower our energy resonates. The whole universe is comprised of these particles, and they are sometimes referred to as energy or spirit; life itself."

Gabriel continued, "Let me flesh this out for you. We angels are currently in the fourth dimension. This lesson that Michael, Raphael, and I are teaching is taking place in the fourth level of existence. However, when we are on Earth in human form, we live within the third dimension, and our light is covered by the clay and water that is the human body. And more importantly, our consciousness is constrained by this physical form. The body acts as a barrier and limits our access to the higher dimensions. Our energy therefore exists in a lower state and vibrates at a slower pace."

"Energy is vital to the evolution of Earth, for it is this force that animates the physical world. Without it, there would be no life on Earth – nothing would grow, move, or change states; it would be sterile. The planet would be just a barren, dry mass, similar to the many millions of planets found in other parts of the universe."

"To be clear, this energy, this consciousness, is what animates the human body. And you are this energy, this spirit. Without you, the human body would die and decay very quickly, returning to its original state of dust. The human body requires your presence to survive, but you do not require the human body to be alive."

One of the angels, named Myriam, raised her hand and asked, "Does this mean that we angels exist in the fourth dimension, and human beings exist in the third dimension?"

Gabriel answered, "Yes, we angels are currently in the fourth dimension. When we decide to be born on Earth, we clothe ourselves in a human body, are called human beings, and exist in the third dimension."

Myriam further inquired, "Does this mean that all human beings on Earth are angels, just like us, but have chosen to be born on Earth to experience God's creation?"

"Exactly," answered Gabriel, "All human beings are angels." Murmurings erupted all around and Gabriel listened carefully while the angels conversed amongst themselves.

"They sure are not acting like angels," said one.

"Are not we angels meant to be good and gentle beings?" said another.

"Angels are supposed to love one another and spread kindness and warmth!" exclaimed yet another.

Once the commotion subsided, Gabriel continued, "I want to clarify that as angels, we can still visit Earth and remain in our fourth dimension state of being. However, if we want to experience the physicality of the world, we must be born as human beings. And as human beings, if we are able to maintain our higher consciousness, or even raise our level of consciousness, we can link into the fourth dimension. This is how some human beings are able to communicate with us, and we are able to influence their lives for the better."

"Now, let us turn to the other dimensions of existence: the fifth dimension is at a much higher vibratory level than the fourth, and the sixth dimension vibrates at an even faster rate than the fifth. These are all higher levels of consciousness, or put in other words, these are deeper levels of awareness. God, the quickest and purest vibrational energy, Love itself, exists in the seventh dimension."

"I do not understand these other dimensions," said Jonah, another angel. "Why do they exist, and who or what resides there?"

Gabriel continued, "These other dimensions are just

purer states of existence. We are the ones who reside there. But we can only exist there if we have achieved the required level of consciousness. Let me explain this with an example: water is ice in its solid form and it exists in the physical world. You can hold it, see it, smell it, and taste it. When you apply heat, it changes its form and melts into liquid; it now exists in another state – you can still see, smell, and taste it, but you cannot "hold" it – you need a physical container to capture the liquid. When it then evaporates, it exists in yet another state – you cannot see it, taste it, or contain it – but it still exists. And you know it still exists, for it forms vapours and clouds, and eventually rains down. In all its different states of being, the substance is still the same – it is water – but it exists at various vibrational, energy levels – solid, liquid, gas."

"In this same way, we exist at various states, depending on our vibrational levels. It is we who choose where to be: the third-dimension world as human beings, where our physical bodies contain or hold our spirit; the fourth dimension where we are now, or in the higher dimensions. The faster our energy vibrates (in other words, the purer our state of being, or the higher our consciousness), the higher the dimension in which we exist."

Jonah asked, "I understand that there are many levels of existence and it is our choice to decide in which dimension we would like to exist. But what are the advantages of existence at each level? Why would we choose one dimension over another?"

Gabriel said, "We originate from God, the source of all life. We surged forth from His Light, and are various versions of Him. Our purest form is to be like Him, within Him, in the seventh dimension. This dimension provides the greatest peace; it offers unconditional love and contentment. Fear and worry do not exist, only peace exists."

"But let us begin with the third dimension and work our way up: If you were to ask a human being what he or she craves the most, each would likely respond that happiness is what he or she desires, free from all worry and stress. This is what it is like in the seventh dimension. Human beings mistakenly believe that they must acquire wealth and material objects to be peaceful, stress-free and happy. They strive to be successful in life in order to have an easier material existence, and thus, achieve happiness. They also want to attract attention from others – they want to be recognised and adored – and the root of this is love. Human beings crave love. So basically, all men and women on Earth want to be loved and want to exist in a perpetual state of happiness. But whatever each human being achieves in the world, whether it is material wealth, happiness, love, or even a combination of these, it is never enough. Human beings are never satisfied, they always crave more, in the mistaken belief that if they obtain more of whatever it is they desire, they will then be loved unconditionally, and be content. But what is remarkable is that the type of satisfaction that human beings desire does not exist in the third-dimension world. It is only found in the higher dimensions. And whatever little satisfaction human beings do achieve in the world (be it material wealth, happiness or love), it is actually temporary, for life on Earth is finite. When life comes to an end, the human being sheds his or her body, and the essence, his or her energy, moves up to the fourth dimension where we are now, and they leave everything and everyone behind."

A bright and colourful angel, named Indra, exclaimed, "But I do not understand. I had visited Earth as a human being and realised I would only achieve the happiness I desired once I returned to my original home, which is here. And even though I am an angel here in this fourth dimension, I am not at complete peace!"

Gabriel continued, "As you have realised, Indra, existence is not perfect in this fourth dimension. While it is purer than the third dimension given that our physicality is removed, there are matters that still weigh on us; we are therefore not content. This is because elements of our ego still exist, such as pride and fear; we still regard each other as separate beings, albeit in angelic form. But we are connected and we must strive for complete unity: we must see each other as one and the same in order to achieve the ultimate peace and happiness. And we can only do this by raising our consciousness, our spiritual, vibrational energy, and move up through the dimensions of existence closer to God."

"But how do we increase our vibration levels and move up? And why would we want to be born on Earth and step backwards to the third dimension, when we already exist in the fourth dimension?" asked Sarah.

"I will answer your second question first," said Gabriel, "God created the Earth as a form of expression, as a way to convey His qualities of love, power, strength, and compassion, similar to the way an artist creates a painting. He breathed His Life Force into Earth's creation. He then allowed us angels to experience His artistic creation by becoming three-dimensional human beings, for a very brief period of time, in order to know and understand the full breadth and scope of His wonder. In other words, God allowed us to "step into His painting". So rather than calling this a step backwards to the third dimension, it should really be labelled as a step sideways, a temporary experience. We do not change who we are, for we are still beings of light; we have just clothed this light by donning a human body to experience the painting from within. The painting is not reality, it is just a reflection of the artist's creativity."

"And when we step back into the reality of the fourth dimension, we return to our normal state of existence. It is only when we are ready to enter the fifth dimension that we begin to change who we are. For it is at this stage that we start to lose our individual persona, our ego, and truly begin to merge with each other in unity. If we look back to the third dimension and Earth, we can observe that the coupling of human beings is to procreate, and further, it is a means to enable them to feel closer to one another. But human beings never truly touch each other, for their physical bodies act as barriers. The intoxication that is experienced by the coupling of human bodies on Earth is a mere fraction of the elation achieved in the fifth dimension by the merging of our energies. And this, in turn, is just an element of what is experienced in the sixth dimension. The further we progress up the dimensions, the closer we are to achieving complete peace and love. And finally, when we merge into God, the Great Universe, we are in our purest and most powerful state, free from all worry and stress – we are LOVE itself."

"As for how to increase our vibration levels so that we may move closer to God in the seventh dimension, as I stated earlier, this is done by letting go of your persona, the ego, and moving towards a higher state of consciousness. This means releasing or letting go of all that hurts you, troubles you, worries you. By peeling away all the layers of your wants and desires, you will allow your spirit to break free from its bonds. Hatred, greed, jealousy, resentment, anger, and an unforgiving nature, especially when one is vindictive or is generally vengeful, these attributes are amongst the greatest barriers to allowing your energy to move freely. They sap your energy, and tire your spirit. By loving all life forms, allowing each to have its space in the universe, and generously giving and empowering all with your light, love and energy, you will invigorate your own vibrational level."

"Do you understand this basic concept of where, how, and why we exist?" asked Gabriel. A wave of whispers and murmurings floated through the atmosphere, and Gabriel gave the angels a few minutes to absorb the teachings.

"We have another question," said Yuri, "We sort of understand why we exist: God created us, we burst forth from Him. We also understand that God created the universe, including planet Earth, and created man and woman in order to provide us with a means of experiencing His creation. We also accept that to achieve complete peace, happiness, and love, we must return to our source of being, to God, the Beginning. But what we do not comprehend is where does God come from? Was He created by another being or energy? Why does He exist? What is His purpose?"

Gabriel, Michael and Raphael smiled and gave each other knowing looks.

"Do either one of you want to take this question, or shall I continue?" asked Gabriel.

"Where would we even begin? How does one articulate this answer?" responded Michael, "It is incapable of being described in words."

"Only when you reach the seventh dimension and experience God, the Life Force, will you then be able to understand the answer," said Raphael, "and each one of you must resolve this question for yourself."

"Exactly," agreed Gabriel, "There is an answer to this question, and you will answer it for yourself once you reach the vibratory level of the seventh dimension, and "meet God face-to-face". Those of you who wish to "meet God" must do the necessary work to move up through the dimensions. It is only in this way that you will be able to comprehend." Gabriel gave the angels a few minutes to contemplate the matter and listened to their discussions.

"Can you imagine meeting God face-to-face? It would be wonderful!" said Angelica.

"I want to be like Gabriel and have the ability to speak directly with God," said Elias.

"Then you must emulate him and listen to what he says, so that you can travel up to the seventh dimension," responded He-Ping.

"We must all make the effort to reach our highest levels of consciousness and awareness. It is the only way to achieve the ultimate peace and to restore harmony," said Dawood.

"But there is something that I still do not understand," said Ezra, "You have explained that God exists at a higher consciousness, what you call the seventh dimension. But I thought God was everywhere, and not just in one place. It does not make sense to me."

"Both statements are true," said Gabriel. The angels looked at one another in confusion.

"But how can that be?" questioned Lhakpa.

Gabriel continued, "It is because God's consciousness is omnipresent. He exists everywhere. Most do not see Him, but some do feel Him and are aware of His presence. However, to fully experience Him and be like Him, your level of consciousness must be attuned to His level in the seventh dimension. It is there that you will experience the full extent of His presence and power. Let us use the example of a radio. You must tune into a particular radio frequency in order to listen to your chosen station. If the sound is not clear, you adjust your settings on the radio to fully capture the particular frequency. Other radio stations exist on different radio wave frequencies. Whether or not you tune into a particular station, the radio waves still exist everywhere. In this same way, God exists everywhere, like the radio waves. However, in order for you to tune into Him, you must adjust your consciousness. While you will find Him at every level (or at every frequency), His purest presence, with laser sharp clarity, is experienced by you at the moment you reach the seventh dimension. And to push the metaphor further, when you reside with Him in the seventh dimension, you become the radio waves themselves."

The angels looked at one another in amazement, and Gabriel knew it would take some time for all this to sink in.

Gabriel said, "Now let us move on with the practical lessons. Raphael, would you please take the next session?"

Raphael gathered the angels even closer. "Let me summarise the current situation on Earth. Many of us are choosing to enter Earth as human beings, but are forgetting who we really are. And because of this forgetfulness, many are treating our fellow human beings, our sibling angels, very badly. People are hurting each other through words and actions; our egos are taking over our personalities. We are becoming possessive of all that the Earth contains, many believing that we own the wealth and resources God created. Now, would you all please follow me?"

As they hurried after Raphael, the angels suddenly realised

they were heading to Earth. Raphael gravitated straight to the home of a family of eight – a father, a mother, and their six children.

The home contained a large common room: a huge fireplace and chimney rose from the back wall, flanked either side by shelving piled high with pots, plates, and utensils of all kinds. A massive wooden table anchored the room, circled by rugged carpets and thread-bare cushions dotted all around. The children were preoccupied; the younger ones absorbed in their play, the older ones concentrating on their studies. A warm fire crackled underneath a boiling pot of stew, sending tantalising aromas into the air.

Suddenly, the mother ran into the room, followed by the father shouting, "I told you that I did not want this for dinner! Yet you defy me and cook it anyway!"

"But we didn't have anything else! Do you want the children to go hungry?" said the mother.

"Are you saying that I cannot provide for my family?"

"No I'm not! This is all we had today. If you want something else then bring it home and I'll cook it!"

"I work tirelessly every day and all I want is a good meal and some respect! Can't you even do that?"

"What do you want me to do? I'm not a magician who can conjure up food from nothing!" The father's face reddened with rage and he rushed at the mother.

The children instinctively ran towards him shrieking, "Father! Stop!"

"Don't tell me what to do!" He grabbed a long-handled spoon from the sideboard and turned towards the children. The mother stepped in between as his arm came down, and she took the full brunt of the father's blow. The mother cried out in pain, and the children screamed. The father tried to get at the children.

"You will respect me even if I have to beat it out of you!"

"No!" shouted the mother as she fought back, preventing the father from reaching the children.

"Run outside!" she yelled at them.

The angels could not believe what they were witnessing: some were paralysed with shock, while others rushed to protect the mother, however, they could not prevent all the blows from striking her.

Raphael began to pray and invite peace and love into the house, willing the father to remember that he was better than this; the angels joined Raphael in a chorus of prayer. A warm energy began to permeate the room. The father stopped and tried to calm himself – he fell to his knees and began to cry.

"Why are you crying, when I'm the one who's been beaten?" asked the mother.

"I don't know," sobbed the father, "All I know is that I feel the pain of every blow, deep inside of me." The mother took the father in her arms and held him close: they closed their eyes, both exhausted from the encounter. Raphael then moved away, the angels following him.

"What is particularly sad about this situation," said Raphael, "is that all eight members of this family are the closest of friends in the fourth dimension. They are angel friends who decided to experience life on Earth together, so that they could look after one another and enjoy each other's company. They wanted to discover the wonders of the world together. Because most of this group were apprehensive about visiting Earth, two of them went ahead to become the mother and father so they could provide a safe environment for the rest to be born as their children; they promised to protect them. They have all forgotten who they actually are and why they chose to be together. The father has found life difficult and is obsessed with material wealth, and the mother and children are too blind to see how strong and powerful they really are. All eight have been mesmerised by the physicality of Earth in different ways and have let fear grip them and get in their way."

One angel was particularly disturbed by what she witnessed and tentatively stepped forward. "Excuse me, Raphael, but why is the father so aggressive?" she said, her eyes welling up.

Raphael reached out to comfort her. "While the father is able to provide a basic living for his family, he is not able to acquire the luxuries his neighbours have. This causes him a great deal of frustration, for he feels humiliated and disrespected, even though his family is content with what they have. It is his own feeling of inadequacy that is manifesting. Unfortunately, he takes his anger out on his family." After a short pause to recover and centre themselves, the angels were ready to continue with the lesson. "Please follow me," said Raphael.

He took his students to visit other situations. The angels witnessed human beings cheating one another, stealing from each other, forcing one another into slavery, and maiming and killing for one reason or another. In many parts of the world, whole tribes of people were warring with each other, and all for personal gain in a fleeting, physical world. Could they not understand that whatever they gained on Earth was temporary, and would be left behind once their physical lives came to an end?

During each encounter, the angels became more and more emotional, and their auras (the light emanating from them, and which some human beings called "halos") became dull and heavy with grief.

"Raphael, we need a break. Can we please stop for a while?" asked one angel. Raphael led them to a beautiful wooded area filled with plants and all manner of vegetation. A rainbow of flowers decorated the surrounding fields as the tall grasses swayed in the breeze. A lovely scent infused the air and they felt God's spirit all around, working through the life forms as the plants grew and the flowers blossomed. They rested in His Presence.

Some distance away, the angels saw a lady merrily humming a tune while planting seeds. She quietly stopped and scanned around her, as if she sensed the angels. She smiled and looked towards the sky. "Thank you for the lovely day," she said to no one in particular and resumed her work.

The angels continued to rest, and once all felt slightly recovered, Raphael resumed his lesson. He explained that when these human beings returned from Earth to the fourth dimension and "woke up", many regretted their behaviour. They tried to atone for their actions and seek forgiveness from their fellow beings. "While many angels have forgiven each other, there are some who are so damaged by the treatment their fellow angels inflicted on them while on Earth, that they are laden down with sadness and are unable to rise up. It will take a great deal of time and effort on our part to restore them to their original luminosity so that they may glow brightly again."

Raphael continued, "We have been trying to influence human beings from here, to jog their memories to remember who they are, and therefore prevent them from having negative thoughts or engaging in such destructive behaviour. It has proved very difficult and we have not had the success we had hoped for. So, as God conveyed through Gabriel, we will now work on Earth itself as human beings, so that we may physically teach our fellow angels to remember the truth and lead them back towards God. In this way, they will have a much better chance of choosing to do good on Earth, or at least refrain from doing any harm."

Raphael then led the group back to Gabriel and Michael, who had been observing from afar.

"Do you understand the importance of the work you have agreed to undertake?" asked Gabriel. "There is an urgent need to help our sibling angels and other life forms on Earth. God has called upon you. Do you still agree to be born on Earth, so that God may send guidance through you to awaken humankind and lead them to the Truth? Will you be able to remain strong and steadfast in your mission for God? If any of you have changed your minds, do not hesitate to remove yourselves from this task, for it is a difficult one, and at times, it will be fraught with emotional and physical suffering."

All the angels replied in unison, accepting the responsibility and all the risks therein. They all pledged to do their best. Gabriel glowed with joy, delighted that so many angels were going to help with God's work.

"Michael, please organise these missionary angels so that they may be born on various parts of the Earth, and at various times during Earth's evolution. It is imperative that all of humanity benefits from this guidance. And then we will begin the process."

5 ABUNDANCE

Michael organised everyone into groups. Even though angels had no gender, physical life on Earth necessitated choosing either the masculine or feminine form. It was important that both male and female were represented given that many societies had assigned different roles and responsibilities to each. The angels would also have to pick the geographic areas where each would implement his or her assignment so that the whole of humanity was covered. Michael worked out the detailed plans with every group, as well as with each angel individually, and ran these by Gabriel and Raphael.

"I think we should start slowly, and only send a few angels at a time," said Michael.

"I agree. Let us begin with an initial group," replied Gabriel, "We will likely learn lessons from their experiences."

Upon their plans being finalised, Gabriel withdrew into himself and travelled through the dimensions fully into God.

"In the name of God, the most Beneficent, the most Merciful," invoked Gabriel, "we seek Your blessings before we begin this important work."

God said, "My dear Gabriel, I have watched you all, and I am pleased with your efforts to serve your siblings and see to their welfare. Go ahead with your plans. But remember, Gabriel, it is your responsibility to ensure that each angel conveys the message properly and leads My children home to Me. Where they make mistakes, you must try to rectify these. You have a strenuous road ahead, but never forget, My dear child, that I am always with you, protecting and guiding you. Turn to Me during the difficult times.

Convey My blessings to My angels and relate to them how happy I am to know that they have chosen to help their fellow beings. Tell them to seek My help during their troubles, for I will be with them."

"Thy Will be done on Earth as it is in Heaven," said Gabriel, bowing his head as he descended through the heavens. Michael, Raphael, and the others were all deep in prayer, awaiting Gabriel's return. When he appeared and conveyed God's blessings, the angels bowed their heads in gratitude, individually beginning their inner preparations for the journey ahead. Then slowly, one after the other, the first of the missionary angels began to inhabit Earth.

God began transmitting His message. "Gabriel, convey this to My children on Earth: Do not be taken in by the world around you, for it is an illusion. Remember that physical life is finite, but you are eternal, and that you will return to your original home. Do not hurt one another and do not differentiate amongst each other, for you are the same and originate from Me, the One."

Each missionary angel spent at least one lifetime in the world, with some returning to Earth once or twice over to provide additional help where required. Humankind looked upon many of them as special: depending where each carried out his and her work, they were called prophets, seers, mystics, shamans, saints, soothsayers, gurus, spiritual leaders, maharishis, and many other such titles. Almost all were able to guide the communities in which they were born. These societies embraced the values of compassion and kindness: people began to recognise themselves as spiritual beings of light and energy.

However, some missionary angels were not so successful, either because they did not "receive" the messages from Gabriel accurately, or they misinterpreted some of the messages and led their fellow beings astray. Amongst other unfortunate events were incidents of human beings taking their own lives, sometimes *en masse*, in the misguided belief that it was better to return to their original state than live out an illusion on Earth.

"But taking your own life is so violent!" said Gabriel, "It is the same as taking someone else's life!"

"There are consequences to our actions," said Michael, "Why would you just cut your life so dramatically? The impact of this is devastating."

"Not only are their lives incomplete, but their actions hurt those whom they leave behind in the world," said Gabriel, looking towards Earth.

"They are missing the point," said Raphael, "Are they not in the world to appreciate the power and creativity of the Universe?"

"Exactly. The point of Earth is to experience the full breadth of creation: its complexity and simplicity, from the minute to the colossal," said Gabriel, "Once you decide to live a life on Earth, you must complete it. After all, human life is a gift from God."

A third group of missionary angels also attracted Gabriel's attention. For some reason, they forgot who they really were, and why they had entered the Earthly existence. Gabriel carefully considered these cases. "Are they mesmerised by the world?" he asked.

"Yes. And I think it runs deeper," said Michael, "Their egos seem to be overpowering them. And with their charismatic personalities, they are able to secure all that they require to meet their selfish needs."

"We must work harder to reach these angels so that they can fulfil their promise to God," said Gabriel, "Would you and Raphael put together a special team to deal with this group? We have to concentrate our efforts to at least prevent these angels from doing harm."

Many years passed in this manner, with Gabriel, Michael and Raphael at the helm of this operation to awaken humanity. Millions of angels persevered in guiding humankind from above, while the one hundred thousand missionary angels carried on their sojourns on Earth, born during various times in history and in all geographic areas. Those who remained linked to the fourth dimension and rooted in spirit were able to positively influence vast numbers of human beings and invite a great deal of peace and good will amongst people. These missionary angels distinguished themselves and Gabriel took note of their work; they could prove to be very helpful in the future.

God continued His creation on Earth, evolving all species, both flora and fauna. He allowed for humans to live a better quality of life by inspiring various men and women to invent technology and develop the societies in which they lived. As civilisation progressed, many people advanced and did, indeed, live better quality lives. But many did not, either because they were prevented from developing their cultures by those who were afraid of new ideas and change, or because communities refused to share their wealth and knowledge with others. This created a division in society: the "Haves" and the "Have-nots".

"Archangel Gabriel, why is God granting the world such abundance?" asked one of the missionary angels, "It is stoking greed in many people and making our work that much more difficult."

"I do not know," said Gabriel, looking towards Earth, "I will need to find out."

Just then, Michael and Raphael appeared, and the missionary angel turned to them. "Hello Archangel Michael and Archangel Raphael. Do you happen to know why God is granting such plenty on Earth? People are getting greedy."

"No, we do not," said Michael, "but we will try to determine what is happening."

"Very well," said the angel and he went on his way.

Michael turned to Gabriel. "Are you alright?"

"Yes…," said Gabriel, gathering his thoughts. "Yes, of course. Tell me, why are we being addressed as Archangel, and where did this come from?"

"As far as I can tell," said Raphael, "this term came about

when you returned from your interaction with God. I remember there was a great deal of commotion. You see, Gabriel, you were the first they had ever come across who had spoken to God. It caused a sensation. It had never occurred to anyone that this was a possibility."

"But, both you and Michael have also met God," said Gabriel.

"Yes, but God spoke to you," said Raphael, "and you demystified the encounter and gave it life. You showed them that it is attainable for all. And I believe a few coined this term to not only distinguish you from themselves, but also as a mark of respect. Whether or not it is justified, they are attributing this title to me and Michael, too."

"I see…," said Gabriel, "I do not like this hierarchy that continues to develop. It creates divisions and implies that there are different standards applicable to different groups, which goes against who we are and what we are trying to do."

"I think we all agree on that," said Raphael.

"Yes, absolutely," said Michael.

"Anyway, let us get on with our work. I must consult God to understand why He is granting the world such wealth," said Gabriel, and he began to move away.

Gabriel withdrew into God and invoked, "In the name of God, the most Beneficent, the most Merciful."

"Gabriel, it is wonderful to see you again," said God, "What seems to be troubling you?"

"My Lord, why are You providing such abundance to humanity, when not only do they not remember who they are and what their purpose in life is, but many do not even recognise Your existence? Certain areas on Earth are resplendent with plenty. The more dominant are not sharing the wealth with others; selfishness and greed is taking root."

"My dear child, I want to improve the existence of My

children, and see what they will do with the grace and prosperity that I bestow upon them. I have granted My favour to all of humankind, not just a chosen few. It is humanity who is choosing not to share this abundance with their fellow beings."

"My Lord, it is difficult to manage the greed exhibited by some. Is it really necessary to provide such temptation?"

"My dear Gabriel, I must provoke My children to overcome their darker attributes and rise to the challenge. Otherwise, how will they grow? It is not acceptable to remain static and complacent. Remember, I created Earth as a gift to My children and it is for each who enter physical life to make further choices on how each wishes to behave. Will each choose lightness over darkness in each instance? If darkness prevails, there will come a time when I will take My grace away."

"I understand, My Lord," said Gabriel, lowering his head.

"And Gabriel, do not despair. I see all, and am with each and every one of you. Carry on with your work. And if you are troubled, come and see Me again."

"Thank you, My Lord. Thy Will be done on Earth as it is in Heaven," said Gabriel, as he withdrew and descended to Michael and Raphael.

"This work is going to be harder than I thought. I do not think I realised what I was getting myself into," said Gabriel, as he ushered them to a quiet spot. He proceeded to convey God's words to them.

"I see what you mean, Gabriel. This is not an easy task," said Michael.

"We need to increase our efforts to help humankind comprehend that nothing on Earth belongs to them, and that they must be generous and kind to one another," said Gabriel.

"We are with you. You are not alone," said Michael.

Gabriel embraced his two friends. "Anyway, it is too late to back out now!" They laughed as they made their way towards the others.

As time went on and societies advanced, more avarice set in. It did not matter how much or in what geographic area society developed: humanity was overwhelmed with its desire for more.

With all this abundance, the Archangels witnessed a huge shift in human culture: up to this point in humankind's evolution, people exchanged ideas through telepathy; the projection of thought was part of the normal manner of communication and no physical form was required. However, with their spiritual connection growing weaker, humans were losing their ability to communicate. They had to resort to gesturing with their hands and faces in order to convey their thoughts, and uttered sounds to express their emotions. This evolved into different modes of communication with many populations developing a spoken language. Contact between people became a physical act of gesturing, speaking, and even writing, and had nothing to do with their higher consciousness. This further divided human society, for the body now acted as a real barrier. If a human being could not physically see, observe, or communicate with another, he did not know of the other's existence. Hence, in many instances, the Haves did not see the Have-nots, and more often than not, even if they did see, the Have-nots were ignored. Humankind was becoming more individualistic, disconnected, and certainly more earth-bound.

6 LEARNING

The one hundred thousand missionary angels continued their intercession on Earth and were born into both classes of society. Some suffered greatly during their earthly existence, especially those who chose to live as Have-nots. As human beings completed their physical lives and crossed back into the fourth dimension, they immediately recognised they were spiritual beings. Each took stock of his and her worldly life. As they assessed their conduct and saw how their intentions and actions had impacted their lives and those around them, many showed remorse for their negative behaviour. Some vowed never to return to Earth again as human beings.

"I cannot believe how badly I behaved," said one.

"How could I have hurt my family like that?" said another, "What do I do now?"

"Seek forgiveness from those you harmed," said Gabriel, "That is the first step. And then you must forgive yourself."

"How do I do this?" came the reply.

"Learn about yourself. Learn about your nature and who you really are," said Gabriel, "You emanate from God and are a generous, loving being. Show that love to others as well as to yourself."

The angels turned towards one another and sought forgiveness for any harm each had caused while on Earth. Even though it was difficult for victims to forgive, quite a few pardoned their offenders. But forgiveness did not come easily to most. Many were stuck in their pain, their beings dim with sorrow.

"I just cannot forget what happened to me. It is constantly

with me," said one angel.

"How do I convince you that I truly regret my actions?" replied another.

"I cannot be at peace without forgiveness from my family!" exclaimed a third angel, "I am loath to remain for eternity here in the fourth dimension. I want to rise, but how do I rid myself of this burden? I want to get closer to the Great Spirit. Please help me, God!"

Immediately, a wave of warmth descended on them, and the angels calmed down. God enveloped them in His love and they all relaxed into His grace. It was as if God had engulfed the fourth dimension with His light and energy; it brought peace and tranquillity to their beings. The angels had never experienced such love and harmony before, and wondered whether this was what it felt like to exist in the upper dimensions.

Suddenly, Gabriel, Michael and Raphael were summoned by God and they withdrew into Him.

"In the name of God, the most Beneficent, the most Merciful," they invoked while bowing their heads.

"My beloved children," said God, "I am happy that the three of you are working together so closely. Now, convey these words to all: Not only have you lost sight of the concept of love, but you have placed the notions of generosity and forgiveness outside of yourselves, as though they are something for which to reach. Yet, these qualities are innate to you and are part of the essence of your being, for you originate from Me. You plead with me to shower My love on you and forgive your mistakes, which I always do. Yet you are unable to do the same when others ask you for your mercy and forgiveness. Why such petty, small-mindedness? Do you not see your greatness? You are a part of Me, but I am wholly in you. Many of you who visit Earth as human beings not only forget who you are, but ignore your higher consciousness and fundamental nature. It greatly pains Me when you harm each other, and it hurts Me even more when you are unable to forgive. Hate, resentment, and vengeance have no place in your soul and are foreign to your being. Whether you harmed or were harmed, mercy and forgiveness are intrinsic to who you are. You are light and goodness; you are strong and powerful; you are loving and compassionate, for you are a part of Me."

"Gabriel, you must convey this message to all My children. All three of you must teach them about themselves, so that they may discover who they really are."

"Yes, my Lord," they replied in unison, bowing their heads.

"Thy Will be done on Earth as it is in Heaven," they invoked and made their way down through the heavens.

Once they arrived in the fourth dimension, the Archangels gathered the billions of angels. Flanked by Michael and Raphael at either side, Gabriel transmitted the message from God, and continued, "We must all learn to embrace the virtues of love and forgiveness, amongst other attributes intrinsic to us. We will institute lessons to help those who want assistance. Whoever has remained pure and true to their loving nature and wishes to become a teacher or mentor should present themselves. In addition, for those who wish to visit Earth as human beings, we will explain to you how to remain connected to the higher dimension so that you do not forget who you are." Gabriel turned to Michael and Raphael, "There is quite a bit of work to do. Please begin organising the classes."

Michael and Raphael set about establishing the schools. They recruited teachers and organised the classes according to the lessons each student required to learn. Some were about forgiveness, others about humility, generosity of spirit, and overcoming one's ego. It was important for angels to be made aware of the trappings of Earth and to be instilled with the knowledge of how to remain connected to their own light. All were to be taught according to their needs without the passing of any criticism or judgment. There was a great deal of hustle and bustle as angels fluttered about earnestly, each trying to help the other's light shine more brightly.

During this time, Gabriel noticed another phenomenon

and raised it with Michael and Raphael.

"Have you observed that angels are forming attachments to and favouring either our masculine or feminine traits? Why are we identifying with one or the other?" said Gabriel.

"There seems to be a lack of balance and equilibrium in their beings," said Michael, "Their experiences on Earth have heavily influenced them. Their spirits have absorbed the characteristics of the male or female body."

"We will have to address this, because the whole of our being is both masculine and feminine," said Gabriel, "Gender is a physical concept of Earth, and it does not belong in the higher dimensions."

"Nor should any one character trait dominate a personality; all must be in complete balance," said Michael.

"We are seeing the ego push through quite forcefully," added Raphael.

"I think it is important to provide instruction on balancing the spirit," said Gabriel, "Raphael, you seem to have perfect equilibrium with your masculine and feminine qualities. Perhaps you could lead these classes?"

"I would be honoured," replied Raphael.

Many hundreds of years passed with Michael and Raphael managing the angel schools. During this time, Gabriel continued to direct the special human beings, those missionary angels who had been sent to Earth to help humankind. He also led the millions of angels who guarded individual human beings, and he generally monitored the situation on Earth. Every so often, he cast an eye on the angel schools. Amongst all the activity, he observed what the others had not noticed. Although relatively insignificant given the billions of angels working together, a few hundred or so were standing apart and not participating in the activities. Their attention seemed to be focussed on the third-dimension world. They faced planet Earth and had, in fact, "turned their backs" on the rest of the angels. Their beings were thick with darkness.

Gabriel's heart sank with disappointment. "These angels seem to be completely mesmerised by Earth," he thought, "They are so overcome with darkness, they literally cannot see they are beings of light. They are entranced by God's creation on Earth. Can they not see that this is just a reflection of God? If only they would turn around, they would glimpse the full breadth of creation behind them in all dimensions. The true beauty is God Himself, not His reflection on Earth."

Gabriel approached them. "My dear siblings," he softly said, "why are you not participating in our work? We miss you and wish you to be a part of us."

"But we are a part of you. We are just waiting to go back to Earth. It is so beautiful there," replied one.

"But it is just as beautiful here, if not more so. Please come with me and I will show you," said Gabriel.

The angels looked suspiciously behind him. "We do not see any beauty. There is nothing there. You are just trying to trick us. We see the beauty that God created on Earth and we wish to surround ourselves with it. In this way, we will be close to God."

Gabriel noticed that a few of these angels were part of the group of missionary angels who had taken an oath to guide humanity. He had to do something to bring them back from the cliff's edge. After all, this was part of Gabriel's promise to God, to guide these particular angels and to rectify any mistakes they made.

Gabriel said, "Yes, God created the Earth and it is beautiful. It is for you to appreciate, and even enjoy God's creation, and more importantly, to honour it in God's glory. But it is temporary and is not all God created. If you re-focus your vision and look closely, you will see that God created everything, including all that is contained in dimensions beyond space and time. He is everywhere, as well as on Earth. But the beauty you experience on Earth is just a ray, one ray, emanating from His Light. It is but a glimpse of the whole. The beauty you will find when you are closer to Him in spirit, within Him, is unimaginable. Come with me and I will show you."

But the angels had already turned their backs on Gabriel, facing Earth again, hypnotised by all it seemed to promise. Gabriel recognised that their lights were so deeply engorged with darkness, they could not comprehend that there was more to God's creation than Earth.

As soon as opportunities presented themselves, Gabriel watched as these souls jumped back into the world as human beings, ready to experience all the pleasures it had to offer, seeking happiness and joy in the mistaken belief that this would bring them closer to God. And Gabriel knew that this spelled trouble.

He kept an eye on these troubled beings and paid special attention to the missionary angels amongst them. This group grew up on Earth and began to preach various systems of belief, for deep within them they sensed their purpose was to teach humankind. They believed that God created the Earth and universe, and that was all; and that if you lived on Earth according to their interpretation of God's Will, you would reach "heaven". They utilised all means available to get their righteous message across, including threats and violence, at the cost of compassion and kindness. While they did not have many followers, they nonetheless influenced a portion of the communities in which they lived, particularly the young and vulnerable. They actually began to harm humanity, all with the mistaken intention of bringing their fellow human beings closer to God. In fact, they were just feeding their own egos.

Gabriel tried desperately to intervene with these angels and transmit God's messages to them. It was imperative that the correct principles and values be conveyed to those human beings who followed their teachings. However, this was to no avail. These missionary angels lost their connection with the fourth dimension and were unable to hear Gabriel. But they had a feeling deep inside them that they were meant to fulfil a mission for God, so they pursued their goals according to their own doctrines.

"How far removed this is from God's wishes," said Gabriel to Michael and Raphael, "God has given free will to each angel, to each human being. It is for each to decide how to conduct themselves, and raise their consciousness and spiritual energy to move up through the dimensions to be closer to God. And this is accomplished through love, compassion, generosity and kindness; not through mental, emotional and physical violence. How do we bring them and their followers back into the fold? How do we convince them of the truth?"

Raphael said, "Shall I gather some angels who wish to help with this problem? We can concentrate our efforts on these groups of people and send special prayers and love to awaken them. And once they complete their earthly lives and return home, we can help them with the transition and counsel them on how to truly achieve the ultimate peace and beauty they are seeking." Gabriel and Michael agreed, and Raphael set about putting this in place.

But Gabriel was not pacified. "These angels are causing havoc on Earth," he thought, "How will I rectify their mistakes? I realise relatively few human beings have been adversely impacted by their actions, but the consequences will reverberate long into the future. God has personally charged me with this responsibility – how will I face Him?"

"God, please help me. I have failed," whispered Gabriel, falling to his knees. Both Michael and Raphael rushed towards him.

"Gabriel!" said Michael, "We are here to help you with this assignment. Remember, you are not alone." They felt a wave of love and warmth overcome them and they knew God had made His Presence felt.

"We are in this together," added Raphael. Gabriel embraced them. He felt comforted, even though he knew he had a long road ahead. Remembering God's words to turn to Him during difficult times, Gabriel prayed for strength.

7 FORGIVENESS

Angels continued to be born on Earth to experience worldly, physical lives. Upon their return to the fourth dimension, they entered their periods of self-evaluation: How did their actions or omissions on Earth affect others? Did they intentionally or unintentionally harm anyone? Were they ever hurt by someone? Were they able to forgive? Did they treat others with kindness? Did they fulfil their responsibilities? Were there missed opportunities in their life's journey?

Each individual was counselled on the power of love and forgiveness to enable them to overcome feelings of anger, resentment, regret, and other emotions tied to their recent lives on Earth. These self-consuming emotions eroded their souls and retarded their advancement to the upper heavens.

Many individuals absorbed the teachings, and began to evolve their consciousness – some even elevated themselves to the fifth dimension. Others, however, could not forgive. Despite all the guidance from God, and all the counselling in the angel schools, and no matter how much the wrongdoers sought forgiveness, the victims held on to their anger and resentment. Their egos were so entrenched and impacted by their Earthly experience, they could not comprehend the freedom provided by forgiveness. This further impacted the wrongdoers who were left bereft with regret and self-loathing, for without this forgiveness, they were unable to evolve to the higher dimensions.

"Please help us, Archangel Michael," said one offender, "we are unable to bear this torment any longer."

"Can you not prevail on these angels to forgive us?" another asked Raphael, "I want to better myself."

"Archangel Gabriel, please ask God to intercede on our behalf," pleaded yet another.

"But you can ask God directly for help," said Gabriel, "Whether in angel or human form, each of you can communicate directly with God, and do not need an Archangel, or anyone else for that matter, to mediate for you or intercede on your behalf."

"Then please pray with us," came a reply from the crowd.

They all huddled together and prayed for God's help, each asking for forgiveness for the hurt they had caused others. As they meditated in silence, they felt a surge of energy tenderly wrapping their beings. After a few minutes, a peaceful glow settled in and the angels relaxed into the warmth.

God called out to the Archangels and they withdrew into Him. "In the name of God, the most Beneficent, the most Merciful," the Archangels recited.

"Gabriel, Michael, Raphael, I am glad you are here," said God, "I know My children are suffering, and are repentant for all their mistakes. I have bestowed My love and mercy on them. But it is not from Me that they require this forgiveness, but from those whom they have harmed. Convey to My children that they must seek forgiveness from the victims. And if the victims do not forgive, they are only hurting themselves, for it is they who are holding on to the hurt and pain. My children must learn to be merciful and forgiving, for if they do not, they will be bound to those who harmed them. And this bind will act as a rod of self-inflicting pain and suffering. I say to all: forgive the perpetrator and release yourselves. Mercy for others is at the heart of who you are. Explain this to My children."

"Yes, my Lord," they replied in unison.

God continued, "If they still do not learn to forgive others for harm committed whilst visiting Earth, then establish a system in the world where each must answer for his or her actions and pay this debt to the victim. But remind the victims that they will be tied to the offenders until every iota of this obligation is met, and there will be occasions when it will be easier to forgive than to go through another experience, or even another lifetime, with the offender. Now go back to My children and help them understand. Tell them that I am always with them, guiding them and protecting them. When they turn to Me in their difficulties, I am there to help them, and they should not be fearful, for My power and strength resides within each of them."

"And Gabriel," said God, "do not regret that you did not notice the troublemakers in the group of missionary angels, for you are not perfect. They are My children and will finally answer to Me. Carry on with your work and fulfil the promise you made to help all My children. But remember, your only task is to convey My message; it is their free will to decide whether they will listen and heed My words. And where you can, rectify their mistakes on Earth; but do not blame yourself for their errors. It is their responsibility and each will be accountable. And remember, Gabriel, Michael, and Raphael, I am always with you and help you with your work."

With these blessings and guidance, the Archangels bowed their heads in gratitude and invoked, "Thy Will be done on Earth as it is in Heaven," and descended to those waiting in the fourth dimension.

When Gabriel conveyed God's message to the angels, many rejoiced with happiness, relieved for a way out of their predicament.

"I am grateful for God's guidance and your help," said one, "for without this, I would have been trapped in my own sorrow and misery. God answered my prayers."

"But I cannot forget the torment and cruelty that was inflicted on me during my lifetime," said another, "I just cannot find it in me to forgive the perpetrators."

"You are holding on to your grief," said Gabriel, "and you are choosing the more difficult path, for you are reliving the cruelty over and over again."

"I do not know how and where to find the compassion to forgive. I have been to the angel schools and have been counselled individually, but I just cannot seem to move forward. I think I need to see the perpetrators experience the pain and suffering they inflicted on me."

"Very well," said Gabriel. He knew he now had to establish the system of debt and repayment. It was the only way to release both the offender and the victim from their obligations to one another, so that each was free to pursue their quest to achieve the ultimate peace and happiness.

Gabriel, Michael, and Raphael discussed how to implement such a system. They remembered God's words that every iota must be paid back, unless the wrongdoer had been forgiven. This required that both the offender and the victim return to Earth together, living lives that would allow for the obligations to be fulfilled. Their paths would have to somehow cross on Earth, either by chance, or they would need to be in a relationship, such as parent and child, husband and wife, siblings, friends, or some other type of association. It was only in this way that each would be able to repay their debt to one another. By experiencing the same wrong, or helping the one he or she wounded, the wrongdoer would work off his or her debt.

The Archangels addressed the group of angels who were still dim with sadness, caught in a dreadful grip of blame and regret.

"It is a pity that you are unable to find it in your hearts to forgive. Mercy is so much a part of your being. But we must move on from this point. Which of you feels a sense of injustice and wants to be recompensed? And which of you would like to re-enter the earthly existence to work off the debt you have incurred?" asked Gabriel. Several angels came forward. Two, in particular, seemed keen to rid themselves of this obligation.

"My name is Arun, and I committed many wrongs against my friend Prakash while we were on Earth. We worked together but I constantly cheated him out of his fair share. I am ashamed to say that in the end, Prakash was left penniless and lived the rest of his life in poverty. Despite my remorse and all my apologies, Prakash is unable to forgive me. I know what I did was wrong, but I do not know what to do to convince Prakash how sorry I am. I am at my wit's end; we must both be released from this tie."

"Prakash, are you sure you do not want to even try to forgive Arun? Perhaps if you talk this through, you may comprehend what fears gripped Arun and why he behaved the way he did. You may find it in your heart to show compassion and mercy," said Gabriel.

"I would prefer for Arun to pay for what he did to me," replied Prakash, "My children suffered in poverty because of his greed." Gabriel looked disappointed.

"This hard-heartedness may land you in deeper waters, Prakash," said Gabriel, "However, if that is your wish, then let us proceed. Do you both agree to be born on Earth again and live out your lives in kindness and generosity, serving one another?"

"Yes, we agree," they responded in unison.

"Arun, you realise that you will have to be generous of spirit, and serve Prakash your whole life, and ensure Prakash is well-looked after and protected? And Prakash, you realise that you will be tied to Arun, and that you will also have to be generous of spirit, and look after Arun? And do you both understand that you must not commit any new wrongs against each other, or else you will incur new liabilities, and will then enter a perpetual cycle of indebtedness, unless each of you forgives the other?"

"Yes, we agree and understand," they both responded.

"We just want to be free from this debt, and we wish this to be done as quickly as possible," said Arun.

"Then search for appropriate parents so that you may be born, one to each set," said Gabriel, "However, Prakash, you must be born female, and Arun, you must be born male, so that your relationship on Earth will be as husband and wife, serving and looking after each other in your new lifetime on Earth. In this way, your obligations will be met quickly. Arun, as the husband, you must care for your wife, protect her, and provide for her throughout her lifetime. And Prakash, as the wife, you must care for your husband and protect him. Be respectful of one another. But you both must remember to be careful not to commit any new wrongs against each other, for you will then initiate a cycle of debt and obligation that may take you hundreds or even thousands of years to complete, unless you forgive each other. Remember to keep your connection strong with the fourth dimension. Be spiritually aware, and do not forget who you are. We will help you from here, and guide you in the right direction, so listen quietly for our presence. And remember, God is always with you; seek His help during your difficulties."

And with these words, Arun and Prakash went on their way. Soon they were born on Earth as babies, with Arun being born a male child, whose parents named him Arjun, and Prakash being born a female child, whose parents named her Priya. Specific angels were assigned to help guide them throughout their lifetime and all prayed that they would succeed in their endeavour.

Another pair of angels came forward and asked the Archangels to help with their return to Earth. "We are Alexander and Benjamin, and we need to work out our quarrels. We each belonged to different tribes who fought each other constantly. We were sworn enemies during our earthly lives."

Gabriel asked, "Are you not able to forgive each other for your bad behaviour?"

Alexander lashed out, "How can I forgive him? He killed my wife and captured my daughter!"

"But do you not see that those souls who were your wife and daughter are here, safe and sound? Do you not realise that you also killed and maimed members of Benjamin's tribe? Can you not comprehend that your earthly battles were immature, unenlightened actions that only resulted in suffering for naught?" said Gabriel.

Alexander retorted, "But I must avenge their deaths! I suffered greatly for many years without my wife and daughter, and Benjamin must experience what this feels like!"

"But I have forgiven Benjamin," said Alexander's wife.

"And so have I," said Alexander's daughter, "In time, I went on to live a good life even though I was separated from you. Can you not see that Benjamin regrets his actions and is remorseful?"

"Do not seek out revenge through another life on Earth," implored Alexander's wife.

"I cannot let it go," said Alexander.

"Very well," said Gabriel, sighing in resignation, "Benjamin, do you wish to return to Earth as a human being?"

Benjamin replied, "I must free myself from Alexander's hold. I committed the wrongs and I must atone for them. Otherwise I will never be at peace. And quite frankly, neither will Alexander!"

Gabriel asked Michael to make the necessary arrangements, with the caveat that Alexander and Benjamin be born into the same family as sisters.

"Alexander, you will have to watch as Benjamin experiences great loss, such as you had experienced at his hand. You will see him lose his spouse and child under dreadful circumstances, but hopefully being sisters, it will also kindle the compassion and mercy that you are unable to demonstrate at the moment. Do you both agree to this?" asked Gabriel.

"Yes, we do," they replied.

"Very well," said Gabriel, "Michael would you please proceed with the arrangements?"

The Archangels oversaw this new system, with more and more angels choosing this method to release themselves from their obligations. Angels felt that it was much easier to obtain recompense from a wrongdoer than to show mercy and walk away. But Gabriel knew that they were treading a more difficult path. And exactly what he feared began to occur: in their new earthly lives, again, angels forgot who they were and were mesmerised by the illusion around them. They became possessive of everything God had placed on Earth, and they succumbed to greed, jealousy and selfishness. They incurred further debt and obligations in regards to one another and were now imprisoned in a vicious cycle of give and take that could persist for thousands of years, unless the victims showed mercy and fully granted their forgiveness.

"How ironic!" thought Gabriel, "In order to break this cycle, the aggrieved angel had to forgive the wrongdoer, which was what God had conveyed for them to do in the beginning. If the angels had only listened to God, and firstly, not committed any wrongs but lived in the spirit of love and kindness, then none of this suffering would have occurred; and secondly, having been the recipient of maltreatment, if the aggrieved were only able to forgive, as God had asked them to do, none of the angels would be caught in this trap."

Many thousands of years passed in this way, with all the angels working hard to help their fellow beings return home and reach God. As time evolved, Gabriel became increasingly concerned that they were headed in the wrong direction: more and more angels were choosing to enter Earth and live worldly lives; very few were remembering who they really were, and most became intoxicated by the world; many committed wrongs against their fellow beings; and compassion and mercy were rare. Love was absent from the world as more fear set in. The world was getting darker, not lighter; and angels were becoming heavier with the burdens they carried within their light.

8 MERCY

Gabriel decided to gather the tens of thousands of missionary angels who had remembered their promise to God, and had indeed fulfilled their purpose. He now needed their help more than ever.

"My dear siblings, we are not as successful as I hoped we would be in our task to help our fellow angels when they take on human form. We need to increase our efforts to help them undo the tangled web they are weaving for themselves. I would like you to visit Earth again, but we need to make a greater impact. We should enter the world in concentrated groups and try to influence humankind. I have decided to join you and will be part of this effort on Earth."

"Archangel Gabriel," spoke up one angel, "If you are with us on Earth, then who will transmit the messages from this side? And more importantly, who will guide us during our physical lives?" Gabriel turned to Michael and Raphael, and they both stepped forward.

"We will divide the work between us," said Michael, "I will transmit the messages as conveyed by God and will also oversee developments on Earth, while Raphael will manage the angel schools and take care of our siblings in these upper dimensions."

"And remember," added Raphael, "God is always with you, and guiding you, regardless of whether Gabriel, Michael, and I are involved."

"Exactly!" said Gabriel, "Each of you has a direct connection to God; it is the link with your higher consciousness, deep within you, and will always guide you forward. You do not require anyone to intercede on your behalf, whether it is me, Michael, Raphael or anyone else, but you must work to tap into this link. Each of you has the ability to access God directly. However, do not make the mistake of linking to your ego, for it will get in the way and will certainly lead you astray." All the angels murmured in agreement, with some not at all confident they could access God directly.

Gabriel picked up where he left off. "We need to understand why people are committing so many wrongs, and why they find it so difficult to forgive one another."

Another angel asked, "Archangel Gabriel, why is God allowing angels to visit Earth, and why has He given instructions to establish the system of repaying debts in our physical lives on Earth? If He forbade us to associate with the material world, then we would obey Him. Would that not be easier?"

Gabriel answered, "Yes, it would. But that would defeat the whole purpose of our individual existence. God has granted us free will: to make our choices both on Earth and in the heavens. Life on Earth is a gift from God, a place where we are able to experience His creation. However, our journey must not allow our egos to break through and take control of us, staining our spirit with selfishness, jealousy, and hate. For those of us who fall into this trap, it is important to recognise our mistake and seek forgiveness."

"Conversely, if we are wronged by someone, we must find it in our hearts to forgive, for it is the only way to be free from this tie. If, however, one or neither party is remorseful or merciful, as the case may be, then God has provided a means to rectify the situation through this system of repayment." The angels discussed these matters amongst themselves and Gabriel gave them the necessary time and space. After a few minutes, he continued, "What is important to grasp is that free will is at the heart of our existence. God does not dictate our thoughts and actions. If He did, what would be the point of our existence? It is incumbent on us to govern our behaviour and take responsibility for our actions."

"We will try our utmost," responded one angel.

"Good! Now, are there any more questions before we proceed?" asked Gabriel.

With nothing more to discuss, Gabriel requested the angels to ready themselves for their assignments. He organised the missionary angels based on where they would intervene on Earth, for there were now several land masses that made up the world. They all split into groups and prepared themselves.

In order to ready himself to take on human form, Gabriel transcended into God and meditated in silence. He was beginning to grow weary from all the effort, and he rested within God until he felt ready for his task. When he finally felt rejuvenated and glowed brightly again, he invoked, "In the name of God, the most Beneficent, the most Merciful."

"My dear child," said God, "You are as true and pure as when you first burst forth. You are My closest child and are the most like Me. Your compassion for your siblings pleases Me, and I am proud of you. And as I have already conveyed to you, do not regret the mistakes you made in not identifying the troublemakers early on – you are the most like Me, but you are not perfect. Perfection only lies within Me, in the highest consciousness."

"And do not be disappointed with your siblings. They will learn and they will return home to Me. But if you are willing and able, you must continue with your endeavours to awaken them. I am pleased that you will enter Earth as a human being again, however, you must be born female, for My children have decided to regard their feminine side as inferior to their masculine. As a female, you will embrace your femininity and allow these virtues to manifest. You will comprehend the pain and suffering that many of My children endure. It will enable you to better understand why many angels find it so difficult to forgive, even though compassion and mercy is intrinsic to their being. Now go forth, and remember that I am always with you, guiding you and protecting you. And during your life on Earth, when you go through your hardships and difficulties, turn to Me and I will help you through these. Remember Gabriel, you are never alone. I am always with you."

Gabriel bowed his head and recited, "Thy Will be done on Earth as it is in Heaven." He descended to the fourth dimension and briefed Michael and Raphael.

"God instructed you to be born female?" said Michael, looking up suddenly.

"But God always leaves such decisions to each individual," said Raphael.

"I know," said Gabriel, "but these were His explicit instructions."

They thought no more about it and initiated their search for parents through whom Gabriel could be born a girl. The Archangels focussed their attention on the Have-nots, for it was only through this half of society that Gabriel would be able to fully experience the necessary hardship. They identified a couple who seemed to be good-hearted even though they did not view women as equal to men, however this was generally the case all over the world. The family had several children and had divided the roles of the boys and girls very clearly in their household and in the life around them. They struggled for basic survival, but this was exactly the type of experience that God asked Gabriel to acquire.

"These are the parents I choose," said Gabriel, "and for all that they will do for me, I will work hard to improve their situation." The father's name was Louis and he toiled daily at the menial jobs he was able to secure. The mother, Chantal, worked tirelessly to provide a loving home for her family. While they were both happy to learn they were to have another child, each secretly worried about having an additional mouth to feed.

"I am looking forward to having all these brothers and sisters," said Gabriel.

"They will be able to guide you in your early years and support you in later life," said Raphael.

"Remember, we will be watching over you," said Michael.

"I will, and thank you," said Gabriel, as he withdrew to prepare himself for his journey.

At the appointed time, Gabriel slipped into the body and patiently waited for the birthing process. When Chantal went into labour, Gabriel invoked God's name and prayed for strength and courage to complete the work successfully; he also asked God to bless this family who were about to welcome him.

"It's a girl!" said the midwife, holding the baby out to Chantal. Gabriel was born a beautiful and delicate baby. She smiled and looked inquisitively at the adults around her.

"A girl?" said Louis, "We don't need another girl in the family! We have enough mouths to feed! I need more boys! How is a girl going to help feed the family? She will just be another burden. Get rid of her!"

"No!" screamed Chantal.

An uproar of voices shocked the baby and she began to cry. Chantal tried to soothe her, but the baby was suddenly wrenched from her arms and whisked away.

Gabriel was confused. Gusts of icy air hit her face, chilling her to the bone. She could only convey her distress by crying. She writhed in discomfort as her tiny hands and feet grew numb with cold.

"This is unbearable!" thought Gabriel, "I am trapped in this body and my nascent brain will not allow me to communicate." Gabriel suddenly felt herself falling and she hit the ground with a thud. Sharp bolts of pain reverberated throughout her body and she screamed in agony.

"Why is it colder? What is bearing down on my chest?" thought Gabriel anxiously, "It's too heavy! I cannot breathe!" She tried to scream louder to convey her anguish, but only managed a gurgle – she gasped for air.

"I cannot see anything!" panicked Gabriel, "why has it gone so dark? My body no longer works but I am trapped inside. What is happening? God! Where are You? Please help me!"

"I am with you," said God, "Do not be alarmed. Just remain calm and I will bring you home."

Suddenly, Gabriel was drawn up in a powerful swoop, and all his pain and discomfort disappeared. Michael and Raphael received him, and cradled him in their light until he was able to reacquaint himself. They waited patiently and continued to project their light and love on him to help him recover. It took some time before Gabriel regained his awareness and was able to get over the shock. He finally began to speak.

"I cannot believe what just happened," he whispered, "It was a terrifying experience. How can one being do this to another? How can one person take another's life?" Gabriel bent heavily with sorrow. He could not stand up; his light had faded into dullness and his energy vibrated very slowly. "I was completely helpless," he said tearfully, "There was nothing I could do to protect myself. I was entirely dependent on those around me. Never before have I been in a situation where I had no control over my fate."

Michael comforted Gabriel and gently said, "You are okay now. You are with us and you are safe."

Gabriel calmed himself and drew in strength from those around him. Everyone sat in silence, continuing to project their light and love on him. After a few minutes, Gabriel said, "I am better now," as he picked himself up and rose to his full height. "What shall we do next?"

"Not so quickly, Gabriel. Strengthen yourself further," said Michael, "and then you know you will have to find it in your heart to forgive them."

"Yes, I know," sighed Gabriel, "Maybe I do need more time to recover from this incident." He made his way to a quiet corner. He allowed his tears to fall, and then closed his eyes and meditated silently. When he felt at peace again, he slowly stood up, and with all the strength and determination he could muster, he uttered, "God, please help me to forgive. Bless me with a soft heart and generosity of spirit to show mercy to those who wronged me, including my father, my mother, and those who attended my birth, for none prevented the incident from occurring. And especially help me to forgive the one who buried me alive."

Gabriel knelt down and prayed in silence. After several minutes, he raised his head and declared, "I forgive you all for the wrongful act you committed against me. God, please bless all of us with Your mercy and grace."

Michael and Raphael came towards Gabriel; they were pleased that he was able to look past the cruelty and overcome his ordeal. The three embraced one another.

"What do you want to do next?" asked Michael.

"We continue with our task," replied Gabriel, "for I still need to be born female." They smiled warmly at one another, and once again commenced their search for a new set of parents. Even though it would take time to find parents in the appropriate circumstances, they did not let this setback thwart their plans, and they continued their quest in earnest.

Then one day, after what would have been a few years in Earth time, an angel rushed towards them, imploring Gabriel to forgive him. The angel was distraught and dark with despondency.

"Please forgive me, Gabriel!" he pleaded, "I did not know it was you who was born as my baby girl! If I had known, I would have never had you killed! Why did God not intervene to stop this? Why did He let this happen?"

Gabriel recognised his father Louis, and felt anger rise within him. "It does not matter whether it was me or another! Would you really have no remorse if you had killed another? You committed a grave offense by killing a human being. You must understand that each life form has its reason for being, and must be respected and treated with kindness and love!" shouted Gabriel. Louis looked down in shame.

Gabriel was enraged. "You question why God did not stop you? What has God got to do with you rejecting and killing your child? God gave you free will. It is you who chose to be born on

Earth, it is you who chose to venerate the male gender over the female, and it is you who chose to reject the baby girl and take her life away! You made these decisions, not God!

Gabriel's anger exploded. "In life, each situation and circumstance with which you are presented happens for a reason, and how you choose to react will set in motion a series of events that will not only affect you, but those around you and beyond! So do not put the onus on God for your narrow-mindedness, for your spiteful behaviour! With free will comes responsibility! You are responsible for your actions, as well as all consequences that result from them, not God!"

Louis was desolate and grew greyer with shame; he bent down in despair. Michael and Raphael held Gabriel and tried to calm him by projecting their light and love on him. They placated him and prayed to God to bless Gabriel with love and mercy. They also projected their light and love on Louis, trying to raise his spirit.

Gabriel finally managed to centre himself, and gently said to Louis, "If you approach each situation with good intentions and love, you will never go amiss."

Gabriel knelt down and asked God for strength to overcome his anger, rise above his ego, and express his love. He prayed in silence for a few minutes and then rose to address Louis, "I have already forgiven you, so raise your head and arise." Gabriel moved towards Louis and lifted his spirit to embrace him. Gabriel soothed Louis and conveyed his forgiveness and love. Both began to shine brightly with relief and tranquillity.

"Thank you, Archangel Gabriel," said Louis, "thank you for being so generous with your mercy. If you had not forgiven me, my bad deed would have weighed heavily on me and plagued me for hundreds of years, if not longer."

Gabriel smiled. "We are finished with this incident, but you must learn from it and not make this same mistake again. Remember, femininity and masculinity are equally important, and make up the whole of our being. God created both the male and female form on Earth, and neither is superior to the other. Now, I advise you to attend the angel schools so that you may learn more about love, kindness, compassion, and mercy." With these words, Louis twinkled and sparkled towards the schools, grateful that he had been forgiven by the Archangel.

Michael and Raphael realised that with all that had transpired, they were experiencing what effort it took to be merciful. They also noticed that despite his joy, Gabriel was not completely himself.

Michael turned to Raphael and said, "I wonder whether I should volunteer to be born on Earth, and give Gabriel a break. What do you think?"

"It is a good idea, but only if you wish to do so," said Raphael, "I, myself, have no desire to be born on Earth and physically experience God's creation. My ethereal existence is enough for me. I really do not think I can go through some of the hardships that physical life on Earth entails. And I agree, Gabriel needs a break. If you want to do this, then go ahead. I will support you." They approached Gabriel with this idea.

"You are both very astute at reading me," said Gabriel, "I suppose I know what courage it took for me to forgive Louis. It is harder than you think. I had to reach deep into my being to find love and mercy. I am worried that many will not have the courage and determination to do this. As we have seen, our siblings are choosing to enter life again to repay their debts, for at first blush, it seems like the easier path. But in actuality, it is the more difficult one. In the end, everyone must forgive. If only we all recognised that."

"But Michael," continued Gabriel, "are you sure that you wish to take human form? Do not do this as a sacrifice for me, for even though I had a terrible experience, I am strong enough to withstand a lifetime on Earth."

"You must rejuvenate, Gabriel," said Michael, "It is my

choice to enter life on Earth, and I wish to do this to help with God's work. It is a promise I also made."

"Very well, Michael. Thank you for giving me this opportunity," said Gabriel, who was genuinely grateful for the respite.

The three Archangels began looking for a set of parents through whom Michael would be born on Earth.

9 MICHAEL

Life in the heavens continued as normal, with angels attending the angel schools, and others choosing to be born on Earth. Raphael took on greater responsibility for the schools, practically managing them on his own. He also counselled those who wished to evolve their consciousness even further. This greatly assisted Gabriel, for his energy was consumed with supervising the millions of guardian angels, transmitting messages to those missionary angels who took physical form on Earth, and monitoring the evolution of the world.

Their search for suitable parents for Michael finally resulted in identifying a couple who were of modest means but were part of a loving family. Michael chose this couple, and to be born male.

"Do not forget who you are, Michael," said Gabriel, "I will be close to you throughout your lifetime." Even though Michael had been assigned a guardian angel during his physical life, Gabriel wanted to keep a particular eye on him and help him through his first experience in human form. "God will be constantly with you," continued Gabriel, "And through your hardships and troubles, turn to Him and seek His blessings for strength and courage."

"Thank you, Gabriel" said Michael, and he withdrew into God to prepare himself. When the appointed time arrived, Michael slipped into the body and was born a hearty, healthy boy.

"What a beautiful baby!" said the midwife, as Michael squirmed and fussed in her arms. She handed him to his mother, who tried to pacify him. He began screaming incessantly.

"Why is he crying like this? Is something wrong?" asked the father.

"Maybe he's hungry," said the mother. They tried to feed him but he would not latch on. They tried layering him with blankets to keep him warm, but he struggled against them.

"Let's try rocking him," said the mother. Both the father and mother took turns, but he sobbed relentlessly regardless of what they did to appease him. They examined him closely and found nothing wrong, yet Michael seemed tormented.

Gabriel watched from above.

"I think Michael feels trapped in his human body. He probably finds the experience suffocating," said Gabriel, remembering the sensations he experienced the first time he was born. "Poor Michael! Maybe this was a mistake. I should never have let him take my place. I know how difficult and confining it can be to live in a human body."

"But it was Michael's choice," said Raphael, "He will seek God's help and establish the link. Let us pray to God to help him."

Suddenly they heard Michael call out, "God, please help me!" God slowly began wrapping His light around Michael and he began to calm down. Both Archangels were relieved and remained with baby Michael, willing him to remember they were right there beside him. Michael began to re-establish his link with the fourth dimension.

"Gabriel! Raphael! You are both here," said Michael.

"Of course, Michael," said Gabriel, "we are all here for you. Be calm and confident knowing you are not alone. You are well-protected by us and your parents, as well as by God."

"Thank you both, and thank God! I will try to do my best in this world," said Michael, and he finally settled down in his body, turned to his parents, and smiled.

"Go ahead and return to your work, Raphael. I want to watch over Michael a little while longer," said Gabriel.

As time marched on, Michael grew to be a very strong boy, and finally matured into an even stronger man. His robust physique betrayed the gentility of his soul.

He took responsibility for his family's welfare and cared for those members of his community who were particularly vulnerable. He was regarded as a dependable man of good character, and many looked up to him as a leader amongst men.

His tribe worked hard to secure their living and maintain a decent existence. Michael worked the fields and tended the animals, and tried to be helpful to all those around him. He seemed genuinely happy and content in his life.

He often spent time alone to ground himself spiritually, and continued to maintain the link with the fourth dimension. Michael learnt a great deal about the trappings of the world and taught those around him about their true inner self, with Gabriel guiding him every so often.

Then one day, Michael's life dramatically changed.

As he tilled the fields with his fellow tribesmen, a neighbouring tribe attacked the community. Michael dropped his tools and rushed to the village to protect the women and children. He tried to stop the aggressors by appealing to their good conscience.

"Why are you hurting these people?" shouted Michael, "They have not done anything to you! These women and children are innocent. Your behaviour is reprehensible! Do you not understand that none of us is your enemy? Ask us for what you want. Let us talk about whatever is troubling you." But the aggressors were not ready to listen, and shouted something about revenge for something someone had done, and the situation deteriorated very quickly. A mob of men pounced on a group of women and children, striking out with their knives and machetes. One after the other, children fell to the ground while their mothers tried to shield them with their own bodies. Gabriel watched in horror as Michael picked up an axe and jumped into the fray.

"God! Help them! Calm them down so they can talk through their problems," said Gabriel, as he himself flew in to protect the women and children. Michael fought off the attackers and protected the victims with his body. Suddenly, a knife cut across Michael's arm spurting blood everywhere. He instinctively struck out with his axe, knocking his attacker to the ground. The attacker did not get up – blood poured from his crushed skull.

Michael screamed. "Why? Why did this have to happen? I have taken a life! Please help me!" said Michael, falling to his knees.

Gabriel and Raphael rushed towards the scene as Michael lay sobbing beside the lifeless body. Gabriel comforted Michael while Raphael received the attacker as he crossed over into the fourth dimension. Both Michael and the attacker were in shock: Michael, for the blood on his hands, and the attacker, for his violent actions that resulted in the loss of his physical life. While Raphael helped the attacker reacquaint himself in the fourth dimension, Gabriel tried to calm Michael down on Earth.

In the meantime, the battle raged on. The marauders vowed to avenge the death of their brother-in-arms.

"Help me!" shouted a woman, as a man tried to assault her. Michael jumped to his feet and ran to defend her, as well as all the women and children caught up in the violence. He maimed and killed many assailants. Gabriel looked on in renewed horror, terrified for Michael, for he knew that Michael would be badly affected by this. Gabriel especially worried that the people involved in the carnage would be burdened with anger, resentment, and grief. He sent a flurry of angels to help soothe their souls.

The battle lasted several hours, and when the few remaining attackers fled, Michael finally stopped. He was surrounded by death and destruction. He fell to the ground and wept uncontrollably, devastated by the brutality: the people had inflicted great pain on one another. Gabriel knelt beside him and tried to heal his soul, whispering to him, "I am here with you. Remember that God is ever-present, and that all will be well again." But Michael was inconsolable.

Gabriel and Raphael called upon more angels to assist with

this terrible situation, and hundreds of them descended on Earth. They helped all those involved in the conflict, both aggressors and victims alike, endeavouring to bring love and peace into their hearts and heal their souls. Hatred and fear could not be allowed to take hold.

Gabriel watched as a few villagers assisted Michael and carried him home. Michael isolated himself, weeping and crying for hours at a time. He refused to interact with his family or friends, and had sunk so profoundly into his grief that he could no longer hear Gabriel – the link with the fourth dimension was severed. But more alarmingly, Michael was too devastated to even reach out to God. Days, then weeks passed in this manner, with Michael refusing to eat, or even help with the recovery efforts. His moods were unpredictable; he would get angry very easily, and many people kept their distance. Gabriel tried to reach Michael, to jolt him awake, so that he would remember that he was really an angel and could overcome this awful experience. Gabriel was desperate to establish the link with Michael, but despite his efforts, Michael did not hear him: Michael was too deep in sorrow.

Years went by with Michael barely interacting with the world, too broken to deal with the loved ones around him. Finally, one day, Michael was so desolate and miserable, he seriously considered ending his life. Gabriel tried valiantly to link with Michael to discourage him from having these thoughts, for killing himself was as violent an act as killing another human being. Gabriel wanted to help Michael realise that he must forgive the attackers, as well as forgive himself for violence. He would otherwise enter a vicious cycle of debt and obligation that would take many years to complete. But Gabriel also knew that to forgive one's self was even more difficult than to forgive someone else. The pain of guilt and self-loathing was an unbearable existence. How would Gabriel prevent Michael from going down this nightmarish path?

Gabriel appealed to God. "Please help Michael. Tell me what to do to reach him. He only entered the earthly existence to help me. Can You not open his eyes to see us? Please open his heart so he can feel Your presence! He cannot be left to suffer like this!"

"My dear Gabriel," said God, "Michael must choose to open his own eyes and heart. I will not force him, nor will I do it for him. Only when he takes a decision to reach out for help will I intervene – I have already bestowed My love, grace and mercy on him, but will only raise him from his suffering if that is what he wishes. Remember Gabriel, I have granted free will to all My children, whether they are in angel or human form, including to Michael. It is his free will to choose love over indifference; to choose compassion over apathy; to choose forgiveness over guilt and resentment. Every soul has the capacity to reject violence and work towards peace; and Michael has the ability to work through his despair and turn towards hope. He just has to want to."

Gabriel understood God, and realised that he could do nothing more for Michael other than continue his efforts to re-establish the link with him. Gabriel also remembered that when all else failed, prayer and meditation always seemed to work, even if it only provided respite and serenity for a few moments. Gabriel gathered some angels who wished to help and they formed a prayer circle around Michael. They showered him with love, and prayed for his strength and courage to recognise all the hope and good will around him, for many wanted him to recover: not just the angels, but also his friends and family on Earth.

Then one day, Michael sat at his window and watched the children at play. The sun beat down on their bodies as they chased each other about, but they did not seem to notice the heat.

"How wonderful not to have a care in the world," thought Michael, as he moved to his bed and got under the covers. The four walls seemed to be closing in on him. He shuddered, and quietly whispered, "Someone, please help me. I don't know what to do; I don't know who I am. I don't understand what occurred and why, but I know that it was senseless. What happened to me? I'm sure I have a purpose in life, but I don't know what it is. Someone help me..." Michael gradually fell into a sound sleep. He slept for hours, and when he finally opened his eyes, he felt a profound sense of peace: he felt somehow released from his anguish.

Day by day, and little by little, Michael began to feel better. He slowly began to connect with those around him and recognised that his friends and family were there to help him. He also felt a presence, a palpable stillness that seemed to be with him wherever he went. As the months passed, he gradually increased his interaction with the world and even resumed some of his duties in the fields. However, he refused to pick up any sharp tool or instrument, and worked solely with his hands.

Michael also began to pray and meditate on a daily basis in order to ground himself. During one of his meditation sessions, he felt someone calling out to him, an inner voice gently beckoning him into recognition. Michael allowed himself to be drawn in.

"Michael, it is I, Gabriel. Do you remember me?" Michael began to tremble.

"Gabriel?" thought Michael. His anxiety grew and Michael tried to control his breathing, taking deep, long breaths to settle his being. The name sounded familiar, and he knew not to be afraid. He relaxed and let himself be drawn in further. His awareness gently deepened, and he began to remember.

"Gabriel...," thought Michael, "From where do I know this name?" Suddenly, his memories flooded in at once and he began to put the pieces in place.

"Gabriel! Is it really you?"

"Yes, Michael! It is me. Do you remember who you are?"

"Yes, Gabriel, I remember everything. I'm so happy to be reacquainted with you." Michael hesitated, "But I'm ashamed of my behaviour. I was so violent, Gabriel." Michael held his head in his hands. "I became so melancholic I withdrew from those around me. I even contemplated killing myself. I'm ashamed of my conduct."

"Never be ashamed, Michael. Do not be so hard on yourself. You were put in harm's way by others, which necessitated you defending and protecting the weak and vulnerable around you. Things got away from you. You must learn to forgive the tribesmen for what they did, and you must learn to forgive yourself for your own actions and how you dealt with the situation."

"I know, but that is very difficult to do."

"Yes, it is. But as a first step, ask for forgiveness from those whom you have harmed. It is the only way to relieve yourself of your burdens. Ask for forgiveness, and also forgive others. Then forgive yourself. And remember, God has been with you, and will continue to be with you throughout your life. Seek His help. And your guardian angel is constantly with you, too. Do not break the link with our dimension. And I am also here. If you need my help, just call out to me."

"Thank you, Gabriel." Michael remained in quiet contemplation for a few minutes and then arose from his meditation. He looked around him and took in the view. "I have a lot of work to do."

Michael began interacting with the world more fully. With little acts of kindness, he worked daily to open his heart and forgive all those who had caused him harm. He sought out those whom he had hurt and asked for forgiveness, although it was still too dangerous to approach the neighbouring village: the communities held on to their resentment and grief. Forgiveness from those whom he had injured would have to wait.

As time evolved, Michael lived a productive life, but was never fully recovered from his experience. He still went through bouts of depression but managed to lift himself out of these with the necessary help. He could never return to the joy of his youth, but his life was manageable and had its moments of happiness.

As Michael grew old, he found life more difficult to live.

"Gabriel, I am done with life. I want to come home," said Michael.

"You must live out your existence," said Gabriel, "You have not finished your work."

"But I am so tired. I am ready to come back."

Gabriel knew Michael was fragile, and not wanting him to cross over by his own hand, Gabriel encouraged Michael to turn to God for guidance. "It is the only way, Michael. Do not waste this life by not completing your work. But seek guidance directly from God."

During his meditation, Michael implored God to bestow His mercy and return him home.

"My child," said God, "you have not completed your mission yet. Reflect on it further. If you are still insistent on ending your physical life, then I will bring you home. But by no means should you take your own life – it is violence. There is no difference between killing yourself and killing another. In both cases, you harm your soul."

Michael took the time he needed to reflect upon all that had transpired. In the end, he realised he could not let everyone down, especially Gabriel, and so decided to finish his work. He remained resilient in his commitment to God and continued to teach those around him about the importance of love, compassion, and kindness. Eventually after several years, Michael began to suffer from ill health, and he finally passed on and returned to the fourth dimension.

Gabriel, Raphael and others welcomed him home and helped him with the transition. They let him rest and recuperate from his experience while shining their light and love on him. Gabriel, in particular, waited patiently until Michael was ready to speak. After a great deal of time, Michael finally arose.

"Dear Gabriel, I am so sorry it has taken me so long to recover. I am not quite okay, but I know that you must get on with your work with the missionary angels. Let me relay to you what I learnt."

"I am just so happy to have you back with us," said Gabriel.

Michael continued, "Life on Earth is very difficult now, with many warring tribes inflicting harm on each other, justifying this in the name of one cause or another. In many instances, one does not have a choice but to enter into these battles, just to protect the innocent and vulnerable. While many choose not to behave violently, they still get caught up in the wave of violence. It takes only one person to initiate violence, and it also takes only one person to stop it. The difference between them is that the former is goaded by fear, and the latter is fuelled by courage. However, to have the courage to overcome one's fear is not easy. All I know is that it is extremely difficult to exist peacefully when confronted with cruel circumstances."

"People are becoming more and more possessive of the material wealth found on Earth, and are becoming more selfish and self-centred, ready to indulge in violence in its many forms to protect themselves and their possessions from "the other". Not a thought is being given to the condition of their soul, the only part of them that is eternal. Most do not even know that they are spiritual beings who normally exist together in a higher dimension."

"Gabriel, I know it was my choice to visit the world and help you with God's work in this manner, but I never want to return to Earth again as a human being. I found the experience gruelling. I suffered too much, either by my own hand or because of others. I do not think I can withstand a life on Earth, at least not for the time being. I still wish to help you and God with the efforts to awaken humanity, but I wish to do it from here, in the upper dimensions. I do not want to return to Earth again."

Gabriel reached out to comfort Michael and said, "Of course you may continue your work from here. It is always your choice whether you wish to visit the world in human form. There is much unhappiness and suffering in the world, but there is also great joy and goodness, for the world is full of God's greatest creations. Life on Earth is a gift from God for each of us to explore our souls and express our spirits. It provides us with the possibility to raise our consciousness, and with our free will, to choose to be our better selves. The hope and possibility for peace and tranquillity is ever-present in the world. You experienced some harsh episodes and entered a particularly difficult situation. But I am glad that you will continue your work from here."

"Now, you must rest further," continued Gabriel, "Withdraw into the higher dimensions so that you may reinvigorate yourself. Evaluate your life and determine whether there is any unfinished business. Return to your work only when you are well-recovered. Raphael and I will carry on with our efforts while you are away."

"Thank you, Gabriel." Having conveyed what he needed, Michael withdrew straight into the seventh dimension to rest within God.

Gabriel was relieved that Michael had pushed through his difficulties and was feeling better, although there existed a blight on his soul, for there were some who still had not forgiven him for his actions. Michael indeed had some unfinished business.

10 COMPASSION

Gabriel turned his attention to the missionary angels. He gathered them together, and with Raphael at his side, said, "As you observed, Michael had a very tough time on Earth and is affected by his experience. Life on Earth can be harsh, and you can easily succumb to the situation in which you find yourself. Your task is now much harder than when you first volunteered for this assignment. Earth's population is growing, and people are becoming rooted in the material. Your purpose has not changed: teach humankind about their true nature, however, you may likely face greater personal struggles. Do you still wish to continue with your commitment? Will you be able to stay true to God and to your promise to Him? There is no dishonour in refusing this next assignment. It is always your choice."

Gabriel gave the group time to reflect upon their decisions. He and Raphael moved to a quiet corner.

"I hope Michael is okay," said Gabriel.

"He will be fine," said Raphael, "He just needs time to recover."

"I still feel bad about him taking my place," said Gabriel, "I should never have let it happen."

"You cannot take responsibility for Michael's experience, Gabriel. It was his choice. Remember, we are all in this together," said Raphael.

"I know," said Gabriel as he looked towards Earth and scanned the heavens, "but it was I who triggered all this."

"And I volunteered to help you," said Raphael, "And so did Michael. Neither one of us was under any illusion that this was going to be easy. Michael will be fine, you'll see."

"I certainly hope so," said Gabriel. One of the angels waved to them. Raphael nodded in their direction.

"It looks like they are ready for us – let us get back to the group," said Raphael.

Gabriel and Raphael sat with the missionary angels and reviewed their assignments to confirm whether each was ready for the work ahead. Some angels opted to recuse themselves, given they had already undergone several lifetimes on Earth. Most, however, wanted to continue with additional worldly tasks. When the time came, they set off again on their missions and were born on Earth in various geographic areas. Gabriel continued to transmit messages to them from the fourth dimension. As they taught their fellow human beings about the importance of kindness, compassion, humility, and generosity, and indeed the meaning of love and forgiveness, there seemed to be a great awakening in the world. Vast swathes of humanity changed their behaviour, and peace began to permeate the atmosphere. A gentle, yet powerful presence settled in; there was an absence of fear in the world, a general feeling of acceptance. Life began to flourish in balance, with each life form making space for the other. Flora, fauna, and humans lived in harmony.

"Do you see, Raphael?" said Gabriel, pointing excitedly to Earth, "When humanity overcomes its ego and works together in harmony for the good of all, we can achieve what we thought was impossible: a perfect balance, an equilibrium of peace and contentment."

But it did not last long. A few who had not embraced the teachings, and indeed, did not believe there was more to their existence than life on Earth, created a backlash. They let their egos get the better of them. Selfishness set in – the one became more important than the many, and the balance shifted. Jealousy, greed, envy, and a host of negative qualities resurrected themselves, leading to corruption and injustice throughout the world. As a result, several missionary angels experienced great hardship.

Gabriel and his team tried desperately to protect the missionary angels and keep them from harm's way. Those who held strong to their spiritual links were able to overcome their trials and lead their communities towards peace. However, others became disoriented and the same patterns began to emerge.

Some missionary angels lost their courage and withdrew into solitude. Others lived in fear and became puppets of society, parroting whatever the powerful wanted to hear, and a few took advantage of their charismatic personalities and held themselves out as special people, chosen by the Almighty to lead humankind – but here was the problem: they were not chosen, rather they volunteered to help God. It was not their message that was to be conveyed to the people, but God's message. Their intentions were wrong and self-serving. In their haze and separation from their spiritual essence, they led groups of human beings astray. Some even held themselves out as demi-gods, as they began believing their own narrative.

As time evolved, humanity assigned various qualities to these demi-gods: the fire god, the rain god, the god of food and plenty, the god of fertility, the sea god, and many other such denominations. God the Creator, that ethereal spiritual energy, was far removed from their belief, if He existed at all. Everything became anthropomorphised.

"How could this happen?" said Gabriel, as he sat down in disbelief. "How could these angels encourage people to worship them as demi-gods? How can these angels propound and accept the belief in a plurality of gods? In my wildest imagination, it never once occurred to me that humankind would go down this path!"

As time evolved on Earth, humanity began to engage in senseless, irrational rituals. People made material sacrifices appealing to these gods, in the hope that they would grant them wealth and fortune. Some even sacrificed their fellow humans, believing this would appease their capricious gods. Humanity moved away from kindness and compassion, and fixated on their superstitions, which developed into traditions. Very few focussed on their own light, that energy and spirit that was part of God Himself.

This upset Gabriel to no end. These few missionary angels had set in motion a series of superstitions, rituals, and traditions that would take millennia to correct. And it was now up to Gabriel to rectify these mistakes. When these culprit angels crossed over to the heavens, Gabriel took them aside, and in no uncertain terms, expressed his displeasure at the havoc they had caused on Earth.

"Do you realise what you initiated? It will have far-reaching consequences, influencing humankind for many, many years. You have further entrenched humanity in the material world," said Gabriel.

"I do not know what happened to me," said one.

"Things just got away from me," said another.

"My ego got me. I started believing my own words," said a third, "Please forgive me."

"You must ask God for forgiveness," said Gabriel, "for you have led His children away from Him. Not only did you not fulfil your promise, but you did more harm."

The angels knelt down with Gabriel and prayed for mercy. God enveloped these angels in a wave of love and warmth. His voice called out to them: "My dear children, you need to learn much about yourselves so that you may evolve your consciousness closer to Me. Evaluate your recent lives on Earth and assess where you went wrong. Of course, I forgive you, but also seek forgiveness from those whom you harmed." With those words, the angels bowed in gratitude and began their soul-searching.

While these particular angels had made some huge mistakes, others had distinguished themselves. Gabriel gathered these few thousand missionary angels and thanked them for their hard work. They had remained true to their commitment to God and had managed to awaken portions of humanity under some very difficult circumstances.

Several hundred years had passed, and throughout this time, Raphael had been busily at work in the upper heavens, helping each angel in one way or another to evolve their spirituality; Gabriel was grateful to have Raphael with him. Gabriel also continued with his own duties, and especially intervened in the tough cases on Earth. Michael finally returned from the seventh dimension, freshly rejuvenated and ready to join them. All three were delighted to be together again, and diligently set about helping all those who required assistance, angels and humans alike.

Then one day, an angel approached them. "Michael, you maimed me when we were on Earth together. I lost my legs as a result of your violent actions. I lived a miserable and pitiful life!"

"I am sorry for the harm I caused you," said Michael, "Please forgive me. I would never have hurt you had you not been one of the aggressors who attacked my village."

"I will never forgive you!" said the angel.

"But you were part of the marauding gang that attacked the village!" intervened Gabriel, "Your intention was to harm Michael and the other villagers! Michael was only protecting the weak and vulnerable. And moreover, Michael has forgiven you for your actions."

"But Michael is an Archangel, and he should have known better," said the angel, self-righteously. "I will never forgive him. Michael, you owe me and you should be punished!"

"Why are you holding Michael to a higher standard?" asked Gabriel, "We are all equal and originate from the same source. Just because Michael has evolved to the higher dimensions does not mean he cannot make mistakes. By you calling him an Archangel does not mean that he should not be forgiven. You have chosen not to evolve to a higher consciousness, but that does not absolve you of responsibility for your actions. Nor does it mean that you should not show compassion to others."

"Please forgive me," begged Michael.

The angel scoffed. "No, I will not. You will have to suffer

for your actions, just as I had to suffer during my lifetime." And with that last remark, he turned his back and smugly flitted away.

"I simply cannot go back to Earth in human form to repay this debt," sobbed Michael, "what do I do? How do I alleviate this burden?" Gabriel and Raphael tried to console him.

Gabriel knew that many were finding themselves in this situation – on the one hand, they had not been forgiven for their actions in the world, but on the other, they did not want to go back to Earth to repay this debt – they could not bear another lifetime.

"We have reached an impasse," said Gabriel, "and we have to find a way through this. Perhaps I should consult God. Raphael, remain with Michael and wait for my return." Gabriel made his way to the seventh dimension.

"In the name of God, the most Beneficent, the most Merciful," invoked Gabriel.

"My dear Gabriel," said God, "why are you so anxious and troubled?"

"My Lord, I am afraid for those individuals who find themselves in a position where they are unable to forgive," replied Gabriel, "They cannot find compassion within them. And I am also worried about those who have sought forgiveness but have not been forgiven. Many of them do not want to return to Earth to live out a life and repay their debt. Michael is one of them who is in this position. What shall be done to help them out of their predicament?"

"They cannot be forced to live on Earth," said God, "To take on human form must be a voluntary act. Establish a system in the heavens where these angels may work off their obligations. They may accept extra duties as guardian angels and guide human beings on Earth, especially those to whom they owe a debt, if the victim chooses to live another life on Earth. In other cases, it may be to act as a guardian angel to those who are suffering from the same afflictions that these angels caused while on Earth."

"But Gabriel, be relentless in teaching about the power of forgiveness, for without it, the victim creates his own miserable existence. My children cannot be so hard-hearted, for this is far-removed from who they really are. Insist on refraining from misdeeds in the first place, and remind My children to allow for compassion and mercy to manifest in their hearts. My children should not let pride and ego blind them into a false sense of justice. But for those who are stubborn and trapped by their ego, permit this system of debt and obligation to also begin in the upper dimensions."

"Yes, My Lord," said Gabriel.

God continued, "But warn Michael and My other children that it will be quicker to get rid of their debt by being born on Earth. Although it can be a harsher, more challenging existence, it is a much shorter time span. If, however, they cannot bear another lifetime on Earth, they can repay this debt in the upper dimensions – but they must be mindful that it will take a great deal longer to rid themselves of their obligations. It will be painstakingly slow. And unless they repay their debts, and just as importantly, learn from their mistakes, My children will not be able to raise themselves to the higher dimensions, closer to Me."

"Thank you, God. I will convey Your message," said Gabriel. Then he continued, "God, we have another problem on Earth. While You have graciously conveyed to me to forgive myself for my naivety in not identifying the troublemakers, I cannot help but regret my mistake. Some of them have caused more havoc on Earth. Instead of bringing human beings closer to You, they have led them astray. Humanity has conjured up a plurality of gods of all shapes and sizes, with various characteristics and qualities. Humankind is engaging in irrational, superstitious behaviour and is doing real harm to themselves and to others. I am afraid for my brothers and sisters, for it will take thousands of years to correct this and bring them back to the truth. It seems that we have taken a few steps backwards."

"My dear Gabriel," said God, "I am aware of all that happens, both on Earth and in all the dimensions, for I am Omnipresent. There is nothing that happens that I do not see or about which I do not know, for I am Omniscient. Yes, many of My children have gone astray. Unfortunately, they do not remember who they are and they do not recognise their power within: the core of their being is like Me, made from My light. When My children first burst forth from Me, I not only granted them free will, but I also bestowed them with intellect – irrationality is not part of who they are - they are supposed to apply their intelligence in their daily lives on Earth as well as in their existence in the higher dimensions. Their intellect and spirit must work in tandem to evolve to the higher dimensions. I have given My children free will: they must take responsibility for how they wish to conduct themselves and how they wish to treat each other. They must not cause harm, and if they do, I am still giving them an opportunity to redeem themselves. If they do not heed My words, I will remove all the beauty and possessions on Earth that influence and prevent them from treating one another with kindness, compassion, and love. Now go and continue your work and help My children, for I am giving them this last chance. Gabriel, remember I am always with you, as I am with all My children."

With these words, Gabriel bowed his head in gratitude and invoked, "Thy Will be done on Earth as it is in Heaven," and returned to the fourth dimension. He conveyed God's words to Michael and Raphael. Michael, in particular, wept with relief and was grateful for God's grace, for he now had a chance to lift his burden without having to return to Earth as a human being; he had been afraid that he would forever carry the weight of his wrong-doings.

The next few years were taken up with the Archangels preparing and organising the system of debt and repayment in the upper dimensions, as well as continuing with all their other work. Michael identified a situation on Earth where a child had lost her legs in an accident, and agreed to be one of her guardian angels throughout her lifetime, which would require him to be present at every moment of her physical life, without taking his eyes off her, even for an instant. He would also have to help other human beings in the same situation for a few hundred more years before he would be able to rid himself of this particular burden. And finally, he had to wait for the opportunity to act as the personal guardian angel for the one whose legs he had originally damaged during his lifetime on Earth. When that angel was reborn as a human being, Michael guided and protected him throughout his lifetime. When Michael did eventually finish with his obligation, he withdrew into God in the seventh dimension and thanked Him for providing a path back to his higher consciousness: it had taken several hundred years.

In reviewing my formative years, I understand now that I had taken on a great deal of responsibility, and without me realising it, I was at the helm of a complex, sophisticated system, managing and coordinating billions of beings, whether they chose to be born on Earth for a period of time or remained in the heavens. How did I get into this situation? I had never planned to be a leader of any sort. All I wanted was to help out a few of my siblings who seemed to have landed themselves in a bit of trouble on Earth. Now I was considered to be a higher being, given the title of Archangel (and I am still not sure by whom), with billions of beings looking to me for advice and direction.

And instead of being just a speck in the universe where all of us could experience God's creativity and "view the painting from within", Earth had become a destination for many souls who had become addicted to the physical world, and where many lowered their spirit to be less than who they were. God provided the opportunity, both on Earth and in the heavens, to reclaim the whole of our being, and it was up to each individual to do so, for God consistently conveyed that He would not take away our free will. He would allow each of us to choose our course of action without intervening. At least, for the moment.

11 OMA

The Archangels carried on working for many hundreds of years, but Gabriel realised there was little progress. The obsession with ritual and superstition gripped humankind, and even though human beings realised their mistakes when they crossed over to the fourth dimension, people continuously lost their spiritual connection when they revisited Earth. The ritualistic beliefs perpetuated themselves.

"I think I should be born on Earth again to try and shake humankind out of their reverie," said Gabriel, "If I can make an impact with my ideas, then maybe it will release some of the people from their preoccupation with these superstitions."

"Are you sure, Gabriel?" said Michael, "Things are even more difficult now than when I was there."

"Yes, I do realise this," said Gabriel, "But I must do something to correct this situation. I made a promise to God to rectify any mistakes the missionary angels made. Whether or not I succeed, I must at least try."

"Gabriel, do what you must," said Raphael, "Michael and I will help you from this side, and also keep watch over everything."

"Thank you, Raphael," said Gabriel, "And Michael, please do not worry. I am strong. My light is powerful and will shine brightly, no matter what my circumstances. And I know that God is with us all the time and helps us through our difficulties. Of this I have no doubt."

"I will support you in all that you do," said Michael.

"Thank you," said Gabriel, "If I manage to convince a few, then we will have an opportunity to work with these enlightened people to influence others. Perhaps this will allow for a new path."

"Do you really think it will work?" said Michael.

"I do not know, but I have to try," said Gabriel, looking towards Earth, "I want to be born a girl, since my previous life was cut short by my then father, Louis. I was never able to experience life as a female. And you will recall that God advised me to be born female so that I could allow my feminine virtues to manifest."

Gabriel frowned and took a step closer to Earth. "I find it very peculiar. Humankind still seems to value the male over the female, which, of course, is absurd. Our light is both masculine and feminine. And on Earth, one literally cannot exist without the other; you need both male and female to propagate the species. In any case, I need to be born into a family that allows me to flourish as a girl so I may reach adulthood and actually fulfil my purpose. Let us begin our search for suitable parents."

They scoured the world from north to south and east to west, and finally found a couple who not only seemed open-minded enough to relish a female child, but would also nurture and encourage her. Gabriel began his inner preparations and waited for them to conceive. At the appointed time, he slipped into the body and was born a beautiful baby girl.

The parents were delighted at the birth of their first child. They named her Oma. They seemed to sense that a strong soul had entered their home and were grateful to the gods for this gift.

Oma was a quiet, serious girl and never seemed to be interested in playing games or running around with other children. She enjoyed conversing with those around her and was curious to learn anything new. She was also a good listener and soaked up information like a sponge. She was an unusual child by society's standards, for her intelligence and curiosity distinguished her not only from her peers, but also from many of the adults in her community. The elders all looked upon her with careful regard, suspicious that she may be one of the gods who had come to Earth in disguise.

Her parents allowed her the freedom to evolve into a strong-willed girl, understanding that this was her nature, and she could not be stymied and made to fit into a certain mould. They, however, kept a close eye on her, as not everyone in the community accepted her atypical behaviour.

Oma's community was not immune to the inter-tribal wars that occurred frequently. Most tribes were insular in their outlook and distrustful of others; they never ventured far from their own, unless they were in need of additional resources, be it water, food, or land to support their growing populations. During such conflicts, warriors usually pillaged the area and captured as many women as possible, which helped to populate their tribe and provide the needed labour for the more arduous work. During her childhood, one such battle reached Oma's village. The men came barrelling down the hills, brandishing all sorts of weapons.

"Oma!" shouted her father, "Oma! Where are you?"

"She's near the tree!" screamed her mother, "Oma, come here!" Oma's parents scooped her up and climbed down into the underground shelter they had dug for just such a purpose. It was dark and damp, and smelled of wet dirt. Oma shivered with cold. Tears ran down her cheeks – she prayed to God to help them through this situation. Guardian angels hovered closely to protect them.

Outside, the battle raged on. Women screamed as they watched their husbands, brothers, and sons killed as the assailants destroyed everything in their path. Michael sent a flurry of angels to help protect all the victims, and Raphael readied his team to receive those who lost their lives.

"If only they remembered they were all siblings-in-light," said Michael, as he watched the savagery unfold – he worried for Oma and her family.

Inside, the hatch was suddenly yanked open from above and the warriors reached down groping for people. Oma's mother clamped her hand over Oma's mouth to keep her quiet, and backed her into the far corner of the shelter out of view. A warrior scrambled down into the hole, and Oma's father ran towards him.

"Please don't hurt me! I will go with you to your village! Don't hurt me!" The warrior pulled him out and then climbed back in to check for more people. He caught sight of Oma and her mother.

"Get out!" he yelled, brandishing a long, sharp blade stained red with blood. The mother carried Oma towards the entrance. The warrior grabbed Oma's mother and held her tightly, locking Oma within her arms. He pushed them up through the hatch. The surface was chaotic. People ran in all directions, screaming and shouting; there was carnage everywhere. In all the commotion, Oma's father saw his chance and ran towards the warrior, tackling him to the ground.

"Run! Run!" the father yelled. Oma wriggled herself out and ran as fast as she could. Her mother also managed to free herself from the warrior's grasp and ran after Oma.

"Oma! Oma!" shouted the mother. Oma stopped and turned around. Her mother caught up to her and Oma leaped into her arms – the mother ran towards the forest to hide from the brutality – but not before Oma saw the warrior raise his weapon and strike her father dead.

"Papa!" she screamed, her face contorting in agony. Michael and Raphael draped a veil of protection around Oma and her mother while she ran as fast as she could. The warrior gave chase and nearly caught up with the pair, but he tripped and injured his leg on a jagged rock.

Still clutching Oma in her arms, the mother ran for several minutes until she found a secure hiding place amongst the trees. Michael remained with Oma and her mother and shielded them from the elements, while Raphael rushed to receive all those who crossed over as they lost their lives. The conflict lasted for hours, and when it finally abated, Oma's mother came out of the trees. When she saw it was safe, she and Oma walked towards the village and joined other families who had come out of hiding. As they surveyed all the destruction surrounding them, it slowly dawned on Oma and her mother that without the father to provide for them, they now had to fend for themselves.

In the fourth dimension, Raphael received Oma's father and helped him with the transition. Oma's father was sad that he had to leave his family, but he was pleased that he was able to save Oma as well as her mother.

"Oma is really Archangel Gabriel?" said the father in disbelief.

"Yes," said Raphael.

"But why would he choose me as his father? I am nobody special."

"Yes, you are. You are kind, compassionate, and open-minded to things unfamiliar," said Raphael.

"I am so honoured to be chosen," said the father.

"Every parent should feel honoured that a child, a particular angel, has chosen them. Families are not created by an accident of birth. A lot of people say 'I did not choose my relatives' – but they did," said Raphael, "They just do not remember."

"May God look after Oma and her mother," said the father, "If you permit me, I would like to watch over them."

"Of course," said Raphael, "Join their guardian angels."

Back on Earth, Oma's mother was overcome with the shock of losing her husband and found life strenuous, but she carried on for Oma's sake. It was a much more difficult life for Oma, too, but she was grateful to have such a good and hard-working mother. Soon Oma reached the age of thirteen and began teaching those around her about the importance of treating one another kindly. She helped wherever she was needed and never refused a request for assistance. She had a sage maturity about her, and the elders became fond of her, although they still remained suspicious about her origins.

Oma's mother was tired and worn out from her hard life, but she lived just long enough to ensure that Oma could fend for herself. When the time came for her passing, Oma's mother readily accepted her fate. Oma was grateful that her mother was able to look after her for as long as she did and asked the angels to help her mother with the transition to heaven.

As Oma grew older, she became a well-respected member of the community, and many individuals sought her advice. She was frequently requested to intervene and mediate during small disagreements and disputes. Oma married one of the boys with whom she grew up, who also happened to be the son of the high priest. She fitted in well with the family and led a normal life by society's standards. Even though her family and community were part of the Have-nots, they worked hard and managed to exist comfortably: they had enough to eat and were well-sheltered in their homes.

Many people increasingly sought Oma's counsel, and her husband and in-laws were proud to have such a highly-regarded wife and daughter-in-law. Her presence also augmented the attendance at the high priest's daily ceremonies for the gods, which made her father-in-law particularly happy.

Then one day during the evening meal, Oma began to question her father-in-law on the meaning behind these rituals.

"What purpose do these ceremonies serve?" said Oma.

"You know they are for the gods," said her father-in-law.

"But isn't it irrational? Some of the ceremonies really are silly. Like sacrificing an animal just to pour blood at the gods' feet. That's just inhumane."

"How could you be so wicked and disrespect the gods?" challenged her husband.

"How could you believe in gods who are angry and merciless, and who apparently are fickle enough to make people suffer if they are not appeased?" retorted Oma, "It makes no sense at all!"

"Hush! The gods may hear you and bring bad fortune to our house," said her mother-in-law. She looked around nervously.

"A god should be loving, kind, and forgiving, not ill-tempered and reckless. I will only pray to one god, and that is God, the Creator, the Great Force, who and which is compassionate and merciful." Oma stood up from the table, leaving her family speechless.

"Who does she think she is?" said the father-in-law, "I have allowed her to have a life outside of the household and counsel people, but I will stop her if she gets too bold."

"I told you not to give her so much freedom. She should be helping me in the house," said the mother-in-law. She turned to her son, "Can't you keep her under control?"

The son looked exasperatingly at his mother and left the table.

From that day onwards, Oma began to pray in her own manner, alone and silently, refusing to participate in the daily offerings and rituals to the gods of her family. Many of those who sought her counsel joined her in her prayers, and soon, many villagers, especially the young, began to follow her teachings.

One day, the elders visited the family.

"Welcome to my home," said the high priest.

"Is your daughter-in-law here?" asked one elder.

"No, Oma is out," said the high priest.

"Good, because we want to speak to you about her. We're concerned that she's spreading all sorts of ideas that are destabilising the community. We don't know where she's getting these ideas from, but as you know, women are not rational creatures. We almost need to protect them from themselves!" said one elder.

"And she's even influencing my daughters. How will I find husbands for them if they try to follow that hysterical woman? Really, Oma should know her place and do what she's good at and born to do. Women must provide stability in the home and leave us to manage our lives and the community," said another elder.

"I will try to reign her in," said the high priest.

Over the next few weeks, Oma and her father-in-law argued constantly, with the rest of the family intervening to calm matters down.

"Oma, can't you just give in to my father?" asked the husband, "You can still believe and practice what you want. Just don't spread your ideas around the community."

"But that would be hypocritical," said Oma, "and I can't live two separate lives to please your father and the elders. In any case, I have to speak the truth. There is only one God, who is a kind, compassionate, spiritual energy."

In time, Oma became estranged from her husband and decided to return to her own home. Eventually, the villagers divided their loyalties, with some following the high priest with his daily offerings and sacrifices to the gods, while others followed Oma's teachings, which were rooted in principles: compassion and kindness to all, to live with integrity, to serve others, and to show gratitude and appreciation for the Universe by respecting all life forms around them. Oma worked hard to instil these values and lead her followers towards the truth. She found it very difficult at times, for in addition to her role as a counsellor, she supported herself and earned her basic living. She worked her small field to grow her food, and many times held her teaching and counselling sessions there. It was not unusual to see groups gathered around her while she toiled away at the dirt; she always planted extra in order to share her harvest. Eventually, Oma came to be regarded as a high priestess in her own right.

From the other side, Michael and Raphael supported Oma and provided her with moral courage during the very difficult times. When Oma began to age, she asked them to send a few missionary angels to be born in her village, so that she could train them to take over and continue her work once she departed from the world. Many years passed as these students grew and matured into adults, and when they were ready, several of them left the village to travel and see the world, carrying her teachings to other societies. As the knowledge began to spread well-beyond her community, Oma knew she could let go: the time of her passing was near. When it finally came, Oma was relieved to have completed her work and was ready for her departure – her body was exhausted with the physical labour.

"Welcome home!" exclaimed Michael and Raphael, as Oma crossed over. They gave her time to get reacquainted with the fourth dimension. Many angels gathered round and projected their light and love on her.

"I am so happy to be home!" said Gabriel, as his full awareness manifested, "Although I am tired, it was good for me to experience such a life."

"You did it, Gabriel!" said Michael, "You managed to accomplish your goals as Oma."

"Even though my body was not regarded as beautiful according to society's standards, it was strong and healthy, and it served me well. I am, however, relieved to be rid of it – it is wonderful to be light and free again! Anyway, the important thing is that the teachings spread far enough on Earth. Humanity may just have a chance to redeem itself."

"Things are working well on this side, too. We have managed to help many angels evolve to the higher dimensions," said Michael.

"The angel schools seem to be achieving their purpose. But we will brief you later. It is time for you to relax and recover from your ordeal," said Raphael.

"Thank you both for your help, protection, and support during my lifetime," said Gabriel. And with these words, he withdrew into God.

12 HUMILITY

Gabriel rested within God and meditated for quite some time. Once he felt well enough, he raised himself and invoked, "In the name of God, the most Beneficent, the most Merciful."

"My dear child," said God, "are you well-recovered from your sojourn?"

"Yes, My Lord," replied Gabriel.

"Good. Now tell Me, what did you learn?" said God.

"I learnt a great deal, My Lord," said Gabriel, "A lot of fear has entered the world – people are gripped by fear. It is the basis for all their decisions and actions. They are scared for their well-being, so they become selfish and possessive. They are scared of others because they do not know them or understand them, so they become unkind and hostile. This fear has led to a great deal of violence, suffering, and injustice. If only human beings would embrace love rather than fear, they would experience a much more pleasant life and could really concentrate on achieving the peace and happiness they so desire."

"Very well. Now tell Me about your experience as a female," said God.

"My life as a female was challenging," said Gabriel, "I had to overcome the many obstacles put in my way by society's attitudes. Rather than assessing my abilities and skills, I was constantly consigned to particular tasks and prevented from doing others, just because I had a female body. And what really hurt, and certainly frustrated me, was people's assumption that I did not have the intelligence to undertake a certain responsibility, just because I had female form. While I rebelled against every prejudice and overcame these obstacles, it took tremendous effort and strength of spirit – I had to be relentless."

"I see. Did you achieve your purpose?" said God.

"My Lord, I am confident that my objective to establish a new path was accomplished, where human beings embrace their intellect and refrain from irrational rituals, and where values such as love, generosity, and kindness towards one another take precedence over their traditions or belief systems," said Gabriel, "If this change takes root, humankind may just be able to succeed and achieve enlightenment. I am, however, still concerned about the troublemakers, those angels who are still mesmerised by Earth and its materiality. They have grown dark with greed and jealousy, and they must be awakened to their true selves."

"My child, I watched over you throughout your lifetime," said God, "and I am happy with your progress. But you must not be complacent. Continue your efforts to awaken My children to their true, powerful selves, and do not be disheartened if some remain unenlightened. My children will return home to Me one day. Help them to follow the path you established on Earth. However, this is their last chance to heed My words. If they continue to harm each other, I will remove all the beauty and possessions on Earth that intoxicate My children and prevent them from treating one another with kindness, compassion, and love."

"Yes, My Lord," said Gabriel.

"And remind My children: I am always with you and watch over you. When you are in difficulty, seek my assistance and I will raise you from your troubles," said God.

"I will, My Lord," said Gabriel.

"And convey to all My angels that I am proud of the work they are doing and all that they have accomplished," said God, "Michael and Raphael have done particularly good work and have managed to help many of their siblings raise their awareness and come closer to Me. Convey my special blessings to them all."

"I will, My Lord," said Gabriel.

"And Gabriel, remember that of all My children, you are the most like Me, but you are not perfect," said God, "Neither are the rest of My children. So do not be disillusioned if your efforts to help your siblings do not take hold. To change people's beliefs requires perseverance: it is a difficult task. Do not underestimate the allure of the physical world."

"Yes, My Lord," said Gabriel.

"Now carry on with your work, Gabriel," said God.

"Thy Will be done on Earth as it is in Heaven," said Gabriel, as he descended to the fourth dimension.

"We have been anxiously waiting for you," said Raphael.

"I have a message for you from God," said Gabriel, and he proceeded to convey all that God had said.

"So we must not underestimate the allure of the physical world. I suppose this is what grips the dark angels," said Raphael.

"We need to convey the message to the missionary angels," said Gabriel, "Michael, would you please gather them?"

Once the ten thousand missionary angels arrived and settled down, Gabriel addressed them. They were elated to receive, and readily accepted, God's blessings. When everyone dispersed and returned to their various duties and assignments, Michael had a private word with Gabriel.

"It is good to have you here," said Michael, "Even though you undertook some much needed work on Earth, Raphael and I missed your presence."

"I am glad to be back," said Gabriel, "I just hope the new path takes root and guides humanity in the right direction."

"We will work hard to make this so," said Michael, "Though I am a bit concerned for Raphael. He has been working very hard for many thousands of years now and seems tired."

"Yes, I noticed that he is not shining as brightly as he normally does," said Gabriel, "He probably needs a break."

"With you back in this dimension, we can manage the

work and let him take some time away," said Michael.

They looked over at Raphael, who was busy flitting around from angel schools to Earth and to the higher dimensions, helping everyone along the way. Gabriel and Michael looked at each other in amazement, for it was a sight to behold the beauty of Raphael: he emanated pure love.

"How can God call me His closest angel, when Raphael has the very qualities that I feel when I am within God?" said Gabriel.

"I know exactly what you mean," said Michael, "the purity of his light is astonishing. I feel rejuvenated just by standing next to him. But Gabriel, do you not realise how powerful your light is?"

Gabriel scoffed. "No more powerful than yours and Raphael's. Now come, let us relieve Raphael." They made their way towards him.

"Raphael," said Michael, "it is time to take a break and rest within God. Gabriel and I will manage the work."

"But I am fine," said Raphael, "I love to serve my fellow beings. It is my greatest joy and happiness."

"I see how much this work pleases you," said Gabriel, "but that is not the point. It is time to rest. There is much work to do in the future, and all three of us will have to be strong and able. Take the time now."

"Very well, then, I acquiesce," said Raphael, as he bowed his head. And in a flash, he withdrew into God.

Gabriel made his way to the angel schools. Over the years, he had visited them many times, but had not focussed his attention on their development and had generally left it all to Raphael. This was Gabriel's opportunity to evaluate the system and also teach a few classes.

When he arrived, Gabriel was thrilled to see so many angels willing to learn. He began by giving several lectures and augmented these with extra lessons. He also provided specialised tutoring for those angels who were on the cusp of evolving to the fifth dimension but needed a boost to help them overcome those qualities that held them back. Gabriel enjoyed the interaction with the students but then grew restless; he was curious to see how many angels had evolved into the higher dimensions.

"Michael, is it okay with you if I visit the higher dimensions?" said Gabriel, "I want to see what is happening."

"Of course," said Michael, "I have everything under control. I can manage on my own for a little while."

"Okay, I will return soon." With Michael securely at the head of all operations, Gabriel commenced his ascent. As he arrived, he was surprised to see the number of angels residing in the fifth dimension, and they all rushed to greet him.

"Oh Archangel Gabriel!" they exclaimed, "How kind of you to visit us! We are delighted to see you. We now have a chance to thank you for all you have done to help us develop. It set us on a course to achieve the ultimate peace and contentment. We say a prayer for you every day." This brought a tear to Gabriel's eye. He did not realise that so many were crediting him with their achievement.

"I am humbled by your prayers for me," said Gabriel softly, "but it is you who have done the work. I only conveyed God's message to you; it is you who have taken heed and absorbed the teachings."

"But you are the one who volunteered to help God with His work. You cared about our well-being and took responsibility. Without your love and care, we would never have reached such heights." Gabriel felt his aura swell with brightness. "Will you please teach us to evolve further? We want to reach the sixth dimension."

"Of course I will." Gabriel spent some time with them, coaching them on how to meditate deeply and release their ego. "The more you open up and let go of any fear lurking within, the closer you will be to your light." Once he completed his tutorial, he took their leave and ascended to the sixth dimension.

"We are happy to see you, Archangel Gabriel," said the angels in the sixth heaven, receiving him warmly. "We keep you in our prayers every day for all your selfless service. You are our role model, and we hope we can progress to the seventh dimension and meet God "face-to-face" as you have." They tilted their heads forward and knelt down. Gabriel was taken aback by this gesture, and his aura inflated and intensified in brightness. He suddenly realised that all this praise was feeding his ego, and he immediately knelt down to level himself with the others.

"Oh God," prayed Gabriel, "Please help me to remain humble. Keep me grounded in the knowledge that I am but one of Your children, and that I am neither above nor beneath but am equal to my siblings, as they are to me." Gabriel meditated for some time before he raised his head. The angels were struck by his actions; they were eager to learn from him.

"Archangel Gabriel," said the angels, "how do we take the final step and evolve to the seventh dimension? Please teach us what we are supposed to do. We have let go of our egos, we pray in silence, and we have been meditating for many years now. But we cannot seem to reach the final goal. What do we do?"

"My dear siblings-in-light," said Gabriel, "before I help you with your quest, I want to talk to you about something. Please come and sit with me." The angels circled round him and seated themselves. "I must ask you to refrain from venerating me so," continued Gabriel, "You and I are the same, we are equal. To this day, I do not understand why I am being called Archangel, nor do I understand from where this term originated."

"But we only want to convey our respect for you," said one angel.

"Respect is one thing, but veneration is quite another. Do not worship me, for it contributes nothing: it does not help me, nor does it help you. Respect me as I respect you. Have confidence in me to guide you, but have faith in God. Venerate God, and worship Him," said Gabriel.

"We understand. But please permit us to continue addressing you as Archangel. It is our way of conveying respect."

Gabriel sighed in resignation. "Very well. Now, let us turn to your desire to reach the seventh dimension. Continue as you have been: pray and meditate, and you must have the courage to persevere. When God believes you to be ready to meet Him, He will open up the heavens and allow you into His abode. But remember one thing: just because you attain such a high level of consciousness does not mean you cannot, and should not, serve others. Enlightenment is truly achieved when you are able to maintain your high level of awareness and still love and serve others, regardless of their station: this is the destruction of the ego. It is godliness."

The angels looked at each other, for finally, the penny dropped. They had spent a good part of their existence in the lower dimensions working hard to serve others and internalise the qualities of love, compassion and forgiveness. This, in turn, raised their awareness so that they were able to exist in the higher echelons away from the chaotic lower dimensions. But in order to progress to the seventh, they had to be able to serve their fellow beings and maintain their higher consciousness: It was not one or the other, it was both!

Things had come full circle. "How do we serve? What shall we do to help our fellow angels?" they asked.

"There are many opportunities to help those in the fourth and fifth dimensions. And when God requires help and word is sent out, then volunteer for the assignments, even if they take you down all the way to life on Earth. For nothing is more loving and generous of spirit than helping those who are in the depths of despair," replied Gabriel.

"Thank you for your counsel," said the angels, "We will always keep you in our prayers."

"As I will keep you in mine," said Gabriel, and he bowed his head in gratitude.

As Gabriel looked around, the heavens seemed to glow more brilliantly and the angels appeared to sparkle more than usual. Gabriel sighed with relief: for the first time in many thousands of years, there was real hope and optimism.

Before returning to Michael, Gabriel thought he would indulge himself for a little while longer. He withdrew deeply into his light and transcended to the seventh dimension. For a few seconds, he basked in the glory of God, and then noticed Raphael in deep contemplation. Not wanting to disturb him, Gabriel quietly settled into his own spirit and withdrew deeper.

"I wish I could remain here for eternity," thought Gabriel.

"You are not ready yet," said God.

Gabriel smiled. "My Lord, You were not supposed to hear that."

"But I am All-Knowing. I am Omniscient," said God, "and you know that."

"I suppose I do, My Lord," said Gabriel.

"My dear Gabriel, you have much work to do to fulfil your promise and commitment to Me," said God, "To be forever within My Love is something that I desire for all My children, including you, for it means that My children will finally acknowledge that they are light and love itself – it is their very essence. You promised to guide My children towards Me, to awaken them from their slumber, to help them achieve the ultimate peace and contentment. Once you feel this commitment is fulfilled, I will open that space for you, that window of opportunity that will allow you to remain within Me for eternity. But until then, you may only meet me "face-to-face" for a short period, to rest and rejuvenate yourself."

"My Lord," asked Gabriel meekly, "Do You promise that I will have the chance to remain with You permanently when I feel that I have met my commitment? I wish to merge into Your light, just as the river merges into the ocean. It is the only thing I truly desire."

"Yes, My child, it is a promise that I make to you," said God, "But you must understand that in order to merge with My light, you must undergo a process of purification – there will be trials and tribulations that you will have to overcome in order to remove any last vestiges of your ego. It is only in this way that we can merge into One. However, I will provide you with the opportunity, if this is what you want."

Gabriel bowed his head in submission and said, "Yes, it is, my Lord. Thy Will be done in and through me each day; Thy Will be done on Earth as it is in Heaven."

Having witnessed the conversation from his corner, Raphael was absolutely stunned.

"God actually made a promise to Gabriel," thought Raphael, "Not only had God never allowed anyone to remain permanently within His Light, He had never even offered this as a possibility." Raphael relaxed and patiently waited for Gabriel to arise.

Gabriel remained cloistered in God and meditated for some time. When he finally surfaced, he saw Raphael waiting quietly beside him.

"Raphael, how nice to see you. Have you rested enough?" asked Gabriel.

"Yes, and I am ready to return to the fourth dimension. And Gabriel, I witnessed your interaction with God. I will do my utmost to help you fulfil your promise to Him and attain that which you desire most."

"I am touched by your sentiments," said Gabriel, "Your love and selflessness is an example to us all."

"It is I who is amazed by your strength, power, and sense of purpose," said Raphael, "You are relentless in your determination to help our siblings – yours is the true example of love and service to others."

The two Archangels knelt in a prayer of gratitude, and then together, they descended through the heavens eager to connect with Michael.

13 FENG

"We have returned," said Gabriel, as he and Raphael approached Michael.

"Thank God both of you are here," said Michael, "It was getting tough to handle this on my own. Raphael, I am glad to see you looking much better."

"Thank you, Michael," said Raphael, "I suppose I did not realise I needed the rest. So, what shall I take over?"

"Please oversee the angel schools," said Michael.

"I will concentrate on Earth," said Gabriel, "I want to observe how the new path evolves."

"Very well," said Michael, "I will manage the transitions as people cross over."

The Archangels worked diligently to help individuals on Earth and those dispersed throughout the heavens. Gabriel paid particular attention to the happenings in the world. He watched carefully as the values and beliefs he established as the high priestess, Oma, began to spread. This new way of life seemed to suit many societies, and people who absorbed the teachings thrived: knowledge and creativity flourished, coupled with the realisation that there was more to their existence on Earth. Idolatry and mindless rituals were on the decrease, which was particularly encouraging to Gabriel. He was delighted with this development and hoped it would extend to those parts of the world whose inhabitants were still mired in materiality. Many years passed in this manner with the Archangels sharing the responsibilities, each taking turns to watch over humankind.

Gabriel also kept a close eye on the troublemakers in the

fourth dimension and convinced them to refrain from returning to Earth as human beings for the time being, which effectively blocked their ability to influence humanity. These angels were particularly heavy with darkness. They clung together and stared intensely at the world below. From afar, this group resembled a dark bubble in a sea of light, almost creating their own domain of existence within the fourth dimension.

"I will have to get through to them one day," thought Gabriel. He almost dreaded the encounter. He still could not comprehend how any being could turn against their own nature and choose darkness over light.

One day, Michael came rushing to Gabriel and said, "We have a problem. Selfishness is starting to settle in again on Earth. The greed for material possessions is growing. Individuals are letting their egos take over their personas."

Raphael joined them on hearing this news. "Oh Gabriel," said Raphael dejectedly, "I so hoped we would succeed. Perhaps it is a disadvantage that I have never experienced life on Earth. I just cannot comprehend why people are mesmerised by the physical."

"Would you want to be born on Earth?" asked Gabriel.

"I have no desire to take on human form," said Raphael, "I prefer my authentic existence."

"I completely understand. Nonetheless, do not be disappointed with humanity," said Gabriel, "It is very difficult not to be drawn in by the world. Self-preservation is a compelling force – it is borne out of fear. A person will do almost anything to ensure he or she is well-protected and has the necessary wealth to sustain them. The question is, what is an individual's definition of wealth and how much of it do they require to feel secure and content?"

"A human being requires bare necessities for survival," said Michael, "These are water, food, and shelter. Where individuals get into trouble is in the desire beyond this. Some people are satisfied with minimal amenities, while others crave much more. And it is all relative: it is how a person sees himself in relation to another."

"That is why this task is so challenging," said Gabriel, "To pry a person away from their materially-driven life to consider who they are and where they come from is extremely difficult. Yet knowing answers to these very questions will ease their way through life. In any case, God warned me to not be disheartened if this new path did not succeed. And He asked me to persevere and not be complacent. So if you are both willing, we should attempt yet again to push humanity in the right direction."

"Absolutely," said Michael and Raphael.

"But we require reinforcements," said Gabriel, "Let us see whether there are any angels who would like to help us." Raphael put the word out, and many angels came forth to volunteer their services. Gabriel recognised some of them from the sixth dimension. Several thousand missionary angels also came forth for another assignment. Gabriel greeted them all warmly.

"Our dear siblings-in-light," said Gabriel, "If you are willing, you must visit Earth again and take on human form so that you may directly influence humanity. I will join you and be born again on Earth." Michael and Raphael turned to Gabriel in astonishment.

"So I will be with you in the world," continued Gabriel, his eyes twinkling at Michael and Raphael. "I refuse to be complacent and will do whatever is within my capacity. Michael and Raphael will guide us from this dimension, together with those of you who wish to remain here." Gabriel scanned the crowd. "Who is willing to be born on Earth?"

A majority of angels stepped forward.

"Excellent," said Gabriel, "let us split into two groups. Those assisting from this side should assemble around Michael and Raphael for your briefing, and those bound for Earth, please gather around me."

Once everyone sorted themselves, Gabriel addressed his group. "As you all know, I had visited Earth many years ago in order to try and establish a new path, a new way of thinking and looking at things, as a way to jolt humanity out of its traditions of mindless ritual and superstition. I wanted to put the emphasis on love and compassion, rather than the strict dogma and inflexible customs that gripped humankind. While this new path seemed to take root and spread, it is now evident that many have let their egos get the better of them. Greed and jealousy have set in as humans try to out-do each other in order to accumulate wealth and attract love and adoration from their fellow beings. And many still try to appease false gods. They have missed the point of true peace and contentment, and successive generations are falling deeper into this trap. We shall all go together to Earth to try and arrest this development and lead humanity in the right direction."

"You must all choose in which gender you wish to be born, and also in what geographic areas," continued Gabriel, "But you must be born together in groups so that you may impact your particular communities. I, myself, will be born male this time around."

With the briefing complete, the angels worked out the details and put their plans in motion. Gabriel also identified the region in which he wished to be born and chose his parents.

"We are ready from our side," said Michael, as he and Raphael approached Gabriel, "All the guardian angels are assembled and have their assignments."

"Good," said Gabriel, "Now I need to begin my inner preparations."

"We will take over now, Gabriel," said Raphael, "We will ensure all of you get the necessary help from here. Turn to us and we will guide you."

"And remember, God will be with you, so look within," said Michael.

"Thank you both," said Gabriel, and he withdrew into himself in quiet contemplation, readying himself for his journey. When the appointed time arrived, he slipped into the body of the infant and rushed through the birthing process. He flew out quickly and smoothly, as if he had the wind at his back, and was born a beautiful robust boy. His parents named him Feng.

Feng grew into a strong and forthright toddler, tearing around, always in a hurry to get things done. As a young boy, he stood out from his peers, always at the centre of attention, instructing those around him. He was confident, self-disciplined and obedient, but did not follow his parents' ways blindly. He always questioned the meaning or rationale behind something – the word "why" was exasperatingly part of his daily vocabulary.

Feng distinguished himself with his ideas and his ability to communicate them. The elders of the community were impressed with him but felt threatened by his views.

"Where has Feng picked up these rebellious thoughts?" asked an elder.

"Not from us," said the mother, "we have always taught him about our ways."

"Is he somehow possessed?" said another elder, "Maybe he is under some malevolent influence."

"But his ideas are not harmful," said the father, "On the contrary, he wants us to be kind to one another and not be tied to ritual."

Feng did not fear the elders, for he knew his way was correct – he had maintained his link with his inner spirit. His young life very much mirrored that of Oma, the high priestess, who lived a long time before. As Feng grew into a young adult, he began openly discussing his views.

"We cannot just blindly follow," said Feng to his peers, "We must think and engage our intellect."

"But for what purpose?" asked a friend, "We are content where we are. Why destabilise the community?"

"Are you not even mildly curious about who you are and where you come from?" said Feng, "Do you not wonder whether there is more to our existence? And perpetuating all these rituals –

do you not ask who established them and why?"

Feng constantly debated with his friends, provoking them to think about their intentions and actions. Some opened their minds to new ideas and many began to embrace his teachings. These spread to neighbouring villages and regions, and as time passed, a multitude of people moved away from mindless ritual and engaged their intellect to focus on critical aspects of human life: to be kind, compassionate, and caring, and to search within for their true selves.

Several individuals came forward to help Feng – he recognised them as the missionary angels who had volunteered to help – and together, they persisted in trying to awaken humanity. Nevertheless, and regardless of their efforts, the majority ignored Feng's philosophy. Missionary angels born in other geographic areas made some gains, but not enough to make a sea-change to humanity. Humankind remained steadfast in its traditions of superstition and ritual, and well-entrenched in its quest for material gain. From their vantage point, Michael and Raphael realised that the effort was to no avail, especially when the troublemakers became restless.

"We will have to let Gabriel know that the dark angels have entered the world again," said Raphael.

"And that very few people have embraced the teachings imparted by him and the others," said Michael, "He will be upset by this news, but we must bring it to his attention. His body is getting old on Earth and will not be able to sustain him for long."

Michael and Raphael communicated with Feng during one of his meditation sessions and conveyed that some of the troublemakers had entered Earth as newborns. They also briefed him on the lack of progress of the other groups of angels in various parts of the world. On hearing this news, Feng seemed to lose his strength and his spirit weakened. He eventually left his physical body and transitioned to the heavens. Michael and Raphael received him and helped him reacquaint himself.

"How can humanity engage in superstition and ritualistic behaviour without thinking?" said Gabriel, "How can they turn their back on God, the Almighty? I had hoped that we would be able to set humanity on the right course."

One by one, as the groups of missionary angels returned to the fourth dimension, Michael and Raphael helped them with the transition. Once everyone was fully reacquainted and settled, they gathered around the Archangels.

"My dear siblings-in-light," said Gabriel, "you have all been exemplary in your respective assignments. While we have not been able to move the whole of humanity in the right direction, we managed to help a few human beings. We will need to reflect on what to do next to make a greater impact. Now, get some rest and work on your own well-being and higher consciousness."

"We are grateful for the opportunity to serve our fellow beings," said one angel.

"Many of us would like to continue with our task," said another angel, "For some reason, the people in the areas in which I was born are obsessed with wealth and power. Try as I might, no one listened to what I had to say."

"When the time comes, you will have more opportunities to continue your work," said Gabriel, "Right now, we need to determine how else to change the course of humanity, as our intervention did not make much of an impact. In the meantime, get some rest and rejuvenate yourselves." The crowd began to disperse as Gabriel, Michael, and Raphael watched in silence.

As the last of the angels disappeared, Raphael turned to Gabriel and said, "A few of the missionary angels who were on Earth have really distinguished themselves. They are close to reaching the seventh dimension."

"I am particularly impressed with how they handled their lives on Earth," said Michael, "Some entered hostile communities, and many suffered great hardship. Yet, they were steadfast in their loyalty to God and their mission to help," said Michael.

"We may be able to rely on these angels to undertake even greater responsibility," said Gabriel, "If they so choose, of course. However, I must now obtain God's guidance as to what He wishes us to do. I do not know about you two, but I have certainly run out of ideas on how to open humanity's eyes."

"I agree," said Raphael, "I do not want to admit defeat, but I think we are at that point."

"Go ahead, Gabriel," said Michael, "We will manage here." With a nod, Gabriel stepped back, and withdrew into God.

14 SUBMISSION

Gabriel meditated in silence. Once he felt ready, he invoked, "In the name of God, the most Beneficent, the most Merciful."

"My dear Gabriel, how nice to see you," said God.

"My Lord, I have returned from my sojourn on Earth, and I am afraid I have failed in my task. My siblings refuse to heed Your words, and are too mesmerised by physical life and material wealth. They do not see who they really are, and are not interested in their essence. They are short-sighted and cannot see further than their own lifetime. They also continue to worship gods made of stone and engage in irrational rituals. They just cannot comprehend that You exist and are the only god, the Universal Force who is loving, benevolent, and omnipotent. Idolatry has gripped humanity again, and they focus on the form rather than on substance. They do not realise that this is abhorrent to their higher selves. Michael, Raphael and I are at a loss as to what to do. Please guide us and provide us with direction."

"My dear child, you have not failed in your task. All I had asked of you was to do your best to help awaken your siblings. I did not stipulate that you had to succeed, but only to persevere in your efforts to help My children. Remember, I had conveyed to you to not be disappointed if they do not pay attention to My guidance. I granted My children free will, and it is for each to choose how to behave. I also conveyed to you that I was giving My children one last chance to heed My words. And since the vast majority is still blinded by the allure of the physical world, I will remove all the physicality I created."

"Dear Gabriel," continued God, "I create and give, and I also take away and destroy. I will now purge the world of all that it contains. I will remove the knowledge, know-how, and inspiration I granted My children to improve their lives. All physical life that I created – be it mineral, plant, animal, and human – will be obliterated from the face of the Earth. All life spirit will return to its natural state in the higher dimensions, including that of My children: their physical bodies will be destroyed, and My children will exist in the fourth dimension in their true and authentic state – beings of light, shining brightly with love – My angels. They must remain in this way for many years, until every being has rid themself of their desire for material gain and wealth. They must overcome the hatred and selfishness within. They must understand that nothing is more important than love and kindness towards one another, for they are siblings-in-light and originate from the same source. They must learn to not debase themselves by worshipping gods made of mud and water – these are graven images – and their veneration does not reflect the eminence and intelligence of My children. The true self is spiritual, not physical, and life on Earth is but a temporary existence. Regardless of their physical appearance on Earth, or their station in life, or their belief systems – all My children are equal – they are equal on Earth as well as when they return to their essential, spiritual form in the higher dimensions."

"Gabriel," said God, "while I intend to purge the world, I will keep a few life forms alive on Earth. And if you accept, I want you to return to Earth as a human being and save these life forms from destruction. These life forms will repopulate and reinvigorate the planet when the time is right and I am ready for this to happen. It will be a very difficult task for you to complete, for I wish you to experience life on Earth as most of My children do: in a blind, unenlightened state, where they have forgotten who they really are. Up to now, you have maintained your link with the fourth dimension – which is what most of My children have failed to do – and benefited from the help and guidance provided by

Michael and Raphael. If you accept My terms, you must undertake this work without the benefit of having direct access to the fourth dimension. In other words, you must experience life and take decisions based on your instinct and how your spirit moves you from within, rather than knowing your purpose and seeking help from Michael and Raphael when you require it. You will recall that Michael experienced this for a very short time when he lost the link and sank into a deep depression during his life on Earth. It took a great deal of courage for him to look within and find Me. It was only when he took that decision to seek My help and return to Me that he was able to recognise himself and arise. Gabriel, I will block your memory so that you do not know who you really are. Will you still choose to follow Me? Will you still choose to do good, and be loving and compassionate toward your fellow beings? Will you demonstrate how pure your light really is when it is influenced by all those around you? Will you still be true to your spiritual self when you are thrown into the centre of darkness?"

Gabriel was stunned by God's guidance. He remained silent for some time, trying to comprehend what he had just heard. God allowed him the space to absorb His words.

"My Lord, may I please call on Michael and Raphael to join us so they may hear Your words first-hand?" asked Gabriel, "I am shocked, not to mention reluctant to visit Earth under these conditions. I have never been in a situation where I have lost the connection with the fourth dimension, and I certainly have always known who I am."

"Yes, certainly, My child," said God benevolently. Gabriel reached out to Michael and Raphael.

"Michael! Raphael!" called Gabriel, "Would you please join me here? Come quickly."

The two Archangels were busy at work when they heard Gabriel.

"Raphael, I believe Gabriel is calling us!" said Michael.

"Yes, I heard him, too," said Raphael, "We must appoint

an angel to supervise things while we are away. Perhaps one of the special missionary angels in the sixth dimension can help. I will see whether anyone wishes to volunteer." When Raphael offered the temporary assignment, a shimmering angel named Kibwe came forward.

"But I must be permitted to revert to the sixth dimension once you return," said Kibwe, "I am working on my spirit to attain my highest consciousness and I am at a critical juncture."

"Of course, Kibwe," said Michael, "We should only be a short while." Michael and Raphael withdrew into themselves and began their ascent.

"In the name of God, the most Beneficent, the most Merciful," they invoked as they arrived, "we are present." They saw Gabriel and placed themselves beside him.

"My dear children," said God, "I am delighted to see you here. I am very happy with all the work you have done, and am proud of the way you have helped Gabriel. Your selflessness and generosity of spirit pleases me so, and I have witnessed the fruits of your labour – many of My children have raised their awareness and have moved up through the dimensions closer to Me. They have internalised the concepts of love and forgiveness, which they now realise are innate to them. I only wish that more of My children had listened to you and heeded My words. Nonetheless, as I conveyed many times before, I granted free will to My children and it is up to them to choose how they wish to conduct themselves."

God then explained to Michael and Raphael what He had earlier said to Gabriel.

"My Lord, are You really going to destroy everything on Earth?" asked Raphael, astounded by God's plans.

"Yes, I am," said God. The Archangels glanced at one another in disbelief.

"My Lord, why have You placed these conditions on Gabriel?" asked Michael.

"My dear Michael," said God, "You may not be aware that

Gabriel elicited a promise from Me to grant him that which he desires most: to merge with My light and permanently reside with Me. As you know, I have never granted this privilege to any of My children. When you first burst forth from Me, My intention was to let you exist as free spirits, for in your essence you encompassed every part of Me – you were no less than Me. I designed the universe and all it embodies, including Earth, so that you could experience creation in all its forms, but you became intoxicated by this and began to degrade your soul. Rather than shine brightly, your light began to fade. You moved away from the purity that is in Me and became less than you were. And in order for any one of you to merge into My spirit, you must exist in your original, purest form. Gabriel, I have already conveyed to you that of all of My children, you are the most like Me, but you are not perfect. There are vestiges of your ego that still exist. You must polish your light to such an intensity that it will be able to freely unite with Mine. Gabriel, if you still wish to do this, then you will have to meet My conditions and pass My tests, for it is not possible for any impurity to enter My light – such impurity means that your ego is present, however minutely. Any one of My children, should I grant them this opportunity to merge with Me and become One, will have to undergo such trials to purify their light."

"My dear Gabriel," continued God, "you are not obliged to do any of this. I am happy with you just the way you are. I could not be prouder of your conduct and behaviour towards others. It is your free will, your choice, as to how and in which dimension you wish to exist. Should you want to carry on with your work as you have been, I am fine to continue. Should you wish to lessen your responsibility or curtail your engagement in any way, I am fine with this also. You may meet Me any time in this seventh dimension, and as often as you like. But to reside permanently within My light is quite another matter, for it is then that you become Me."

God allowed Gabriel to take in His words. Gabriel slowly grasped what God was trying to explain to him: in order to merge with God and remain permanently with Him, Gabriel would have to let go of his ego. But it was not just a simple release – it had to be a conscious decision to invite the Whole to take over the Part – in order to become the spirit that is God, Gabriel had to be willing to sacrifice his own existence. He would no longer be a separate entity – Gabriel would become the Universe itself – he would be the Alpha and the Omega, but Gabriel, the persona, would no longer exist.

"My Lord," said Gabriel, "it is my greatest desire to become one. But it is a momentous decision, something that I am only beginning to understand. I am also frightened to lose my memory and link with the higher dimensions during a lifetime on Earth. I cannot comprehend what this would be like."

"My Lord," said Michael, still not quite believing what he was hearing, "is there anything that Raphael and I can do to help Gabriel with this?"

God looked at them kindly. "One of you may agree to be his personal guardian angel during his lifetime on Earth. But you are forbidden to jog his memory. You see, Gabriel must search within himself, and come to his own conclusions and take his own decisions in his life on Earth. It is only in this way that he will be able to demonstrate that he is ready to proceed to the next step."

"I would like to take on this responsibility," said Michael, "if Gabriel still wishes to advance and accepts me to be his guardian angel."

"I can take full charge of Gabriel's work in the upper dimensions, and if God grants me permission, I will request other angels to assist me while Gabriel and Michael are on their assignments," said Raphael.

"My dear Gabriel," said God, "what are your thoughts?"

Gabriel seemed burdened by the weight of this decision. What should he do? He was being given a chance to be one with God, to reside in His grace for eternity. But now that he understood what this meant, that he would no longer exist, was this what he really wanted? And his resolve would have to be tested. Would his ego get the better of him?

"My Lord," replied Gabriel, "I require some time to reflect upon this. Will You allow me a short respite before I take my decision?"

"Of course, My dear child," said God, "All three of you should return to your duties and think about what it is that you would like to do. As soon as you decide, return to Me. I am ready to implement that which I wish to do on Earth, but will nonetheless wait for your return." The Archangels bowed their heads.

"Thy Will be done in and through us each day; Thy Will be done on Earth as it is in Heaven," they recited, as they withdrew and began their descent.

15 SURRENDER

"Gabriel, do you really desire to be one with God?" asked Michael, as they approached the fourth dimension.

"I do," said Gabriel, "but I did not realise it would require such surrender. I do not know if I have the courage."

"Remember, it is your choice," said Raphael, "God reiterated He is happy where you are, and will be fine with whatever you choose."

"Raphael, did you know about this?" asked Michael.

"I witnessed Gabriel's conversation with God when Gabriel first raised it," said Raphael, "You know, it never occurred to me to even consider becoming one with God."

"Well, it is a major step, so Gabriel, take the time you need to reflect upon it," said Michael, "But whatever your decision, both Raphael and I will support you."

"Thank you both," said Gabriel. He remained preoccupied with his thoughts.

Michael and Raphael saw Kibwe coming towards them.

"Hello Kibwe, is everything alright?" asked Raphael.

"Nothing has changed since you left," said Kibwe.

"Very well," said Raphael, "thank you so much. Will you stay and continue to help?"

"If you do not mind, I would like to return to the sixth dimension," said Kibwe.

"That is fine," said Raphael, "thank you once again."

"Let me know if you require help in the future. I am happy to assist for short periods of time," said Kibwe, and she began her ascent.

Michael and Raphael resumed their work and allowed Gabriel the space to reflect upon everything God had conveyed. Gabriel decided to observe the happenings on Earth for a while and then visit the fifth and sixth dimensions. He needed to resolve whether he would be satisfied existing in any of these states. He began by descending on Earth to scrutinise the actions taken by humankind. While there were pockets of joy and generosity peppered around the world, he witnessed a lot of selfishness, greed, hatred, and violence, all doled out in various forms and to varying degrees. Families were fighting amongst themselves; tribes were warring with one another; and lying, cheating, and stealing were rampant. And what particularly irked him was the mindless sacrifices to gods made of stone.

"I cannot stand to watch people debasing themselves like this. Nor can I bear to see people suffer," thought Gabriel, as he moved around, "Earth cannot be left to rot like this; something must be done."

Gabriel turned his attention to the fourth dimension. "Let me see what is happening in the angel schools," thought Gabriel. He approached the schools and began to look around.

"It is nice to see you here, Gabriel," said Raphael, as he made his way towards him.

"There are so many more here than when I last visited!" said Gabriel.

"Many are trying to learn about themselves. Would you like to teach a few classes?" asked Raphael.

"Yes, I really would," said Gabriel, "Where shall I start?"

"You would be best placed to take the advanced classes, Gabriel. They would like to learn about stillness," said Raphael.

"Very well," said Gabriel.

Raphael escorted Gabriel to the classes and left him to begin the lessons. Needless to say, the students were ecstatic to have the benefit of Gabriel's guidance, and he remained at the schools for quite some time. Eventually, Gabriel realised that while this work was satisfying, he was restless and needed something more fulfilling.

"Perhaps the work and counselling I can do in the higher dimensions will serve me better," thought Gabriel. He moved on to the fifth dimension, where he was welcomed by all who resided there. Gabriel was pleasantly surprised to see so many more angels at this level.

"Michael and Raphael have really done a wonderful job in helping so many graduate to this dimension," thought Gabriel.

Gabriel settled in and counselled the angels on the various impediments that prevented them from attaining their higher consciousness. The most prevalent of these was the ego: it crept back in every so often and prevented the spirit from advancing further.

"Try to step out of your being and observe yourself," said Gabriel, "Watch how you react to situations. Are you led by your emotions, your insecurities, your fears? From the outside looking in, what causes this momentary assertion of the ego? What are its triggers? When you can answer these questions, you can determine how to overcome the obstacles."

Gabriel remained in the fifth dimension for some time and was glad to assist the angels, but he could not shake off his restlessness. He finally moved up to the sixth dimension to examine whether this was a better fit. The angels welcomed him and shone their light and love on him to help with whatever it was that troubled him - they could sense he was heavy with burden. Gabriel remained alone with his thoughts and meditated in silence. Every so often, an angel approached him for some advice and guidance, but he largely remained deep in contemplation. He began to realise that while he had attained the highest consciousness and was able to maintain his being at this level, he still had not achieved the blissful, peaceful existence he craved – there was something missing.

"I am the most content in the full presence of God. Anything less is inadequate," thought Gabriel.

He considered this very carefully. First, to become one with God meant surrendering his ego; Gabriel would no longer exist as a separate entity but would merge with God, just as a drop of water merges with the ocean. One would not be able to single out Gabriel's light from that of God's. Gabriel would become the all-encompassing Universe – he would be Nothing, yet he would be Everything. Secondly, if this was what Gabriel decided to undertake, the path would be riddled with challenges that would test his faith, his resolve, and his strength of character. Did he have the courage? Would his ego dominate by letting fear get in his way?

Gabriel prayed and meditated for a length of time, and when he finally resolved his dilemma, he made his way to the fourth dimension to consult with Michael and Raphael.

"I have made my decision, but want to obtain your views before we revert to God. While it has been my choice, an honour for me, to help my siblings, I am not content with remaining in these dimensions for eternity. Even before my promise to God, when I twinkled and sparkled throughout the universe, merrily observing and experiencing God's creative force, I knew in my heart that I would eventually return to my origin. I also knew that this was something that I would ask God to grant me. However, I did not know what this would entail, and how much determination it would take to make the final journey home." Michael and Raphael waited anxiously, their souls heavy with expectation.

"But, I still wish to surrender myself and exist in my purest form within The Light," said Gabriel, "My soul will not accept anything less. This is now my chance to do just that and I must at least try. In any case, what do I have to lose? If I do not succeed, I will just remain where I am and continue to do God's work. After all, meeting God "face-to-face" every so often is not a bad position in which to be!"

Michael and Raphael wiped away their tears. This startled Gabriel.

"Why are you crying?" asked Gabriel.

"Because in your desire to merge with God, we will lose you," said Raphael. Gabriel was taken aback.

"I suppose I did not think how this would affect you. I am being self-centred and only looking at my needs," said Gabriel.

"As you should, in this case," said Michael, "This is a very personal matter. We are just being selfish and possessive. Of course, we understand that your merging with God will bring you great happiness. It will even bring you closer to us, for your light will be ever-present – we will exist in your light," said Michael.

"And when it is our time, we may also take the decision to merge with God," said Raphael. They embraced Gabriel.

"While you skim over the enormity of your decision, we understand its seriousness," said Raphael, "Know that we will support you throughout your trials, and we will do whatever it takes to help you attain your goal."

"Yes, Gabriel," said Michael, "you are very dear to us. Your strength, determination, and sheer power never cease to amaze us. While you do not seem to recognise this yourself, the light that emanates from your being is the purest and brightest of all, other than that of God Himself. Whatever you wish to do, we are with you every step of the way."

Gabriel embraced them again. "I am eternally grateful to you. How fortunate I am to have you beside me. Now, if you agree, let us withdraw into God, for He is waiting to implement that which He wishes for Earth."

The three Archangels swooped upwards, after requesting Kibwe for her help again. They arrived in the seventh dimension and invoked, "In the name of God, the most Beneficent, the most Merciful."

"My dear children, I am happy to see you again so soon," said God, "Gabriel, I believe you have come to a decision."

"Yes, My Lord," said Gabriel, "I cannot give up the opportunity with which You have presented me. I must at least try."

"Very well," said God, "Now I want the three of you to come closer to Me so that I may explain to you what I will begin to do on Earth."

The Archangels drew nearer and waited patiently for God to begin. All three were aware of the magnitude of what was about to happen and felt privileged to be in God's Presence. Gabriel, in particular, knew that his existence would never be the same from this moment on, and while he was adamant that he wanted to pursue the opportunity to be one with God, he still felt a twinge of fear deep within him. The other two sensed this and threw him sympathetic looks. All of a sudden a wave of love enveloped the three angels.

"My dear children," said God, "fear nothing, for I am with you. And Gabriel, you may withdraw from this process at any time. You must never exist in fear – this is a characteristic of the ego – be joyful and calm at all times. None of you are alone in your work, for it is My work you are doing; you are merely assisting Me out of choice. If at any time any one of you feels that you are no longer able to bear this responsibility, then return to Me and tell me so. I will relieve you of any burdens that you carry."

"My Lord," said Gabriel, "my fear is rooted in the unknown. And I recognise it is my ego asserting itself. I will have to work on this. Also, I am scared to enter Earth with no memory of who I am. I have existed for millions of years, yet this is the first time that I will lose my direct link with You."

"Ah, but Gabriel!" exclaimed God, "You have misunderstood! You will not lose your link with Me, but only to the upper dimensions! You can never lose your connection to Me, for you are part of Me and I am wholly in you. It is for you to look within yourself and recognise Me." Gabriel felt relieved; he grinned at the other two.

"You are My children," said God, "and I will never leave you bereft of my support and grace, for I cannot. So be at peace within yourselves and let go of any fear lurking within."

Gabriel felt a little foolish at his anxiety and realised that he would have to be much braver if he was going to pass the tests that lay ahead of him. He silently asked God for strength and courage. God smiled benevolently and cradled the three Archangels in a loving embrace.

"Now, let us turn to the matter at hand," said God, "I have granted humankind a lot of leeway. I have watched human beings destroy each other and all that I have created. I have provided opportunity after opportunity for humanity to redeem itself, but this has been to no avail. I intend to purge the Earth and begin again. Gabriel, I wish you to enter Earth as a human being, and try one last time to awaken humanity. This unintelligent, irrational idolatry is a blight on their souls and they must be jolted out of this reverie. Gabriel, I want you to take on male form and try your best to teach My children the truth. If they do not listen, and I suspect they will not, then I wish you to build a sea-faring craft, one that will float in water and that will have room to shelter and protect enough human beings, both male and female, who would be capable of repopulating the Earth. This craft must also be able to house animals and various species of plants and roots so that flora and fauna are able to propagate themselves. Take with you enough grains and seeds so that you may sow the land once it is prepared and fertile again. This will take many years, as the soil will be saline and brackish, for I will send a deluge of sea water, the likes of which have never been witnessed on Earth before. Everything will be razed to the ground, and that which is not razed will sink into the depths of the ocean. In one swipe, I will rid the Earth of all that troubles it. All My children who have chosen to be born on Earth will be brought back to the heavens, save those whom you choose to keep with you, Gabriel. I want My children to return *en masse* to their spiritual self so that we may begin again."

"My children are spiritual beings, and they must be taught to remember this and not become mesmerised by the physical. Every last one of My children will remain in the heavens until they learn and accept this. They must acknowledge and embrace the principles and values that are the basic tenets of their existence, whether they choose to be born on Earth or remain in the heavens, and I will no longer tolerate this wanton behaviour to which they have become accustomed. Hostility, ridicule, vindictiveness, jealousy, and greed: these traits are as vicious as maiming and killing one another. Not only have they damaged My children's minds, bodies and souls, these behaviours have also disturbed the equilibrium of Earth. And now this disturbance has wound its way into the heavens, for My children have brought these attributes home with them. When one hurts another, I feel that hurt in the depth of My being; and when one cannot forgive another, My pain knows no bounds. Love, forgiveness, kindness, compassion: these are the qualities that are innate to My children, and must be resurrected within them."

"Gabriel, teach all these tenets to My children on Earth, so that we may begin again. Your life on Earth will be fraught with difficulties, and you will have to remain strong and steadfast in your work for Me. You will be tempted by the physical world around you and you will make mistakes, because you are not perfect. Perfection only lies in My light, within Me. You must endeavour to remain as true to the essence of your being as possible."

God turned to Michael and Raphael. "You must help Gabriel from this side, but he cannot know his true identity. Michael, you have proposed to be Gabriel's personal guardian angel, and he has accepted this role. When he makes mistakes, it is for you to attempt to save him from himself and guide him in the right direction. But any decisions must be his and you must never reveal your identity, nor his identity, to him. Raphael, as you had suggested, you will take over all of Gabriel's responsibilities in the heavens while he is on Earth. There shall be no recourse to him for advice or help of any kind, nor he to you. However, I want the three of you to recruit a few more angels, indeed those special angels who have distinguished themselves and who are on the cusp of entering this seventh dimension, so that they may help you with all the work in the heavens. And I warn you now, it will take a host of angels to replace the energy, strength and power of Gabriel alone. From these special angels who come forward, choose the most enlightened, loving beings, for it is only by combining such might that you will be able to make up for Gabriel's loss."

"Gabriel," said God, "you must scrutinise and select these few angels, for not only will they need to help with the heavenly work while you are on Earth, but they will assist you with rebuilding the world after the purge and once you complete your lifetime. Ensure that they are strong in love and compassion to the core of their being, for they will have important work to accomplish in the millennia ahead. Now My children, return to the heavens below, and let us begin our work together. And remember, when you need My help, turn to Me and I will carry you through your difficulties."

The three Archangels bowed their heads, invoking, "Thy Will be done in and through us each day; Thy Will be done on Earth as it is in Heaven." They held one another as they began their descent to begin the world anew.

As they approached the fourth dimension, Kibwe hurried over to welcome them. She briefed them on the happenings on Earth and in the heavens. From what the Archangels could observe, matters remained unchanged.

"Thank you for all your assistance, Kibwe," said Raphael.

"Would you like to reconsider and continue to help us?" asked Michael.

"I am grateful for the opportunity," said Kibwe, "but a return to the sixth dimension is in my best interest at the moment. I need more time to myself. I must attain the highest consciousness possible before I return to God's service."

"Very well," said Raphael, "we pray for your success."

"Thank you," said Kibwe, tilting her head forward as she stepped away from the Archangels. Michael and Raphael turned their attention to Gabriel.

"What is the first step, Gabriel?" asked Raphael.

"Would you please gather the missionary angels so that we may convey God's message?" said Gabriel.

"Yes, of course," said Raphael, and he left to assemble everyone. Gabriel and Michael waited in silence.

"Gabriel," said Michael, tentatively, "Are you ready for this?"

"I believe so," said Gabriel, "but I am still worried about my next life on Earth. I cannot imagine not linking into the fourth dimension."

"I will be with you," said Michael, reassuringly, "I will make every effort to guide you and send you signs."

"Thank you, Michael," said Gabriel, "I just hope that I will be aware enough to notice."

Raphael reappeared with several angels. "The rest are making their way here."

The Archangels waited patiently, and once everyone was in place, Gabriel explained what God was going to do on Earth. A great commotion ensued as they erupted into discussion.

"God is ready to destroy everything He created on Earth, just to put us on the right path?" asked one angel.

"This is really serious," said another, "I knew things had got out of hand on Earth, but for God to take such a drastic step?"

"And in one swoop!" exclaimed another, "How will we cope on this side with so many returning all at once?"

"Archangel Gabriel, how will we manage the transition for such a large number of returning people? What is your plan?" came a question from the crowd.

"I will not be here, because I will take on human form to help with the transition on Earth," said Gabriel, "Raphael will be in-charge here. Those of you who wish to help must make yourselves known to him."

"We all wish to help," said one angel, "I do not think there is anyone here who does not want to participate and be useful."

"Very well," said Raphael, "but it is best to confirm this individually."

One by one, each angel came forward and pledged their support for the work, sealing their commitment.

"Now carry on with your normal activities," said Raphael, "and await further instructions from me. I will call upon you when the time comes."

The three Archangels then ascended to the sixth dimension to seek out those special angels who had distinguished themselves and who were on the cusp of entering the seventh dimension.

"Who would like to assist and take on a much greater role during this critical hour in Earth's history?" asked Gabriel.

Quite a few angels came forward and presented themselves. Gabriel paid particular attention to the group: he identified the purest, and the strongest of faith, and sat down with each of them to discuss their wishes and desires, and why each felt they wanted to take on this responsibility to help God. Gabriel spent a great deal of time with them individually, for he did not want to make the same mistake he had made a multitude of years earlier with the troublemakers – he still had to deal with them and the consequences of their actions.

Gabriel continued his interviews with the special angels, and as the group of eligible contenders began to dwindle, either because Gabriel felt they were not ready for such heavy responsibility or they themselves withdrew from the process, the remaining angels looked very promising. Michael and Raphael also met with each individually and shared their views with Gabriel. The group was finally whittled down to four angels who were on the cusp of entering the seventh dimension, but required more service to others in order to make the final breakthrough. The three Archangels agreed that these four were the most enlightened, and together, like a harmonious quartet, would serve God's work well.

"Before we confirm the appointment of these angels, it will be important to seek God's blessings," said Gabriel. The three Archangels withdrew into the seventh dimension.

"In the name of God, the most Beneficent, the most Merciful," they invoked.

"My dear children," said God, "I believe there is something you wish to ask Me?"

"My Lord," said Gabriel, "we have selected four of our siblings who are the most enlightened, and who wish to help Raphael with Your work during my and Michael's absence. Are You happy with the choice and do You accept for them to take on this responsibility?"

"My dear children, I am very pleased with these four

angels," said God, "Not only am I confident that they will do a wonderful job in helping Raphael, but they will also have the courage to help put My children on the right course on Earth once we begin to rebuild the world. So now go with My blessings and begin your preparations. Gabriel, I want you to be born on Earth as quickly as you can, for My children are suffering, and I want to bring them back."

"Thy Will be done in and through us each day; Thy Will be done on Earth as it is in Heaven," said the three Archangels, and they descended through the heavens to the fourth dimension. Upon their arrival, they gathered all the angels to announce that God had accepted for four of their siblings to help Raphael.

"Please come forward," said Gabriel, as he beckoned the four, "I want to introduce you." Whispers and murmurings permeated the atmosphere as the crowd adjusted itself. Many angels strained to catch a glimpse, for they knew that the chosen ones were very special; they were being given an opportunity to reach the heights of Gabriel, Michael and Raphael.

"May I present to you our four siblings, the Quartet, who will help Raphael in the heavens. Please meet Abraham, Moses, Jesus, and Mohamed."

17 DELUGE

In a quiet corner of the heavens, Gabriel embraced Michael and Raphael, and said, "How I will miss you both! I have come to rely on the two of you as an extension of myself, and to be cut-off from you will be difficult."

"I know I have the Quartet with me, but it will not be the same without you," said Raphael.

"But you will have recourse to me, Raphael," said Michael, "Even though I will be concentrating fully on Gabriel, you can still visit me whenever you wish. We will be able to observe him and help him where we can, and of course, where we are permitted."

"We must help God to put things right on Earth, and if that means that we have to be apart for a few years, then so be it," said Gabriel.

"We will do our best and we will also try to help you achieve your goal to be one with God," said Michael.

"I am very grateful for everything you are doing to support me," said Gabriel, "but my personal goal is secondary. Of primary importance is to ensure that our siblings learn and understand the truth, and rebuild Earth in the right direction. I just hope that during this lifetime, I do not make too many mistakes and set myself on a backward course. Michael, please do everything in your power to protect me from myself."

"Of course, Gabriel," said Michael.

"I will send special angels to be born around you so that you will be surrounded by love and kindness," said Raphael, "and Michael will protect you. But Gabriel, please do not forget that God is with you, so look within."

"I will," said Gabriel, as he embraced Raphael again. They said their goodbyes and Raphael hurried off.

Michael turned to Gabriel, "What is the next step? Do we look for a family who will provide you with the necessary environment to do your work on Earth?"

"Absolutely," said Gabriel, and they set off on their search. They visited many people and clans in different regions of Earth, and settled on a certain family in a part of the world where Gabriel would be able to influence a great number of people.

"This is it," said Gabriel, as he turned to face Michael, "I will now begin my inner preparations. And Michael, even though I will not rationally know that you are with me and guiding me from here, in my heart, I will know that I have someone looking out for me. Thank you for taking care of me."

"I am at your service, Gabriel," said Michael, "You have no idea how much I have learnt from you and what a joy it is to be in your presence."

"You were the first one who volunteered to help me many, many millennia ago," said Gabriel, "and you are still the one personally aiding me in my biggest challenge to date."

"I hope one day to emulate you," said Michael, "I hope I have the courage to take the final step to surrender my ego and become one with God."

Both had tears in their eyes as Gabriel withdrew into himself to prepare for his birth on Earth. Michael stood guard at his side, ready to protect and guide him. The chosen parents on Earth conceived, and at the appointed time, Gabriel invoked, "In the name of God!" and slipped into the body of the baby. He was born a healthy boy, whose parents named him Noah.

Noah was a normal boy, yet like Oma and Feng in years past, there was a maturity about him that his parents could not explain. He played with his many friends but never got into the usual trouble that young boys of his age frequently found themselves. He had a generous, giving spirit and was kind to all. As Noah grew into a young man, he worked tirelessly to support his family and was an active member of the community, providing assistance wherever it was needed.

He was also a devout believer and attended the temple regularly, making the usual offerings to the gods to garner fortune and favour. Nonetheless, as he matured, an unease began to stir within him. He ignored it for a few years, but it was always present, gnawing at him. He still participated in the ceremonies for the gods, but it progressively became an obligation rather than a genuine act of devotion.

His restlessness grew, and so did his discomfort in attending the temples. After one such visit, he could no longer bear it – he was now an adult with a strong mind, and he felt ridiculous making offerings to deities made of stone.

"What do I do?" thought Noah, "I cannot speak to my family. They will not understand. Maybe I should talk to Seth. He is quite reasonable and generally open to new ideas." After one of the ceremonies, Noah asked Seth to join him on a walk by the river. They ambled along quietly, enjoying the fresh air and beautiful foliage.

"It's been too long since we last spent time together," said Seth, "I'm glad you suggested this walk."

"We were inseparable as children," said Noah, "Now our lives are filled with our family and daily responsibilities."

"We see each other often enough – there are so many social occasions!" said Seth, "But we rarely have the opportunity to speak alone."

"Well, this is exactly why I asked you to join me today," said Noah, "I want to talk to you."

Seth stopped abruptly and turned to Noah. "Is something wrong?"

"No, of course not," said Noah, ushering Seth along, "it's just that…I don't know what it is, but I'm not content with these rituals that we perform at the temple. The gods whom we worship don't have spirit, nor do they have rational thoughts. They're just stone and clumps of clay. How can we worship stone? It seems absurd to be devoted to these objects. Aren't we men of reason?"

"I know what you mean. I also find these rituals foolish. But there's nothing we can do about it," said Seth, shrugging his shoulders, "We have to accompany our families, otherwise we will attract a lot of unnecessary attention."

Noah pressed further. "I'm also disheartened by the way everyone is choosing to behave. There's so much cheating and stealing. Why is there so much greed? Shouldn't we care about one another's welfare? People are so dogmatic and steeped in tradition. They are losing sight of what is really important. Our worship should encourage compassion and kindness. Rather, everyone is trying to out-do each other in life and at the temples. Things must change, Seth."

"Even if we wanted to, what changes could we make and to whom would we speak?" said Seth, "The elders will certainly not entertain any new ideas, and the masses will just follow what the elders dictate."

"But Seth, it seems ludicrous to perpetuate this," said Noah, "I certainly wouldn't want my children to follow these rituals. Surely there must be more to life than just existing. The stone gods are inanimate objects, but we men and women have spirit. There is life within us. Don't we think for ourselves and aren't we accountable for our behaviour?"

Seth arched his eyebrow. "Accountable to whom? Who's there to watch over us and judge right from wrong?"

"But, Seth, don't you feel it deep within you when something is right or wrong?" said Noah, "Instinctively you know; you sense what is acceptable behaviour. You're your own judge, your own moral conscience. But where does this instinct come from? There must be more to us than just our physical bodies. And if we're the ones who created the stone carvings and called them gods, then who created us?" Seth turned towards Noah and lowered his voice.

"Noah, you seem to be questioning a lot more than just the offerings we make to the gods. You must be cautious with your ideas, for not only will they upset the elders, they'll disturb the whole community."

"I understand your concerns, Seth. I don't want to defy the elders. Although I do believe things must change. I just don't know what to do about it." Noah looked far into the distance. He bent to pick up a stone and plopped it into the lake. He watched as the water rippled out in ever-increasing circles.

"If you have any ideas about what to do," said Noah, "then please share these with me. In the meantime, let's keep this conversation to ourselves. I don't want anyone getting the wrong idea and creating problems."

"Of course." Seth left Noah deep in his thoughts, considering his reflection in the water.

Noah continued with his daily life and tried very hard to ignore his feelings, yet people's behaviour distressed him, and he found the rituals and superstitions irksome. He realised he would have to take time out every day to control the disquiet within. He began to take long walks along the river, meandering amongst the trees and bushes.

"There must be more to us than our physical existence," he thought, "This can't be it. There must be some purpose to life and why we're here on this land. I know there must be something, or some being, that's greater than us, and it certainly isn't one of those stone gods lying in the temple."

Noah felt hypocritical making the offerings to the gods; he just did not believe them to be deities, nor did he believe in the traditions his family had practiced for generations. He began making excuses as to why he could not participate in the rituals, and increasingly spent time walking along the river, as if searching

145

for something. One day, he came across a humongous tree. Its trunk was sturdy and robust, several times wider than Noah, and its branches spanned out against the sky, creating a thick canopy above. Noah sat under its shade. He looked up at the blue sky peeking through the boughs and said out loud, "Who are you and where are you? You must exist, and if you do exist, make yourself known to me."

Noah thought he heard a faint whisper, and sat upright. He listened quietly for a while, but heard nothing distinctive. "I could've sworn I heard something, or someone, answering my call," thought Noah. He remained under the tree for a few hours, periodically calling out, but nothing happened. "It must have been the wind rustling the leaves," he thought, as he got up. But it still niggled him.

From that point on, Noah took a daily walk and sat under the tree calling out, "Who are you and where are you? Make yourself known to me!" Even though it was preposterous to sit by the river calling out to an unknown entity, it still seemed better to Noah than bowing down to a stone sculpture praying it would bestow good fortune on him.

Then one day, Seth asked if he could join him on his walk.

"Of course," said Noah, "in any case, I want to continue our conversation." The two men strolled down the banks of the river, watching the birds whistling and chirping as they flew amongst the trees.

"There must be some greater force that exists, Seth," said Noah, "How can such spirit manifest itself, whether in birds, animals, or men? It's certainly not the stone gods in the temple who grant us life."

"I know you've been pursuing this question during your walks, Noah. Two or three individuals have apparently heard you speaking out loud, and people are beginning to speculate whether you are gripped by some sickness. This is the reason why I wanted to join you today, to warn you about the talk that's winding its way through the community."

"I don't care what people think of me," said Noah.

"There are many who like to gossip, and right now it's just that: idle gossip," said Seth, "But don't provide them with the fuel to fire up their tongues. You're known as a strong man of great character. With your solid reputation, your ideas will be able to influence many people. But it must be approached wisely. Don't fall at the first hurdle."

"I'm grateful for your warning and will be more careful," said Noah, "But there will come a time when I'll have to forge ahead in my own way, even if people don't understand. I know deep within, there's something I must do. There's a purpose to my life. I just don't know what it is at the moment, but I must follow my heart."

"I understand, Noah, but don't get carried away. Please call upon me if I can help you."

"Thank you, Seth."

"Now let's enjoy this beautiful afternoon before I return to all my responsibilities!" said Seth. They continued their stroll and reminisced about their childhood days.

Noah returned to his tree, but after his conversation with Seth, he realised people were watching him. He shrewdly selected a stone carving from his family's collection and set up a small shrine against the tree.

"This should throw off any suspicion," thought Noah, "Praying to a stone god is completely ordinary and inconsequential. It will not draw the attention of passers-by."

Noah sat under his tree every day, closed his eyes, and whispered his summons, "Who are you? Make yourself known to me."

He continued his vigil, returning every day. Days, then weeks passed by, but nothing happened. Noah began to wonder whether his efforts were an exercise in futility, but he persevered.

"If nothing happens soon, I'll stop all this," thought Noah.

A few days later, as Noah repeatedly called out for the "someone or something" to make itself known, he thought he heard a voice. It seemed to grow louder with each repetition, "I am God, the Almighty. I am the Creator, I am the Great Force; I am the spirit within you. I am that which you seek."

Noah swivelled his head in all directions. "Where are you?"

"I am the spirit within you. I am that which you seek."

"Within me? How are you inside me?" asked Noah, anxiously.

"Look within yourself, and you will find me." Noah tried to steady his breathing.

"I knew you existed…Are you the god of all gods?"

"I am the only god. There are no other gods. The idols that you worship are just stone carvings. There is no god but Me. I created everything, including you. You are a spiritual being, and your physical life is temporary. All men and women are only there to experience My creation and are not there to own and possess, for nothing belongs to them. You must be kind and compassionate towards each other, for you are all siblings. When you die your physical death, you will return to Me. You must convey this to all men and women and teach them the truth." Noah was awestruck, and it took him a few seconds to absorb these words.

"Only one god? And our spirit will return to you after our death?" said Noah.

"You must convey My message to all men and women and teach them the truth," came the voice again.

Noah put his hand on his chest to calm himself. "Did I hear correctly or is this just my imagination?" thought Noah.

"You must convey My message to all men and women and teach them the truth," insisted the voice.

With a great deal of trepidation, Noah replied, "Yes, God, I will." He waited for more, but nothing came. He slowly stood up, and in a daze, made his way home.

In the heavens, Michael and Raphael cried with joy. They were ecstatic with Noah's breakthrough. God spoke to them, "Michael, Raphael, remember you must not reveal your identities, and especially his own identity to him. Gabriel must evolve and progress as Noah."

"Yes, my Lord," said Michael and Raphael, grinning like naughty schoolboys. They composed themselves. "Thy Will be done in and through us," they each invoked and resumed their duties.

Noah returned to his humongous tree every day and continued to ask for guidance from God the Almighty, the only god. "What exactly should I do? How do I approach this? Will people believe me that you exist and are the only god?" After relentlessly probing for many days, Noah began doubting himself. "Did I really hear a voice or am I deluded? I want to believe that there is some higher, powerful force – is my wanting to believe overwhelming my rational mind?" thought Noah, "Is the voice I heard just my own thoughts projecting what I want to hear?"

As days turned to weeks, and then months passed by, Noah grew weak with anxiety. His family began to worry. "What illness has befallen him?" they asked each other. Noah worked less and rested more, and slowly began to withdraw from society. He tried to maintain a façade of normality but he was profoundly troubled. He spent a lot of time under his humongous tree, staring up at the sky and gazing far off into the distance. Hours would go by with him sitting in complete silence.

Then one day he heard the voice again, coming from deep within, "Why do you doubt Me? You know that you heard Me and that I am the Great Spirit who created you. I gave life to you and all that exists around you. I am God the Almighty, and there is no god but Me. When you die your physical death, you will return to Me, for you are My child. You must convey this to all men and women and teach them the truth. Why have you not obeyed

My command as you said you would?" Noah was simultaneously stunned and revitalised by these words.

He vigorously shook his head, as if trying to clear his thoughts. "I know these cannot be my words, for I do not possess such imagination!" thought Noah, "And this feels authentic. My instinct tells me these words are true. I must follow God the Almighty's instructions."

Noah sat up, cleared his throat, and said, "Dear God, I will follow Your words, but please do not abandon me. Do not remain silent when I speak to You. You must continually guide me." Immediately, Noah felt a wave of love and warmth, and a calmness descended upon him. Noah knew God was demonstrating His Presence.

"But He still did not speak to me," thought Noah. He waited for a while, but nothing more came. "Oh well, I have to find Seth and share this good news with him."

Seth was at the market buying fruits and vegetables. He waived Noah over when he saw him.

"Hello Seth, I hope you're doing well," said Noah.

"Yes, I am," said Seth, "and how have you been faring?"

"I am fine," said Noah, "but I'd like to talk to you. Do you have time for a walk?"

"Of course," said Seth. He asked the vendor to set aside the produce he had picked out. "I'll be back for these."

Noah and Seth set off, walking in silence for the first few minutes.

"It's nice to spend time with you again," said Seth, as they strolled along the river.

"Seth, I have found the one god," said Noah.

"What do you mean?" said Seth.

"He spoke to me, and asked me to convey the truth to all people. He is the only god, and it is He who has created us and all living matter, and it is to Him that we will return once we die our physical death. Everything in our lives is temporary, and we must treat each other with kindness, for we are His children and we will return to our true home one day," said Noah.

Seth stopped and grabbed Noah by the shoulders. "This god has visited you?! You have seen him?!"

"No, I haven't seen him," said Noah, "and I don't believe he's a physical being. I just heard his voice from deep within me." Seth's face fell. He was astonished by his friend's claims.

"You heard his voice from within you? But how can this one god be inside you?" Seth could not believe Noah had uttered such words. What happened to his intelligent, rational friend? Perhaps he really was sick. Seth knew that Noah was exploring some new ideas, but maybe it was more serious than he realised, and an affliction had indeed gripped his mind.

"But we are spirit, Seth. We are not our physical body. This spirit that is inside us is somehow linked to the spirit of the one god. There is something much bigger and greater than our mere physical existence here. And I must convey this to our people. There is only one god, and we must all stop worshipping these stone idols," said Noah.

Seth's mouth dropped open. "My dear friend, you know how much I care for you and value our friendship. But what are you saying? Are you feeling well? Maybe you need to get some rest."

"I know this is unbelievable, Seth. But I also know that what I'm saying is true. I hoped you would believe me," said Noah, looking down.

"I'm sorry, Noah. It's just too far-fetched," said Seth.

"And praying to stone carvings in the hope that they may grant your wishes is not far-fetched? Is it not possible that we exist in an ethereal form, and the one god is also ethereal? How else are our bodies animated? There is spirit or some sort of energy within us. Just because we cannot see something does not mean that it doesn't exist. We cannot see the air and wind, but we know and feel it exists. I cannot see this one god, but I hear and feel he exists," said Noah.

"Okay. But why would this god contact you? Has he spoken to anyone else? Why you?"

"I don't know, Seth. Maybe because I called out to him? You know how long I've been meditating on this question. Perhaps it's as simple as that: I approached him."

Seth found Noah's claims unbelievable, but he treaded carefully. He did not want to push Noah away.

"Okay. Maybe I need some time to absorb all this," said Seth, "Let me join you on your daily walk and you can explain it all to me in detail. Who knows, either you'll convince me of this truth, or I'll be able to help you out of this incredulous belief!" They both laughed heartily. Seth hoped that by spending more time with Noah, he would be able to rid him of his dubious notions and perhaps heal his mind.

Noah smiled knowingly and put his arm around Seth. "You're a good friend. Now, go and get your vegetables before someone else grabs them!"

Seth left Noah by the river, contemplating his next move.

After that, Seth and Noah met every day for their walk. As the days and weeks passed, Noah reinforced his arguments that this spirit-god existed and Seth began to understand that what Noah espoused was at least plausible, although he did not wholeheartedly accept it as the truth. The important thing was Noah did not seem deluded in any way, and he had his feet firmly planted on the ground.

"So this one god really spoke to you?" said Seth.

"Yes, I truly believe this in my heart," said Noah.

"What are you going to do about it?" said Seth.

"I have to convey the truth to our people," said Noah.

"But how are you going to do this?" said Seth, "You know that the elders will be very upset and offended, especially because these ideas come from you. They love and respect you a great deal."

"Yes, I know," said Noah, rubbing the back of his neck,

"But I must do this. I think I've found my purpose in life. I'll begin with my family and friends, and then continue spreading this news to whomever is willing to listen."

"It's going to be difficult, Noah, and I'm afraid for you," said Seth, putting his hand on Noah's shoulder, "Most people will not believe you and they will retaliate."

"I know, Seth, but I really have no choice," said Noah, "I won't be able to live a peaceful life knowing this truth and not acting upon it."

"I'll support you as much as I can, Noah. But I cannot allow this to affect my family. I don't want them to suffer any repercussions from the community," said Seth.

"I understand," said Noah, "When you feel you must step away from me or even sever our friendship, then go ahead – I'll understand. I'm grateful to have you as my friend. At least for as long as you're able."

"Even if I don't openly show my friendship, please know that in me you will always find an ally and well-wisher," said Seth, placing his arm around Noah, "I recognise this is cowardly on my part, but I must protect my family."

A sadness encircled the two friends as they hugged each other.

"Goodbye, my friend," said Noah.

Seth turned and walked away, tears streaming down his face – he wondered whether he had made a mistake by abandoning Noah.

Over the next few weeks and months, Noah began explaining his ideas to his family. They did not take him seriously and balked at the idea of there being only one god. To them, it seemed ludicrous to not have separate gods for the sun, the stars, the sea, the wind, and fire, not to mention the many qualities encompassing good and evil. These belief systems had passed down from generation to generation, and the accompanying customs, traditions and practices were the cornerstone of family and community life. How could they abandon these for one god whom Noah alone says he heard speaking to him, but has not, and cannot, be seen?

"This god should show himself if he wants to be taken seriously!" said a family elder, "And this idea of a spirit within us living on after death – what is this spirit and has anyone seen it?"

Noah felt discouraged by his family's reaction, especially when the older members ridiculed him for his ideas. Noah could only listen to their accusations, for he had no proof to present to them. Regardless of the arguments he raised to support the possibility of the existence of a higher being, their minds were closed. Realising that he could get no further with his family, Noah stopped trying to convince them and continued with his daily activities, including his walks and meditations under his favourite tree.

As the weeks passed, Noah's health deteriorated. He carried a heavy burden: even though no one believed him, he knew deep within him that there was only one god. He could not prove it, and it certainly did not help that this one god had not spoken to him again nor shown himself. As Noah grew weaker, he began to spend most of his time under the tree. He sat in contemplation, his mind running amok with his thoughts. He was genuinely troubled by what had befallen him.

"I used to be a strong, capable man," thought Noah, "Now I'm frail and anxious, unable to focus on anything but this one god."

One day as he sat under his tree yet again, seeking and searching for this one god, Noah heard a different voice come through. At first it was very faint, but it grew in intensity as Noah strained to hear it. "Noah, do you hear me? I am with you to help you through your lifetime. Do not be so despondent. All will be well," said the voice.

"Who are you? Are you God the Almighty? It doesn't sound like God," said Noah.

"I am not God the Almighty. I am one of His messengers who is helping you."

"What is your name?" asked Noah.

"You may call me your guardian angel, for that is all I am for you."

"What do you want from me? What am I supposed to do?" said Noah.

"You must convince those around you, your family, your friends and your community, that there is only one god, and they must refrain from worshipping idols. They are debasing themselves by this idolatry and by their reckless behaviour. They will have to account for their deeds."

"But I have tried with my family, and they all laughed at me. No one believes me," said Noah.

"You must persevere, regardless of peoples' reactions. This is your purpose in life and it is important that you fulfil it. Do not worry about the repercussions. God will protect you."

"I will try, but please ask God the Almighty to also guide me. Why won't He speak to me?" said Noah.

"God the Almighty is guiding you. Look within and you will find Him. I will convey messages to you and will protect you throughout your life. I am your guardian angel."

Noah was alarmed by this interaction. He could barely accept that he had had a conversation with God the Almighty. How was he going to explain this new interaction with what seemed to be an ethereal being sent by God? And where did this being reside? It could not possibly be within him. This was all too much for Noah.

"How am I going to explain your presence?" asked Noah.

"I only exist to guide and protect you, so you do not have to explain me to others. I am just another being who will help you with your work. Do not conflate me with God. You know God exists and you must convey His message. Do not doubt yourself and your purpose."

"Very well, guardian angel. But please speak to me every so often. Do not be silent," said Noah.

"I am with you. Now you must commence your work," said the guardian angel.

"Very well." Noah stood up and looked around him. Everything seemed normal; life carried on everywhere not noticing Noah in its midst.

"What am I going to do now?" thought Noah. He slowly began to walk home.

Over several days, Noah reflected upon everything that had transpired and realised he would have to move forward with his ideas.

"My heart leaves me no choice," thought Noah, "it will not leave me in peace."

Noah began to speak openly about the one god. He addressed people at the marketplace, during informal gatherings, and even within the temples after the various rituals and offerings to the gods. He visited families in their homes and sat down with individuals on a one-to-one basis, each time trying to convince them to at least accept the idea that the existence of a singular, spiritual god was possible. But no one was convinced; people were too deeply rooted in their beliefs, traditions, and customs.

As time evolved, Noah's reputation began to tarnish. His ideas created friction in the village. And as predicted, he and Seth grew apart as Noah's beliefs ostracised him from the community. He was alone in his quest and travelled further afield from his village to reach wider society.

When he could, Noah would sit under his favourite tree by the river and meditate in silence. During one of these sessions, he reached out. "Guardian angel, I am not making any progress in my attempts to convince people that there is only one god," whispered Noah, "No one believes me."

"You are doing very well and God the Almighty is pleased

with your efforts. He can see that the people refuse to heed your words, despite all your attempts to convince them of the truth. God the Almighty will now change the course of the world. He will send a deluge of water to rid the land of all that troubles it: the greed and selfishness; and the unintelligent, irrational idolatry. All life forms will be obliterated from the face of the Earth. Life spirit will return to its natural state, including all of humankind: their physical bodies will be destroyed, and they will return home to exist in their true, spiritual form."

Noah could not catch his breath; the words frightened him and he became apprehensive.

"Noah, you must not worry, for I am with you throughout your sojourn," said the guardian angel, "You will live a very long life, for you must help God during and after the great deluge. You will be saved, as well as other men and women. God also wants you to save some animals and plants so that these may serve your needs after the waters recede."

"But how can God destroy all that he has created? And how will I be saved?" said Noah, breathing heavily. He put his hand to his chest.

"It is God's wish. He can create, and He can destroy. And He can recreate, again and again. You must build a sea-faring vessel that will be strong enough to endure the calamity, and big enough to house men and women, as well as animals, plants, and seeds. Chop down this humongous tree and begin to build your ark. It must float on the river."

Noah was shocked into silence and could not utter a sound. Did he hear his guardian angel correctly? Was this really happening to him or was it just his imagination running wild? Noah lay against his tree trying to regulate his breathing. He finally managed to calm himself and relaxed his body. He was exhausted from his encounter. After a few minutes, he fell fast asleep.

Seth walked home along the river and saw Noah lying against his tree. He missed his friendship, and especially all their interesting conversations. He truly felt remorse for not fully supporting Noah in his quest.

Seth strode towards Noah and bent over him.

"Are you okay, Noah?" Seth asked gently. Noah opened his eyes.

"Seth, how nice to see you," said Noah, rubbing the sleep from his eyes. "I'm actually not sure how well I am. I've been receiving messages from God, and I'm greatly disturbed by what I must do. I don't feel well at all." Seth had never seen Noah looking so ill. His face was sunken and drained of colour; dark circles had formed under his eyes.

Noah tried to stand but could not lift himself. Seth helped him to his feet and propped him against the tree. Noah could not quite get his balance and Seth continued to hold on to him.

"Let me accompany you home," said Seth.

"It's not a good idea to be seen with me, and especially after I tell you what I must do." Noah proceeded to explain about the deluge and all that he had been guided to do.

Seth's eyes widened. "How can this be?! And you have to build a sea-craft?!" said Seth.

"I myself don't know what to make of it, Seth. Anyway, right now I'm really not feeling well and I need to go home," said Noah.

"I'll take you," said Seth, as he held Noah and half-carried him home.

Noah remained in bed for days. He was completely distraught. He still could not comprehend that this one god wanted to destroy everything: it was mind-boggling. Noah began to doubt himself again, questioning whether he had actually heard these words from some higher being, or whether it was his mind playing tricks on him.

"Maybe everyone is right and a disease has indeed gripped me," thought Noah.

Seth came to check on Noah every so often, but found him in generally the same condition: Noah seemed lost in his own thoughts and was physically very weak. It was completely out of character, for Noah's mind was usually sharp, and his body always strong and vibrant.

"I cannot bear to see you like this," said Seth, "What can I do to help you regain your strength?"

"I don't know," said Noah, "If I'm having trouble believing what was conveyed to me, then how can I convince others? I don't know if it's true. If it is, then how will I accomplish all that I'm supposed to? And if it's not true, then what is happening to me, Seth? Either way, I don't understand the turn my life has taken."

"I'm sorry you're going through all this," said Seth, "I don't know what to do and how to help you. But I do know that you must eat something, and get some fresh air." Seth helped Noah out of his bed and called for some food. After Noah ate a little, Seth took him outside. He put his arm around Noah to support his weight and they went for a short walk. As they made their way down the lane, many people stared at Noah with pity; some were spiteful in their remarks.

"Look at him now," said one, "Going around professing there's only one god and insulting all the gods in the temples. Where's his one god now that he's sick?"

"It's the wrath of the gods," said another, "they've struck him down for his insolence and he's now diseased."

Another called out, "You're lucky you have a friend like Seth who's willing to help you despite all your nonsense teachings!" Seth's heart sank with sympathy for Noah.

"Why don't you all go about your business and leave Noah to deal with his problems?" said Seth, "I'm helping to heal him, and will help him find his way to the truth."

Noah smiled and let out a chuckle, shaking his head.

"What is the truth? I cannot tell anymore," said Noah.

"You know that deep within you lies the truth," said Seth, "Continue your search and do not lose your focus, Noah. If this one god truly exists and has created everything, he will not abandon you."

Noah was surprised by Seth's remarks and looked at him quizzically.

Seth smiled. "Let's get you home."

As the days and weeks passed, Seth visited Noah every day and ensured that he ate well and took in fresh air. Noah looked forward to Seth's visits, brightening up whenever he arrived. Slowly, Noah began to recover and regained enough of his strength to take a daily walk along the river. They engaged in many discussions, with Seth prodding and challenging all of Noah's beliefs and assumptions. Noah finally came to the conclusion that he had to persevere in his quest and follow the guidance of the one god: his heart would not allow him to do otherwise.

When Noah felt well enough, he began to regularly sit under his humongous tree to strengthen his spirit and recover his confidence. Many months passed in this manner, and things seemed to return to normal for everyone. His friendship with Seth was also rekindled, only this time their bond was much stronger.

Then one day, as Noah sat under his tree contemplating in silence, he heard his guardian angel call out to him, "Noah, are you feeling better now? Can we resume our work again?"

"Why have you not communicated with me?" asked Noah.

"I have, but you could not hear me," said the guardian angel, "You were too deeply disturbed."

Noah felt a twinge of regret.

"I am sorry that you have suffered," continued the guardian angel, "but please know that I am with you every moment, and that God is with you and protecting you always. So do not fall into a state of melancholy again. Have faith in God the Almighty, and if you need assurance and guidance, just turn to Him and ask. Now, you must start building your sea-faring vessel, for time is running out."

Noah drew in a long breath. "Okay, I am ready to begin the work." After waiting for a few minutes without further remark or response, Noah got up and went home to gather his tools.

Noah stood at the foot of his tree, rubbing his hands over its coarse, uneven trunk. He felt sorry to chop it down. It had sheltered him for many years, not only during his meditation, but also during his darkest moments. Noah sat down against it for one last time and closed his eyes. The leaves rustled as a light breeze flowed through. Noah felt a tingly presence swirling around him. It was almost as if the tree was speaking to him, saying it was born for this reason and had been waiting patiently for the day when it could serve out its true purpose. Noah smiled and stood up. He picked up his axe and began chopping. Seth passed by and was surprised to see Noah hard at work.

"I'm glad to see you've decided to embrace your truth," said Seth.

"It's thanks to you for helping me through my difficulties."

"It's good to see you back to yourself."

"I feel much better following my heart," said Noah, "even though the messages I've received sound outlandish even to me. I suppose it does not matter if others believe me, as long as I am confident in what was conveyed to me."

"I'll always be your friend, Noah. But I must publicly retreat from our friendship again in order to protect my family. They're being harassed all the time and I fear for their safety. If it was only me, I would openly join your cause. But I have to look out for my family."

"Not to worry, Seth," said Noah, "Be on your way so you're not seen with me. In the future, if you wish to join me, I'll welcome you with open arms."

"Thank you, Noah. But please remember that I do support you, and if you need my help, then get a message to me."

They hugged each other and said goodbye. Seth went on his way, and Noah returned to his tree, hacking and chopping with all his might.

Day by day, Noah's ark began to take shape. The work was physically demanding, but Noah did not slow down, for he understood that time was running out. People would walk along the river staring at his ridiculous build. Children passed their hours splashing and swimming in the river, all the while gawking at the strange man named Noah. He was constantly teased, taunted, and bombarded with insults, but Noah was determined to complete the task that had been assigned to him by the one god. When the ark was finally complete, the people in his community gathered around in amazement, gaping at the site, for it was the size of several houses combined. They had never seen such a humongous sea-faring vessel. It peaked their curiosity and they came to inquire what Noah would do with it.

"I will take it out to sea," said Noah, "Will you help me lower it into the river?" Everyone laughed at him, but decided to assist him, even if their only intention was to satisfy their curiosity, or perhaps hasten Noah's departure from their midst: his presence was a destabilising force within the community.

It took the whole village of strong and able men to help Noah get the craft into the water. Seth was amongst them and he grinned at Noah from afar, his eyes congratulating him on his achievement.

The ark was a sight to behold as it splashed into the water. It towered over them and bobbed perilously from side to side.

"Are you sure it will float?" asked one villager.

"We'll soon find out," said another.

"Where are you taking it, Noah? And when are you leaving?" asked somebody, as the crowd roared with laughter. Noah ignored their questions.

"Thank you for your help," said Noah, as he boarded his ark and disappeared into its bellows. He peered through its boards, watching the villagers disperse.

"They ask good questions," thought Noah, "where, and when, am I taking it?"

Noah began to spend his days and nights on the vessel, readying it for the calamity that was to befall them. One night, Seth secretly visited him on the ark and brought him provisions and supplies.

"Let me know what else you need, Noah. I want to contribute to your cause," said Seth.

"Here's a list of all the items I require to fit out the ark's interior, as well as the foodstuffs, bedding, clothing, tools, plants, and seeds I will need," said Noah, "I am grateful for whatever you can contribute."

"I'm so happy that you've actually built your vessel," said Seth, scanning the interior, "It's extraordinary! I admire your conviction."

"It's been hard work," said Noah, looking towards the sky, "Now all I have to do is wait."

Seth put his arm around Noah. "For some reason, I don't think you'll have to wait too long."

"You're a good friend, Seth. But you'd better go. I don't want anyone to see you here." They hugged one another and Seth quietly left the ark, telling Noah that the provisions would be delivered to him over the coming days. And true to his word, Seth was extremely generous with the supplies, and provided Noah with double of everything he required.

And then one day, it began to rain.

It rained incessantly. Days turned to weeks, and weeks turned to months, and it continued to rain. It drowned the crops and flooded the houses. Rivers of gushing water suddenly appeared and flowed down the streets. People moved up to the second story of their houses, at least those who had them, while others relocated to higher ground. By this time, Noah had filled his ark with animals, two by two, and stocked it with plants, seeds and food of every kind. He even brought a cutting from his humongous tree, for he had every intention of replanting it one day, somewhere. When his own house washed away, Noah brought those family members who were willing to accompany him to his ark; the rest moved to higher ground. On one particularly dark and stormy night, he sought out Seth and his family. The lightning and thunder crackled so loudly, Noah's voice was barely audible over the noise.

"Seth! Seth! Move your family to my ark!" shouted Noah, "I'm going to seek out more men and women to join us!"

The waters were rising quickly. Noah thrashed around the village, struggling against the current, searching for people to help rebuild the land after the calamity. He came across some who were strong and of good character, and some who had not been so kind to him over the years, and invited them all onto the ark. They were grateful for Noah's help. Once they were all safely on board, including Seth and his family, the winds and rains seemed to accelerate.

"The gods are angry," said one man.

"Not the gods!" shouted Noah. "There is no god but God the Almighty! It is He who has created us and everything on this land, and it is He who is destroying it all!" Suddenly, a surge of water appeared from nowhere and lifted the ark high above the treeline. Everyone was tossed about and they held on for their dear lives. Wave after wave surged upon them for hours on end. When the tempest petered out and the boat finally stabilised, Noah came up to take a look: the whole village had been razed by the water. No one could have survived such a deluge, unless they were in a sea-worthy vessel.

Noah and his people remained on the ark for weeks, floating and bobbing along. Land was nowhere to be seen, dry or otherwise, only water as far as the eye could see. During this period,

Noah taught his people about God the Almighty, and warned them to leave their idolatrous beliefs and superstitions behind. He taught them the importance of showing kindness, compassion, love, and generosity to others. Months went by, and slowly the people came around and embraced the truth of who they were.

"Are we really spirit beings?" asked one. "If so, then how do I begin to know myself?"

"Sit still, in silence, and concentrate on nothingness. Empty your mind and seek out God," said Noah. The people began to follow his teachings. The months turned into years, and little by little, the people came together to form an even closer community, with God at its centre.

And very slowly, the waters began to recede.

Then one day, Seth shouted from atop the ark, "Noah, I see land! Come and take a look!" Noah hoisted himself up and looked beyond.

"It's time to rebuild, Seth!" said Noah. They both jumped for joy. Hearing the commotion, the people below scrambled to the surface.

"Land!" shouted Noah, pointing towards the mound of earth appearing against the horizon. Noah hurried along the vessel and grabbed the helm with both hands. Slowly, the ark veered towards the terrain as Noah continuously adjusted its course. When they got close enough, he lowered the anchor – the resounding thud against the seabed indicated their arrival – they had reached their new home.

Noah held his hand up signalling all to wait while he climbed down into the shallow water. The people watched silently in anticipation, and when Noah's feet finally stood on solid ground, they wept with relief, many of them thanking God for their good fortune. Then very cautiously, Noah's people and animals slowly disembarked and made their way onto their new homeland.

It was extremely difficult to settle down and establish their new community. They struggled to till the soil, and patiently waited for their crops to yield food. They reared their animals and established homesteads and community services to enhance their quality of life. As time went on, existence became slightly easier, especially when newer generations began to populate the area. Even Noah's family expanded, and he was pleased when some of his progeny joined with Seth's descendants.

Noah continued to instil the values of kindness, compassion, and generosity, and schooled his people in the oneness of God, the All-Encompassing Spirit, and that their old ways of worshipping physical deities was anathema to their spirit. The majority of Noah's people embraced his teachings, however a few secretly continued their rituals and offerings to stone gods, which they had surreptitiously carved from local rock. Noah was disappointed at this development, but relentlessly engaged with his community to ensure they were on the right track.

Over the years, Noah and Seth became inseparable; they provided one another with companionship and a great deal of support, especially as new generations were born. The youth had not experienced the great flood and therefore did not understand what the fuss was about. These younger inhabitants could not relate to Noah and Seth, and nor could they to them. The two old men became just that to the younger community: old men who were to be respected, but who did not understand the modern ways.

"As long as the majority accept that there is only one god, that they are spiritual beings who should be kind and compassionate towards each other, and share the wealth and abundance that God has provided, then my work is done," said Noah, sitting under his tree. He was growing weary with old age. "I'm exhausted and my body no longer sustains me. Not like my tree; it grows stronger with every passing year." He stroked the jagged bark, remembering its ancestor rooted by the river in the old village.

"I, too, am tired," said Seth, "but I must continue to lead

and support my family, for they depend on me for direction," said Seth.

"You may not know this, Seth, but I've been communicating with my guardian angel quite regularly. He also seems to think that my work is done. But he said it is up to me and God to decide when I wish to revert to my spirit form," said Noah. Seth was astonished by Noah's remarks.

"How can you speak like this, Noah? You know there's still much work to do," said Seth, "And I still need your companionship, my friend."

"But I feel my work is done," said Noah, "It's now up to future generations to continue to build their lives and rehabilitate the land. Life has become very tedious for me, Seth. You must understand."

"Of course I understand," said Seth, "but you must not talk like this. I need you to remain strong and continue to lead our people. And I'm not ready to lose you. I will not let you wither away." Seth was going to do everything in his power to take care of Noah. He truly believed that Noah was a special being, for had he not been chosen by God to save the people from the great flood?

From that point on, Seth kept a close eye on Noah. He ensured that he ate well and took his daily exercise. Noah persevered for Seth's sake and carried on for a few more years. But as he grew more decrepit, Noah was unable to withstand life any longer. He slowed down, preferring to remain alone and silent for the most part, and spent his days sitting under his tree. During this period, he conversed with his guardian angel, who provided him with a great deal of comfort.

"I am tired, guardian angel," said Noah, "I want to return home now. I've had a very long and tedious life. It's time."

"I am with you for as long as you are in your physical form, Noah. You are not alone. Continue to pray to God, and ask Him for what is best for you," said the guardian angel. Noah prayed to God and continued to do so for many days.

From their realm, both Michael and Raphael watched Noah with concern, and also prayed to God to do what was best.

"I hear your appeals, as well as Noah's prayers," said God to Michael and Raphael, "When the time is right, I will bring Gabriel home." Michael and Raphael cried with joy, for it had been many years since they had heard Gabriel's name spoken out loud: it made his return seem real.

As the days marched on, Seth noticed Noah's health deteriorating very quickly and he knew the end was near. He sat by Noah's bed day and night and made him as comfortable as he could. They reminisced about their childhood, and laughed at their youthful indiscretions. They fondly remembered their long walks along the river in the old village and spoke about all the hard times they had experienced together. And when the moment finally arrived, Noah took a few long breaths and whispered to Seth, "Do not be sad, for I am happy to return home and meet this one god for whom I have devoted my life. My guardian angel said he would receive me. And when it is your turn to return home, I will be there to greet you. Seth, I am grateful to you for being such a true and devoted friend throughout my life." And with those words, Noah's spirit left his body.

On the other side, Michael waited with anticipation. Many years had passed, and the heavens had felt Gabriel's absence. Finally, the moment arrived. As soon as Noah's spirit began rising, Michael reached towards him.

Noah was overcome with love and affection. He felt as if he was floating in a tranquil sea, with waves of warmth flowing over him. A heavenly, divine being appeared before him and drew him near.

"Hello, Noah," said Michael, as he fought back tears, "I am your guardian angel. Sit here with me until you get reacquainted with this realm." Noah sat down and looked at the divine being.

Noah felt he knew his guardian angel very well, but could not explain how and why. Raphael watched from afar and was impatient to join them. Many angels surrounded Noah and projected their light and love towards him to help him become fully aware. Slowly, he began to shine brightly.

Michael asked gently, "Do you remember who you are? And do you recognise all of us and where you are?"

"Yes, I do" he replied, "I am called Gabriel. And you are Michael. And I see Raphael approaching us, too." Raphael moved closer, with Abraham, Moses, Jesus, and Mohamed following. The four stood back as Raphael rushed to embrace Gabriel; the three Archangels glowed with joy at their reunion. The Quartet moved forward to receive Gabriel and many angels congregated around him, eager to welcome him amongst them.

When the excitement finally abated, the Quartet left to resume their work, leaving the three Archangels to catch up. Michael and Raphael ushered Gabriel to a private corner and began to speak in earnest.

"Gabriel, it is so good to have you back with us," said Raphael, "How we have missed your presence!"

"It is wonderful to be back," said Gabriel, "it was a very long and difficult life. But I feel exuberant! It really is fantastic not to have to carry around the weight of the human body. I am light and free!"

"Your last days were particularly tiresome," said Michael.

"I could not have done this without the two of you. Michael, thank you for protecting me and guiding me along the way. And Raphael, you have always stepped in and allowed me the freedom to pursue greater challenges. I am eternally grateful to you both. But I do not know whether I accomplished the task God set out for me. Did I pass God's test? I must withdraw into Him to find out. But enough about me. How did the transition go when God sent the deluge across Earth? Were you able to receive everyone as they crossed over?"

"It went as well as can be expected given that millions of souls arrived at the same time," said Raphael, "We all worked very hard to help with the transition, and everyone settled in. However, we continue to work with some souls who have found it difficult to forgive themselves, and each other, for mistakes they made during their lifetimes on Earth. But we continue to persevere."

"Good," said Gabriel, "I would like to learn more about this, but first I must report in to God."

"Of course, Gabriel! We will carry on with our duties and wait for your return. Go now and rest," said Raphael, "And Michael, you should also rest. The Quartet and I can manage things. You have been through each and every ordeal with Gabriel. Take some time out for yourself and recover your full strength."

"Very well," said Michael, "And Gabriel, I do believe that you passed your test." Gabriel smiled, for he appreciated Michael's encouragement.

"Let us see what God says," said Gabriel. The three embraced one another before each went his separate way.

Gabriel withdrew into God in the seventh dimension and rested. When he felt strong enough, he raised his head and invoked, "In the name of God, the most Beneficent, the most Merciful."

"My dear child," said God, "are you well-recovered from your ordeal?"

"Yes, my Lord," said Gabriel.

"Very good," said God, "Gabriel, I am so very proud of your accomplishments. You have done extremely well in your duty to rebuild Earth and establish the correct way. Many of My children will benefit from your guidance for generations to come."

"My Lord, not all the people embraced the truth," said Gabriel, "There are still some who insist on maintaining the old ways and continue to engage in superstitious rituals and offerings to gods made of stone."

"There will always be those who are tied to the material,"

said God, "My children are not perfect, whether in physical or in spiritual form. Perfection only lies in My Light."

"Yes, my Lord," said Gabriel.

"Now Gabriel, I am sure you are wondering whether or not you passed the test," said God.

"Yes, my Lord," said Gabriel, tilting his head forward.

God smiled benevolently, and said, "Come closer to Me." Gabriel withdrew into God more deeply.

"I am very happy with your efforts," said God, "and of course, you have passed this test. Even though you encountered many difficulties during your life as Noah, you remained faithful and true to your spirit and to Me. You chose to be compassionate and kind towards others, and forgave when you needed to – you have certainly passed this test. Now we will see how life on Earth evolves as we begin again, and whether My children will take this second chance that I have granted to embrace their truth."

"Gabriel," continued God, "if you are ready and still wish to, I now want you to begin the next phase of our work. I want you to concentrate on teaching and tutoring all My children in the angel schools. Convey My message to them that they must internalise the lessons on love, kindness, and compassion, and they must particularly learn about mercy and forgiveness. Just because I cleansed the Earth in one swoop does not mean that My children are cleansed. Each must atone for all the hurt each has caused, and must find forgiveness in their hearts for what each has endured at the hands of another. If they do not, it will remain a stain on each of their souls, and will prevent them from achieving the ultimate peace. Gabriel, do you agree to continue with this work?"

"Yes, my Lord," said Gabriel.

"Very good," said God, "Now go back to My children and help them. And know that My blessings are continuously over you, and that I am always with you."

"Thy Will be done in and through me each day. Thy Will be done on Earth as it is in Heaven," said Gabriel, as he bowed his head and began his descent to the fourth dimension.

Gabriel noticed that the heavens were radiant with light. It had been an eternity since he had seen the higher dimensions shimmering so brightly, and he glowed with contentment. Many angels became aware of his presence and called out to him, wishing him well, and thanking him for all he had done to help them. Gabriel was taken aback to see the billions of angels acknowledge him, and he said a prayer for them all. When he reached the fourth dimension, he found Michael and Raphael waiting for him.

"How are you feeling?" enquired Raphael.

"I am well and ready to work," said Gabriel. He then told them what God conveyed.

"We are so happy for you, Gabriel. We knew you had passed your test," said Raphael.

"Thank you. And how are both of you? Have you recovered from your gruelling task of guarding me, Michael?" They laughed heartily.

"Yes, I have," said Michael, "but I must admit, at times it was not easy, especially during your bouts of sickness. It took a lot of restraint on my part not to reveal my identity to you to help you out of your melancholy, and to hasten things up on Earth."

"Well, I am just so grateful that it was you who guided me. And what about you, Raphael? How are you and how has your work been proceeding?"

"The work has gone well, although I would never have been able to do this without the Quartet," said Raphael, "They have been indispensable to the workings of all the heavens, and have been particularly supportive in the angel schools. Once we began receiving everyone here after the great flood, it took tremendous effort to ensure that each soul became reacquainted with this realm quickly and settled down. The Quartet basically took charge of the entire process and were critical in guiding each individual to their rightful place within the dimensions. The vast majority are now in the angel schools learning various lessons and increasing their awareness. Many have been able to reach their higher consciousness and are making their way up through the fifth and sixth dimensions. The Quartet have been providing tutorials and helping groups of angels advance quickly."

Gabriel radiated with happiness. "I am so happy to hear of the progress, Raphael. I am looking forward to spending time with the Quartet. If I read between the lines and understand God correctly, there is still a lot of work to do and they will play a pivotal role in the future. Raphael, do you need to rest a little?"

"I am absolutely fine. Compared with what you and Michael have just been through, my work has been extremely easy. I have not had to contend with the physical world on Earth. I really do not know how you both flip back and forth between the physical and spiritual realms and still manage to balance yourselves. In any case, I am ready to continue with our work. I am just delighted to have you and Michael back with me."

"Wonderful! Shall we proceed to the angel schools now? I would like to see for myself what is happening," said Gabriel. During their conversation, an angel had quietly approached them and had patiently waited for them to finish.

"Archangel Gabriel," said the angel, "My name is Esperanza and I am Seth's guardian angel. Seth is approaching the end of his life and is taking his last few breaths."

"Oh! Then I must hurry," said Gabriel, "I must be there to receive him when he crosses over. Esperanza, thank you so much for drawing my attention to this."

"We will accompany you," said Michael. With the two Archangels in tow, Gabriel rushed off with Esperanza to be with Seth, and waited for his final moments. Gabriel saw Seth's whole family gathered around him, and also observed that Noah's family and many villagers waited solemnly nearby.

"I hope Seth's family appreciates all that he has done for them," thought Gabriel, "He worked tremendously hard to ease their way through life."

As Seth's final breaths drew nearer, Esperanza moved towards him and reached out to receive him. With his last breath, he began to rise.

"Seth, I am Esperanza, your guardian angel. Come with me." Seth moved into the warm, loving embrace and steadied himself. Angels gathered round to project their light and love on Seth until he was acquainted with his environment.

"I am happy to meet you, Esperanza," said Seth, "I feel wonderful! I feel so light and free! Thank you for taking care of me." He looked up and saw Noah standing there, with a huge, beaming smile.

"Noah! It is you! You actually came to receive me!" exclaimed Seth. Gabriel embraced him and sat him down, while Esperanza remained close by.

"You must get properly acquainted with this realm," said Esperanza. Many angels gathered round and projected their light and love towards Seth to help raise his awareness, and remember.

After a few moments, Seth looked awestruck and said quietly, "Archangel Gabriel, it is you."

"Yes, it is me," said Gabriel, "I am delighted to see you again, Seth. I am so grateful to have had you as my friend during my lifetime as Noah." They both sat in silence for a few minutes, absorbing the love and affection projected towards them. Suddenly, a wave of realisation engulfed them both and they looked questioningly at Michael and Raphael.

Michael said, "Gabriel, as you have now recognised, Seth is one of the special angels we had sent you. Seth's higher awareness had reached the sixth dimension, and he had especially asked to be born near you so that he could help you with your worldly task. But his memory was also blocked so as not to mistakenly reveal your identity to you. So Seth, also, went through a similar test. He is now on the cusp of entering the seventh dimension."

Gabriel turned to Seth. "Why did you want to help me with this task?"

174

"Because I wanted to serve you and those on Earth," said Seth, "I was there when you visited the sixth dimension a long time ago and advised us to serve others in order to raise our consciousness and enter the seventh dimension. Do you remember? You told us enlightenment is truly achieved when you are able to maintain your high level of awareness and still love and serve others, regardless of their status: this is the destruction of the ego. It is godliness. And then we asked you how to serve? You replied that when God requires help and word is sent out, then volunteer for the assignments, even if they take you down all the way to life on Earth. For nothing is more loving and generous of spirit than helping those who are in the depths of despair."

Gabriel was astonished. This angel had volunteered to help him during his life as Noah, and had been instrumental in Noah's worldly success: without Seth, Noah would never have had the strength to carry on, especially during his bouts of illness.

"I am indebted to you, Seth," said Gabriel.

"No, you are not," said Seth, "We each gained something from our friendship and experience. You have no idea how much I have learnt from you. I am grateful to have had the opportunity."

Gabriel and Seth embraced one another tightly and spent some time discussing how things had evolved on Earth in the few years after Noah's passing. Seth had attempted to continue Noah's teachings, but found that later generations were too far removed from the deluge, and the message of God was diluted with each successive generation.

"Human beings have very short memories and do not seem to learn the lessons of the past," said Gabriel. "Anyway, we tried our best, Seth. I am pleased that you continued the effort. It is now up to each individual to follow his and her inner spirit."

"Yes, Gabriel. And I am happy to be home again." They sparkled with joy as they embraced one more time. Esperanza then escorted Seth up to the sixth dimension to rest, and Gabriel joined Michael and Raphael to visit the angel schools.

Earth was sparsely populated. Very few angels were permitted to visit the planet in human form. The vast majority attended the angel schools learning about themselves and how each wished to develop. Gabriel and Raphael focussed their efforts there, teaching and tutoring at various levels, while Michael monitored the evolution of Earth.

Gabriel also spent time with the Quartet. He mentored each one, helping to strengthen the specific qualities each required to raise himself further. Michael and Raphael also provided them with individual support where necessary. Many years passed in this manner, with everyone settling into a routine, trying hard to advance themselves.

One day, God called out to Gabriel.

"I am being summoned," said Gabriel.

"Go ahead," said Raphael, "we are fine here."

Gabriel withdrew into God and invoked, "In the name of God, the most Beneficent, the most Merciful."

"My dear Gabriel," said God, "I have been observing all the activities in the heavens and on Earth, and it is now time to determine how far My children have progressed. I wish them to purify themselves so that their lights burn as brightly as they originally did when they first burst forth from Me. I will now open up the possibility for many to live Earthly lives again. But I am changing the parameters. No longer will My children be able to visit Earth and unreservedly enjoy My creation; this privilege is no longer theirs. Now, in addition to their learnings in the angel schools, I will utilise Earth and all that I have created within it to educate My children to raise their consciousness: life on Earth itself will be a school to learn lessons."

"For those who wish to, I will make it possible for them to be born on Earth, but I will block their memories so that they do not remember who they are. They will have to rely on their inner self, their spirit, to guide their journey through life. While they will not remember their existence prior to being born, their link with their spirit will be maintained. And this will be crucial: the further they move away from their inner spirit, the further removed they will be from Me. I, however, will always be within them and will never abandon them. Gabriel, during your life as Noah, despite having no memory of your existence before your birth, by listening to your inner spirit and following your instincts, you raised your consciousness and connected with your true self. And there you found Me, the divine within. So, you have demonstrated that this can be done."

"Gabriel, as time evolves on Earth, I will help humankind by sending messages and guidance, sometimes directly, and at other times through those of My children who wish to assist. I want My Message to be continuously conveyed to humankind on Earth. I want it reinforced so that My children will obtain a good grounding in, and will learn to embrace those qualities that are closest to Me: love, compassion, kindness, mercy, forgiveness, and most importantly, that we are all one and the same. From amongst the special missionary angels, at least those who wish to visit Earth again, choose a few to perform this task. They will be My Messengers. They will be critical to guiding My children, and I want them to be born in all parts of the world to convey My Message: east and west, north and south. My Message must not only be taught in the angel schools and in the higher dimensions, but also on Earth, in the life school. And when it becomes necessary, during certain times in Earth's history, I will send distinct and extraordinary Signs to humankind to strengthen My Message."

"My dear Gabriel, I wish you to specifically work with

Abraham, Moses, Jesus, and Mohamed and help them to raise their consciousness even higher. They are on the verge of evolving into the seventh dimension and meet Me face-to-face. Convey to them that I am ready to receive them as soon as they are able to progress through the final stages and raise themselves. When they are ready to take this step, they must let me know. Involve Michael and Raphael in helping them to achieve their objectives."

"Yes, My Lord," said Gabriel.

God continued to give Gabriel specific guidance related to the Quartet, but directed him to keep this part of the message confidential.

"It must only be shared with the four of them," instructed God, "and even then, only at the right time."

"Yes, My Lord," said Gabriel.

"My child," continued God, "I also want you to pay special attention to My children who have embraced darkness. Mobilise all your strength to attract them back into the light so they may begin their journey towards recognising the truth of who they are. You may not be successful in this endeavour, but I wish you to make every effort to try and wrest them from their reverie; they are trapped in illusion."

"I will do my very best, My Lord, but I ask for Your continuous blessings and guidance, for this will be a difficult task," said Gabriel.

"My child, you always have my blessings," said God, "I am with you each and every moment and shower you with all My love and grace."

"Thank you, My Lord," said Gabriel, tilting his head forward.

"My dear Gabriel," said God, "What you do not realise is that I, too, am waiting patiently for the day when you permanently merge with My Light."

Gabriel was taken aback. "My Lord, why would You wish that?"

"My child," said God, "It is precisely at that moment that I will shine more brilliantly; a part of Me will have come alive again."

Gabriel bowed in supplication before God and said, "But I am nothing compared to You."

"My dear child," said God, "You are everything to Me."

God put His hand on Gabriel and raised him to his full height – by humankind's standards, he was gigantic: an imposing, mighty figure whose light illuminated the heavens. He projected sheer strength, but with such gentility that his appearance simultaneously overwhelmed and soothed those around him – his presence permeated the atmosphere with peace.

"My dear Gabriel," said God, "Do not underestimate how much I feel your absence when you are not with Me. Just as it is your desire to merge permanently with My Light and remain with Me, it is also My desire that you return home to Me. You are a part of Me, and I miss your presence within."

"My Lord, I will do my utmost," said Gabriel, "I will put all my strength into the efforts to help my siblings rise to their highest."

"I could not be happier, Gabriel," said God, "Now return to the lower heavens and carry on with your work. And remember, I will be with you every step of the way. When you are in difficulty, turn to Me and I will carry you forward through your troubles. My blessings are with you."

"Thy Will be done in and through me each day. Thy Will be done on Earth as it is in Heaven," invoked Gabriel as he began his descent to the fourth dimension, where Michael, Raphael, and the Quartet waited to receive him.

He conveyed God's message to them, at least the part that was not confidential.

"I am delighted by this news," said Raphael, "Life on Earth will provide more opportunities for individuals to raise their awareness."

"And the planet requires more human beings to develop the communities," said Michael.

"We have a lot of work to do," said Gabriel, "and we must begin in earnest. We should start by announcing that God has provided the opportunity for all angels to resume visiting Earth again in human form.

"Very well," said Michael, turning to Raphael, "Let us gather everyone."

Michael and Raphael called upon the angels. Gabriel and the Quartet watched as thousands upon thousands of angels approached to hear the news.

"Archangel Gabriel," said Abraham, "we are grateful that God is ready to welcome us in the seventh dimension, but we will require your help."

"Of course!" said Gabriel, "Even Michael and Raphael will be present to support you through the final stages. Be assured of that."

"Thank you," said Abraham, as all four tilted their heads in gratitude.

Michael and Raphael made their way back, and once all the angels settled themselves, Gabriel began to speak.

"My dear siblings, God will now permit us to visit Earth again in human form. However, the parameters have changed. We cannot be born on Earth out of curiosity to experience God's creation, or for pleasure, rather our purpose will be to learn lessons quickly, much faster than we would normally learn while here in the angel schools. We will now learn through life experience, from the "school of hard knocks" – the Earth school."

The crowd shifted with surprise as angels whispered and murmured amongst themselves.

"We will begin again on Earth," said Gabriel, "Those of you who wish to be born in human form may do so, but you will have no memory of your prior existence. You will have to rely on your inner self, your spirit, to guide your journey through life. God will always be with you, so look within and you will find Him."

One angel came forward and caught Gabriel's attention.

"Archangel Gabriel, my name is Njeri. There are a few of us who have not been forgiven for the mistakes we made during our last lives on Earth. Are they all wiped out because God is beginning anew on Earth?"

"Not at all, Njeri," said Gabriel, "You must still pay back these debts – these are obligations that will always be with you until you atone for them – they are a blight on your soul and will not allow you to raise yourselves. You may all forgive each other immediately and be done with it, or if you still cannot find it in your hearts to forgive, then you may work off these debts here in the fourth dimension or in Earthly lives. And again, everyone must realise that it is much easier to forgive than to work off these debts. Everyone must open their hearts – it is a mark of your higher consciousness."

"But it is difficult to forgive. How can we allow people to get away with their wrong-doings?" asked Imran.

"Forgiveness does not mean that you condone the action," said Gabriel, "The action is still wrong. Forgiveness is about you and your ability to show mercy. You are raising your being to show compassion. And this not only releases you by unbinding your tie to the wrong-doer and the wrong-doing, it also opens the possibility for the wrong-doer to learn from his mistake."

"But what if the wrong-doer does not learn, or does not even acknowledge his wrong-doing in the first place?" said Imran.

"That is his choice. But do not let his choice control you," said Gabriel, "By holding on to your resentment and anger, the wrong-doer now has power over you. You must break that hold and set yourself free. And the key to this is compassion, mercy, forgiveness. Do not give the wrong-doer the power to set you free. Do it yourself!"

"Thank you for the explanation, Archangel Gabriel," said Imran.

"We will try our utmost to work through our egos and embrace mercy and forgiveness," said Njeri.

"Very well," said Gabriel, as he turned to the crowd and continued, "God has given us a second chance on Earth. Let us not only improve ourselves but also develop the world in a manner that is worthy of who we are. Let our lives and societies reflect our eminence."

"We will," said the angels, as they began to slowly disperse. The three Archangels and the Quartet watched them, silently praying for God to shower His blessings on all.

As the last of them disappeared, Raphael said, "What would you like us to do, Gabriel?"

"We need to focus on the angel schools and provide the impetus for more angels to achieve their higher consciousness," said Gabriel, "Raphael, I especially wish you to drive this forward, for we will require many more angels in the fifth and sixth dimensions to help us with our work on Earth in the future. God indicated He would send messengers to all areas of the world, and only those in the higher dimensions will be able to fulfil these roles."

"It would be my pleasure to do this work," said Raphael.

"Very well," said Gabriel, "Let us begin."

Time marched on with all seven angels working tirelessly in the angel schools as well as monitoring Earth. The Quartet were particularly diligent, and Gabriel kept them close by so that he could guide their advancement. After a few years, Gabriel turned the full management of the schools over to Raphael.

"Michael, let us accompany the Quartet to the upper dimensions. We can concentrate on them and help raise their consciousness," said Gabriel, "You have spent many years watching over Earth and probably need a respite."

Michael grinned. "You know me better than I know myself."

"Are you surprised after all these millennia together?" said Gabriel, and they laughed affectionately.

"Yes, it has been a very long time," said Michael.

"Right from the beginning," said Gabriel, "You were the first one to come forward and help me." They smiled at each other warmly, remembering that time. "In any case, I would like you to remain in the higher dimensions for an extended period and tutor those who reside there. At some point, I will take the Quartet aside and work with them as God had instructed. After we are finished, they will join you to help with the tutoring."

"Very well, but who will monitor Earth?" said Michael.

Raphael called out from the fourth dimension, "I will keep an eye on Earth. Kibwe has volunteered to help, so carry on."

With that settled, Michael, Gabriel and the Quartet made their way up and initiated their activities in the higher dimensions. When the opportunity presented itself, Gabriel took some time out and requested the Quartet to accompany him. He led them to a serene spot, one which had become very reverent for Gabriel: it was the place where he had first met God face-to-face.

Abraham, Moses, Jesus, and Mohamed sat in a semi-circle facing Gabriel.

"It is now time to convey God's message to you in detail," said Gabriel, and he proceeded to utter those confidential words that God had directed him to speak only at the right time.

I fondly remember our conversation, but will not reveal the discussions. It entailed those thoughts and wishes that God had entrusted to me, and the oath each of the four took to do His Will on Earth and in the heavens. I will never forget this moment, for it bound us together in an alliance that exists to this day. I would see my four brothers through great hardship, and together, we would come to watch in horror, and in fact, relive the suffering as humankind twisted and manipulated God's words for their own purposes. These times would reveal some of the worst tragedies I would witness on Earth during my long existence. And they would bring me down to the depths of despair.

19 DARK

Gabriel turned his attention to the work he had been dreading for many thousands of years: he now had to deal with the troublemakers who had ensconced themselves in a dark bubble in the fourth dimension, waiting impatiently to live Earthly lives again.

He made his way to the dark angels. Michael and Raphael detected his movement – they made it a point to never lose their connection with him – they had pledged to help Gabriel with God's work and wanted to be there if he ever needed them.

"Gabriel, are you alright?" said Michael, "do you need our help? Raphael or I can accompany you."

"I am fine," said Gabriel, "I will let you know when I need you."

Gabriel gradually approached the dark angels, for he did not want to startle them. They did not notice him standing there; they faced Earth and had their backs to the heavens. "They are so heavy with darkness," thought Gabriel, "How am I ever going to get through to them?" He took a step closer, and gently spoke.

"My dear siblings, I have come to visit you. How are you all faring?" A few of the dark angels turned and stared at Gabriel's imposing figure; his light shone so brilliantly that it shocked them to their core.

"We are fine, Archangel Gabriel," said one, "but when will God permit all of us to return to Earth? We have been waiting an eternity to appreciate all that He has created."

"But the beauty on Earth is not all He has created," said Gabriel, "There is beauty throughout the universe and in all its dimensions, inside and outside the space/time continuum. The beauty on Earth is a mere reflection of that found in the upper heavens. Please come with me and I will show you."

"How can there be anything more beautiful than the splendour found on Earth?" said another, "The flowers are exquisite; the birds and butterflies are magnificent; how can these be just a reflection?"

Gabriel moved forward and shone his light even brighter. They all took several steps back, awed by its radiance. Gabriel's light dazzled the angels yet it did not hurt their vision – they were transfixed as he held their gaze.

"Life on Earth is physical," said Gabriel, "but it takes the spirit to animate it, otherwise physical form would be lifeless and inert. However, even with the infusion of the spirit, physicality is still limited by its bodily form. In other words, there are limits on Earth. But there are none in the esoteric spheres where we are now. Here, it is boundless and infinite, just like God. Beauty, love, and light are unrestrained. The luminosity that you see glowing from me is not found on Earth, nor is it found in this fourth dimension. It originates from the higher realms. Come with me and I will give you a glimpse of what awaits you if you choose to strive for it."

The dark angels acquiesced and followed Gabriel. He took them to a quiet corner, for many angels had crowded round to observe the goings-on. Gabriel asked all the dark angels to come closer and sit with him. As they drew nearer, he recognised some of the angels who had originally volunteered to help him with God's work many millennia ago. These were the troublemakers whose mistakes Gabriel had so resiliently tried to rectify.

Gabriel opened a portal to allow these angels to peek into the other dimensions. He showed them some of the wonders contained therein.

"Do you see the pure love and happiness that can be found there?" said Gabriel.

They were stunned by the beauty and artistry within. Colours abounded with varying tints and hues, captivating their beings. Vibrations emitted musical tones of deep sensation, gently guiding them into a mystical trance. An energy began to radiate from the opening and enveloped them in a soft tenderness, soothing their souls to the point of bliss. There was a lightness to their being, and it began to dawn on some of them that they had been looking in the wrong place for their happiness.

"So this is what some call nirvana," whispered one, as a few began to weep.

"How could I turn my back on God?" asked another, "It is unforgivable! I have been searching in the wrong place all these years. For me to choose the temporary, physical world over my true and permanent origin is deplorable! I am so heavy with darkness that I do not deserve this light." The angel bent over and began to sob.

"Of course you do!" exclaimed Gabriel, comforting the angel, "You are God's child and He is waiting for you to return to Him. Just ask Him to show you the way; that is all you have to do."

"Is it that easy?" asked the angel.

"Yes, it is that simple," said Gabriel, "Let us ask Him together." They both knelt in preparation; many of the dark angels joined them and formed a prayer circle, but a few were still not convinced.

"I prefer life on Earth," said one, "I enjoy the beauty and attraction there. Peace, happiness, and perfection can be achieved on Earth." A few others agreed.

"How else can I convince you of the truth?" said Gabriel, "What do you need to see or know to turn towards the light?"

"We have turned towards the light, Archangel Gabriel," said one, "We just prefer to exist in the light on Earth. And we will live there for as long as we can, and return again and again, and contribute to God's beauty and perfection on Earth."

"But do you not see that by doing this, you are caught in

an unending loop?" said Gabriel, "You are not progressing, and nor are you really living; you are just existing. It is an illusion. It is like running on a treadmill – you are moving, yet you are going nowhere." Gabriel was met with blank stares. He tried to explain further.

"You are existing in the reflection of the light; you are certainly not living in the light. Do you not want to be closer to God, to your source? You have so much more strength and power than you realise. What you are choosing is weakness and frailty. You are choosing to be tied down by physical form. Why would you limit yourselves like this?"

An angel scoffed. "I am nothing and can never achieve this light close to God. I am not like you, Archangel Gabriel. You are an Archangel, and I could never achieve such heights. I am small and lowly."

"No you are not! You are just like me! We are exactly the same!" exclaimed Gabriel, "There is no difference between an archangel and an angel, nor any difference between angel and human. These are terms that have been concocted, merely because many feel we need to differentiate amongst ourselves; but we are all the same. We all originate from the same source and we all contain the same light. The only variance is how brightly our light shines. It is up to each individual to strive to achieve this radiance, for it is when our light shines vibrantly that we are the happiest and are in our most peaceful existence. And every individual is capable of achieving such heights."

"We do not believe you," said another dark angel, "We do not possess such strength and power. Leave us to appreciate that which we can. Let us just enjoy God's creation on Earth and live there in happiness." The dark angels were restless and began to stand up.

Gabriel also stood up and tried again. "My dear siblings, please remember my words and reflect upon them. Do not discard them so casually. And you should be aware that God is once again permitting us to be born on Earth but has changed the parameters of our visits: it is now a school in which to learn those lessons that will lead us closer to Him. You cannot go to Earth just to appreciate God's creation, because that is no longer possible. You must determine what lessons you need to learn. There must be a purpose to your life on Earth."

"But we will adopt those qualities that will bring us closer to God while we are on Earth," said one angel.

"Yes, and we will help God to create more beauty," said another, "That will be our purpose in visiting Earth."

Gabriel tried one last time as they began to move away. "Be careful not to commit any wrongs. Otherwise you will get stuck in a cycle of debt and obligation that may prevent you from appreciating the very beauty you crave." By this time, the dark angels had turned their backs and were well on their way to their dark bubble, ready to jump into earthly lives as soon as the opportunities presented themselves.

Gabriel was sad to see them go, but was even more worried about the trouble they could stir up. Michael and Raphael had observed the exchange from afar. They came over and took Gabriel aside to have a private word.

"I just do not know what to do to convince these angels that they are more than they realise," said Gabriel, "And I am concerned for the future. These angels may wreak havoc on Earth again. It has taken a purge of the entire planet to cleanse it of the corruption and wrong-doings many of these angels instigated several millennia ago. I just hope that they do not repeat their mistakes and take humanity down the wrong path again."

Michael comforted Gabriel. "We cannot prevent them from committing wrongs. We can only guide them, and try to repair the damage, where possible. None of this is in our control. Each of us has been granted the freedom to choose how we wish to behave."

"But with free will comes responsibility," said Gabriel, "and there are consequences to our actions."

"Do not be disheartened," said Raphael, "We will continue to try to help them. Sooner or later they will turn towards God."

"This is what God assures me," said Gabriel, "and that I should not be disappointed if I am not successful."

"Exactly," said Michael, "and we are here to help you."

"Thank you both," said Gabriel, "Now let us help those who wish to be helped."

Gabriel returned to the angels who had knelt in a circle. He led them in a prayer to God, inviting grace, guidance, and blessings. A loving warmth descended upon them, and slowly they began to lighten from within. The angels were no longer heavy and sombre, for in them shone the glimmer of hope. Gabriel arose and embraced them all lovingly.

"Raphael," said Gabriel, "please accompany them to the angel schools."

Lowering his voice, Gabriel added, "Look after them well. Continue their healing and help them begin their learning. They will need extra special care so they do not fall back into the abyss."

20 MESSAGE

As time marched on, angels began visiting Earth again and the human population began to grow. Gabriel, together with Michael, Raphael, and the Quartet, did their best to ensure that before entering earthly lives, all angels were taught to maintain the link with their inner spirit and to embrace the qualities of kindness and compassion for their fellow beings. As God had instructed, the Archangels selected special missionary angels, the messengers, to be sent to all parts of the world to reinforce these principles.

Gabriel kept a careful watch on the developments on Earth. The part of the world known as the East seemed to be more amenable to the teachings and wholeheartedly embraced these worldly spiritual guides. Truth, godliness, and beauty were aspects of the spirit, and these principles seemed to take hold in certain areas. People began to look introspectively, searching for the true source of their being.

However, some of the dark angels were born on Earth, and as predicted by Gabriel, they began to disturb the equilibrium. Centuries passed with the same patterns beginning to emerge: many people moved towards the truth, but many failed to maintain the link with their innermost self. Thus, a great many did not understand the purpose of their lives nor the reason why they had chosen to be born in the first place. Many began to engage in unethical and immoral behaviour, and even those who embraced goodness favoured physical rituals of worship and reverence. The materiality of Earth once again gripped humanity, allowing greed and jealousy to suppress their better nature: the quest for wealth and power was at the forefront of human endeavour.

And Gabriel warily watched.

Then one day, God called out to Gabriel.

"In the name of God, the most Beneficent, the most Merciful," invoked Gabriel as he ascended to the seventh heaven.

"Gabriel, it is now time to begin sending the Signs to My children on Earth," said God, "My Message must be conveyed while they are in physical, human form, as a reminder to embrace the truth. But My Message must be delivered slowly and deliberately, so that My children have time and opportunity to absorb the teachings through generations. I want each part to be put into practice step-by-step. It is now time to prepare Abraham, Moses, Jesus, and Mohamed."

"Yes, My Lord." Gabriel sensed that this message was particularly significant, and he readied himself to receive it.

God began, "The First Part of My Message to humankind is that there is no God but Me; there is only one God, whether they personify Me as a great Being separate from themselves, or whether they consider Me a vast energy or universal force: humanity must refrain from idolatry and worshipping the physical. The Second Part to be conveyed is that My children must live their Earthly lives within the tenets of kindness, generosity, and compassion for the other. These qualities reflect the ethics and values of their true being and must form part of their code of conduct on Earth. Just because My children take on physical form does not mean they should fall into impropriety. The Third Part of My Message is that My children are all siblings: they all burst forth from Me at the same time, and they are one and the same; they originate from the same light, which is Love itself. Love is the essence of who they are, and forgiveness is its greatest manifestation. They must love one another: hate, prejudice, and indifference are anathema to their spirit. The Fourth Part to be conveyed is that My children are all equal and are a part of Me: each of their accomplishments is not due to them individually, but is part of the creativity of the Spirit that is within us all. Arrogance and selfishness is an expression of the ego, and is not of the true self. Each must annihilate his ego to reach his highest consciousness. That is where they will find Me: they must reach deep into their spirit and submit to their higher, divine Will. It is the only way of achieving absolute peace and contentment. This is My Message to humanity."

"Gabriel," continued God, "transmit My words to Abraham, Moses, Jesus, and Mohamed, and convey to them that it is now time to begin our work. You, Gabriel, will be their direct link and will be responsible for the unfolding of My Message on Earth."

"Yes, My Lord," said Gabriel.

"And transmit My Message to Michael and Raphael," said God, "They will be your greatest support."

"Yes, My Lord," said Gabriel.

"And reinforce this to all My children: I am with all of you constantly, both during hardship, and in times of prosperity," said God, "Turn to Me when you are troubled, and I will carry you through your struggles. And do not forget Me in times of happiness, for it is then that it is most important to hold on to your link with Me, for your ego may reassert itself and tempt you astray."

"Yes, My Lord," said Gabriel.

"Now, My child, go to the lower heavens and return quickly with Abraham, Moses, Jesus, and Mohamed," said God, "I wish to discuss their work with each of them."

Gabriel bowed his head and invoked, "Thy Will be done in and through me. Thy Will be done on Earth as it is in Heaven," and he made his way down through the heavens. Once he reached the fourth dimension, he called out to Michael and Raphael, as well as Abraham, Moses, Jesus, and Mohamed.

"It is time to begin the next phase of our work," said Gabriel.

"What did God say?" asked Michael. Gabriel transmitted everything God had conveyed. Needless to say, all six were stunned by the immensity of the task that lay ahead.

"You are embarking on your greatest journeys," said Gabriel, as he addressed the Quartet.

"We will do our best," said Abraham, speaking on their behalf.

"Gabriel, you will be occupied with this additional responsibility. Michael and I will manage all the ongoing work," said Raphael.

"Yes, concentrate on your new assignments," said Michael, "If any of you need additional help, then call upon us."

"Thank you both," said Gabriel, "You are the pillars on which I stand. You enable me to carry out my assignments. I am and will always be grateful to you for your constant love and generosity." They all embraced one another, and then Gabriel escorted the Quartet to the seventh dimension to receive further instructions from God.

I will not reveal the intimate discussions God had with each, but will summarise the outcome as follows: they would work together to convey the whole of God's Message to humankind, with each taking responsibility to relay a particular part: Abraham would begin and establish the First Part: there is only one God; Moses would unveil the Second Part: the ethics, tenets and laws to govern human behaviour; for the Third Part, Jesus would ignite the spirit of love, forgiveness, and compassion for fellow beings; and for the Fourth and final Part, Mohamed would inspire the virtue of humility (the diminishing ego) and submission to the Will of God to reach the highest consciousness of man and woman, the Divine within. All this, together, constituted God's Message to Humanity, and the new era of truth, wisdom, and peace would arise.

21 SIGNS

God's Message was to be unfolded in one geographic area on Earth, from where it could take root and spread in all directions. The seven angels came together to begin their preparations.

"I will be your guardian angel in each of your lives," said Gabriel to the Quartet, "I will guide you every step of the way."

"Thank you, Gabriel," said Abraham.

"And remember, each of you must convey all of God's Message in its entirety. All four parts must be delivered during each of your lifetimes. Just ensure that the part for which you have taken responsibility is firmly embedded in society. These parts represent the evolution of humanity, and are a metaphor for the growth of the soul," said Gabriel.

Kibwe, who had been working alongside them, approached the group. "Excuse me, Archangel Gabriel. Do you mind if I ask what you mean by this?"

"Not at all, Kibwe. Let me explain. First, an individual acknowledges that she originates from a source, whether she calls it God, the universe, or whatever – she comes from somewhere or something. That is the First Part. Then she looks around her and sees others – she is not alone – so she must govern her behaviour in relation to another. This is the Second Part. Then she begins to mature, realising that she is connected to the other – she is impacted by what happens to the other and vice versa. This is the Third Part. Then finally she asks why, and from where does she originate – who is she? – she begins her search for the source. This is the Fourth Part."

"Thank you, Archangel Gabriel. I will now take your leave

and return to my work," said Kibwe.

"I will join you shortly," said Raphael.

Gabriel turned to the Quartet. "Are you ready to begin?"

"Yes, we are," said Abraham. All seven huddled together, shining their light and love in encouragement. A wave of loving warmth flowed over them, and they thanked God for His grace.

Gabriel moved closer to Abraham and said, "I will never leave your side. And when you are in difficulty, turn to God and seek His help, for He is always with you."

"Thank you, Archangel Gabriel," said Abraham.

His eyes welling up, Gabriel looked squarely at Moses, Jesus, and Mohamed, and said, "Remember these words. You will never be alone." Michael and Raphael glanced at each other, puzzled by Gabriel's reaction.

"Now begin your preparations," said Gabriel.

Abraham took Moses, Jesus, and Mohamed aside to begin their quiet contemplation and ready themselves for the work ahead.

"Gabriel," whispered Raphael, "you are not yourself. Is something wrong?"

"I am fine. It is just that the four of them have made a tremendous commitment to God, and each will have to face gruelling tasks on Earth. It will be difficult to see them go through their trials. It is one thing for me to choose to go through such struggles, but it is quite another to watch a loved one suffer, even if it is his chosen path. It is remarkable what some are willing to do to help their fellow beings."

"Gabriel, they will be alright," said Michael, "Raphael and I will do whatever is required to enable them to fulfil their commitments to God. Remember, you also are not alone in this."

"Exactly, we are all in this together," said Raphael, looking towards the four, "I see that the Quartet is ready. Let us join them."

They all embraced one another, each conveying his love and support, before Gabriel and Abraham left the group and made their way to Earth.

As they moved towards the angel schools, Raphael turned to Michael and said, "Can you believe how humble Gabriel is? He has done the most to help his fellow beings, and is generous to all, yet he is overcome by the commitment of the Quartet."

Michael nodded. "Gabriel has distinguished himself from all of God's children, yet he does not recognise his own achievements. He does not realise that he is considered the most high, and that each of us hangs on his every word."

"Well, he certainly does not recognise the power and strength of his presence. He really is a force to be reckoned with!" They both laughed affectionately and looked towards Earth to watch Gabriel and Abraham: they silently said a prayer for them both.

Gabriel and Abraham were ready to begin their journey. When the moment arrived, Abraham leapt into the body of the baby and was born on Earth. He had an ordinary childhood, growing up in a good family that was well-respected in the area and beyond. Abraham eventually matured into a strong man, tending the sheep and helping those in the greater community. His life very much mirrored that of Noah: in his adulthood, an unease began to stir within him and he refused to worship the idols of his tribe; he followed his inner voice in the face of those who thought him to be of unsound mind.

Gabriel guided Abraham through life, transmitting the necessary missives and even appeared before him in times of particular importance. God tested Abraham's resolve many times, as God said He would, in order to strengthen Abraham: he had to be able to confidently deliver the First Part of God's Message.

Abraham grew weary with life's challenges, yet he persevered in the face of adversity, even when it involved his son.

"God conveyed that I will be the father of many nations," said Abraham to his family, "and I must set humanity off in the right direction. This is my promise."

Many years passed with Abraham following God's instructions: he firmly established the belief in one God, and his descendants began to spread this knowledge throughout their known world.

When the end of his life drew near, Michael, Raphael, Moses, Jesus, and Mohamed joined Gabriel to receive him. By this time, Abraham was old and decrepit, his body worn down by his years of service to God.

At the precise moment when his spirit rose from his body, Gabriel pulled Abraham close and sat him down until he acclimated to his surroundings.

"Abraham, it is wonderful to have you back with us," said Gabriel gently. They all shone their light and love on Abraham, waiting patiently for his full awareness to manifest.

"How wonderful it is to see all of you again!" said Abraham, feeling revitalised.

"You have done very well," said Gabriel.

"I am grateful for your guidance and companionship throughout my lifetime, Archangel Gabriel," said Abraham, "and especially during the harrowing times." Abraham turned to the other five. "Thank you all for your prayers."

"It is now time for you to rest," said Gabriel, "I will escort you to the seventh dimension." Abraham embraced the others and ascended with Gabriel through the heavens.

Following Abraham's work in the world, Michael and Raphael sent many special missionary angels to be born on Earth to reinforce God's Message. Over the years, these missionaries came to be known as prophets, saints, and spiritual leaders. The belief in one God did take root and spread, but not as quickly and widely as Gabriel had hoped. Humanity continued on its treacherous path of selfishness, greed, and corruption. For those who did believe, it did not seem to matter that God was watching them. Gabriel knew that the Second Part of God's Message to humanity would have to be delivered soon.

"It is time to call the Quartet," said Gabriel.

"They are in the sixth dimension, helping those who wish to raise their consciousness," said Michael, "I will gather them."

As soon as they arrived, Gabriel hurriedly said, "Moses, it is now time for you to visit Earth to deliver the Second Part of God's Message."

"Yes, Archangel Gabriel," said Moses.

"Remind the people that there is only one God, and establish the code of behaviour by which humankind must live on Earth," said Gabriel.

"I will, Archangel Gabriel," said Moses.

"Very well. It is time to begin," said Gabriel.

All seven huddled together and expressed their love, support and encouragement. Moses readily began his preparations for visiting Earth, and when the hour appeared, all six angels gathered around and shone their light on Moses, praying to God to bless him.

"I will be with you every step of the way, Moses," said Gabriel, "You have an arduous task ahead of you, and I will guide you continuously. But remember, in times of difficulty, turn to God for help." The seven embraced each other and Gabriel and Moses made their way towards Earth.

Moses had an affluent childhood, but his life gradually turned difficult as the years passed. His was a long, drawn-out, physical suffering, and Gabriel walked with Moses throughout his journey. During his lifetime, Moses constantly reminded the people that there was only one God, and that they must shun their pagan ways. He conveyed the laws by which they were to conduct themselves and censure their behaviour. But not everyone listened. Many ignored the tenets and reverted to the temptations of darkness, while others rejected the laws outright. It did not seem to matter that God was watching, and that they would have to account for their behaviour.

As with Abraham, God tested Moses' resolve to fulfil his commitment. Moses led his people through the harsh terrain, carrying the heavy responsibility God entrusted to him. During a particularly trying day, Raphael joined them to provide support.

"How is Moses faring, Gabriel?" asked Raphael.

"He is growing weary, but is persevering nonetheless," said Gabriel.

They watched as Moses addressed his people.

"Remember, there is only one God, and you shall not take His name in vain," said Moses, "And you shall not steal, nor shall you kill." Moses scanned the crowd, looking for signs of idolatry, especially the golden calf the people forged in his absence during his discourse with God.

"Now it is time to continue our journey," said Moses, as he pointed his staff to the distance. Gabriel and Raphael watched as the people gathered themselves to follow.

"Gabriel, I will accompany you until it is necessary to return to the angel schools," said Raphael. Both Archangels supported Moses' weight as he marched on with his people.

They wandered for many years before reaching their new home. By this time, Moses' people had absorbed the teachings, and Gabriel was confident that their belief and commitment would be strong enough to extend beyond their immediate circle.

At the precise moment when Moses' life finally came to an end, the five angels joined Gabriel to receive him. As his spirit rose, Gabriel pulled Moses close and sat him down until he became fully aware. They all shone their light and love on him.

"I am delighted to be home again and reunited with you all," said Moses, "And Archangel Gabriel, I am grateful for your guidance."

"You accomplished your task, Moses," said Gabriel.

"Now it is time to rest," said Raphael, who seemed especially touched by Moses' travails, "You walked for many years."

"Raphael also accompanied us for a time," said Gabriel, "Raphael, why don't you escort Moses to the seventh dimension? Remain with him until he has regained his strength before you join us again," said Gabriel.

"Thank you Gabriel, I would very much like to," said Raphael, as he and Moses began their ascent to the seventh heaven.

As far as Earth was concerned, Michael again sent special missionary angels to all four corners of the world to encourage people to observe the ethics and morality intrinsic to their souls and remain true to their lighter, spiritual selves. The knowledge and belief in one God finally took a firm hold and began to spread. But Gabriel was wary; he had been down this road before. He watched the developments with a great deal of interest.

Several hundred years passed, with God continuing to grant prosperity in all parts of the world. Accumulation of wealth seemed to preoccupy most people, with corrupt practices further embedding themselves. The gap between those who held wealth and power, and those who did not, grew wider: compassion for one's fellow being gradually eroded.

"Why does humanity repeatedly fall?" said Gabriel, "What does it take for humankind to acknowledge that all men and women are equal, and truly are siblings-in-light?"

Gabriel turned to the other six. "It is time for the Third Part of God's Message to be revealed on Earth. Jesus, are you ready for your work to begin?"

"Yes, Archangel Gabriel," said Jesus.

"Remind everyone that there is only one God, and there are laws that govern their behaviour," said Gabriel.

"I will, Archangel Gabriel," said Jesus.

"Teach them about love and compassion for their fellow man," said Gabriel, "And I will be with you each and every moment of your life, and will not abandon you even during your darkest times. Remember to look within and seek God. He will help you during your difficulties."

They gathered around Jesus, shining their light and love in encouragement, and prayed for God to bless him. When the appointed time arrived, they embraced one another before Gabriel and Jesus made their way towards Earth.

Jesus' birth seemed to attract great attention and people came from far and wide to see him. His childhood was relatively normal, but the unease within began to stir early on in life. As Jesus matured, he began delivering God's Message to all those who would listen: he spoke of the notions of love, compassion, and forgiveness. He strengthened the belief in one God and emphasised the laws by which humanity was to live. He also preached against the corrupt practices that had infiltrated the social order. Again, as with Abraham and Moses before him, God tested Jesus' resolve and commitment several times over.

Jesus drew huge crowds; multitudes of people gathered wherever he chose to teach. Those in power felt threatened and feared that his influence would destabilise the community. They began to work against him, using his own people to betray his trust. As love and compassion dissolved into fear, which incited the desire for blood, Jesus suffered immensely at the hands of the people.

"Such viciousness!" thought Gabriel, as he covered Jesus with a veil of protection, continually whispering words of strength and courage into his spirit. Gabriel held Jesus and guided him through his ordeals. His last days were particularly cruel and the people were ruthless in their punishment.

"Neither Abraham nor Moses suffered such inhumanity during their sojourns on Earth," said Gabriel, as Michael, Raphael, Abraham, Moses, and Mohamed moved to encircle Jesus with light and love: all were struck by the heartlessness of those who claimed to be the followers of God. Abraham and Moses were particularly distressed that their parts of God's Message had not resonated with the people.

"Why have our people become so dogmatic, so rigid?" said Abraham, "I never thought I would witness such brutality."

During his last few moments, Jesus called out in pain to his Father, the One God. Gabriel whispered words of comfort into his spirit, encouraging forbearance. Jesus' anguish greatly affected the angels, especially Michael, for it rekindled memories of his own violent encounters on Earth.

Gabriel remained strong and focussed, supporting Jesus to lessen his agony. Suddenly, God sent a force of energy and lifted Jesus from his body. As he rose, Gabriel drew Jesus into his arms and cradled him for a few minutes; the six angels, together with the many who had gathered round, showered their light and love on him to strengthen his spirit.

During this time, Mohamed's eyes locked with Gabriel's, and an understanding passed between them: "I will be with you during every moment of your life, too," conveyed Gabriel silently.

Jesus finally recovered and became fully aware.

"I am glad to return home and be amongst you again," said Jesus, as his light began to burn brightly.

"You have done well," said Gabriel, "I am just so sorry you had to suffer."

"Thank you for guiding me throughout my life," said Jesus, as he embraced Gabriel.

"It is now time for you to rest," said Gabriel, readying himself to ascend. As the Quartet embraced one another, Gabriel noticed Michael's tears.

"Are you alright, Michael?" asked Gabriel quietly.

"I am fine," said Michael, "it is just that Jesus showed great fortitude in the midst of cruelty."

"Why don't you accompany Jesus to the seventh dimension?" said Gabriel, "Remain with him until he has regained his full strength before you return."

"I would be honoured," said Michael, as he and Jesus began their ascent.

Gabriel turned towards Earth to monitor its evolution.

"I am disturbed by what humankind did to Jesus," said Gabriel, as Raphael came towards him, "Humanity is not absorbing the essence of God's Message. Already three parts have been revealed on Earth, yet many still do not believe in one God and people continue their immorality."

"I see it, too, Gabriel," said Raphael, "Power, corruption, and violence continue to rule humankind."

"Will humanity ever grasp God's Message?" said Gabriel.

"We still have to deliver the Fourth Part," said Raphael, "so there is hope."

Just then, Mohamed appeared and moved towards them.

"May I join you both?" said Mohamed.

"Of course," said Gabriel, "we are observing the happenings on Earth."

They quietly watched as human beings continued their destruction and carnage, warring with one another in their quest for dominance. Every so often there were those who took a step closer to God by being kind and compassionate, but most remained mired in materiality and ignorance.

"Archangel Gabriel," said Mohamed, "when it is my turn to enter the world, I will do my best to reinforce all of God's Message to humanity. We still have a chance."

"I fear that humankind will not comprehend the full Message, let alone put it into practice," said Gabriel, "And I am also concerned for your life on Earth. We have seen what was done to Jesus. Are you sure you wish to continue with this commitment?"

"Yes, I am. My brothers have fulfilled theirs, and I must fulfil mine. Otherwise the Message is incomplete," said Mohamed.

"We will all be there to help you," said Raphael.

"Thank you, Archangel Raphael," said Mohamed, "And I know God will also be with me. And Archangel Gabriel, if you guide me during my life, I know I will be able to bear whatever comes my way."

"I will accompany you throughout your lifetime, just as I did with your brothers," said Gabriel, "I will counsel you through all your difficulties, and will remain with you through your darkest moments."

"Archangel Gabriel, I await your call to enter Earth," said Mohamed, as he embraced the two Archangels and made his way to the sixth dimension to join the others.

"I must return to the angel schools," said Raphael, as he looked towards Earth, "Will you be alright, Gabriel?"

"Yes, of course," said Gabriel, "I will watch over Earth and will call upon you and Michael if need be."

Gabriel continued monitoring the world. He closely watched the unfolding of the first three parts of the Message to Humanity and observed its expansion across the lands. He sent many missionary angels to be born into societies that had known Abraham, Moses, and Jesus, and dispatched others to different parts of the world to reinforce the principles of oneness, of love, and of respect for all beings. Many civilisations accepted, and in fact, incorporated these universal truths into their belief systems, and Gabriel glimmered with optimism at this development.

Then Gabriel witnessed the stark divisions between those who aligned themselves with Moses and those who followed the teachings of Jesus. They seemed to believe that the messages were different, that they were distinct, rather than just portions of the whole of God's Message to Humanity. Gabriel consulted Michael and Raphael.

"I do not understand why two separate paths are developing. It is one God, with the same Message, and Moses and Jesus both originate from Him. Why would people create separation and harbour disdain for the other?" said Gabriel.

"It is very disturbing to see what is happening," said Raphael, "I would understand if those in far-off lands not exposed to the message of Abraham, Moses, and Jesus established a different path. But for the people who have embraced their teachings, it is ludicrous to disparage and alienate each other, preferring one messenger over the other."

Michael pointed to a section of the world and said, "They are even resorting to violence. They are actually fighting each other for dominion, each believing in their righteousness."

The Archangels watched as the divisions widened and positions became further entrenched. The Quartet joined them and watched in horror as their parts of God's Message were distorted and manipulated to serve the egos of those craving power and influence: a great deal of destruction and violence was committed in the name of the One God, and in the names of Moses and Jesus. Many angels in the fourth, fifth, and sixth dimensions gathered around the seven angels and watched the happenings on Earth with a great deal of concern.

"We need to do something to stop this behaviour," said Abraham, "Have our people not understood any part of God's Message?"

"They are not following the laws," said Moses dejectedly, "They are killing, stealing, and lying."

"They have no love and compassion for their fellow beings. Of what use were our visits to the world?" said Jesus, with tears in his eyes.

Gabriel realised that hopelessness was beginning to set in the group. He first pulled himself together, and then moved them to a quiet corner.

"Do not be distraught," said Gabriel, "We will need to be patient. It will take time for humanity to absorb the teachings and apply them with understanding to their daily lives. Remember, life on Earth is now much harder, given people have no memory of their true existence – they do not remember that they are spiritual beings who have been born on Earth for a particular purpose. We will need to give them the time and space to learn their lessons and raise their consciousness. They will need to reach deep within to find the link and truly know themselves, and as a consequence, know their siblings-in-light. Once they recognise "the other" as their own, it is then that they will truly be able to follow God's Message. And remember, not all of God's Message has been conveyed yet."

"We may need to strengthen Mohamed's role to consolidate God's Message," said Raphael. All nodded in agreement.

"I am ready for this," responded Mohamed. Suddenly, a wave of loving energy enveloped the seven angels, and they heard God calling out to them.

They ascended through the heavens and invoked, "In the name of God, the most Beneficent, the most Merciful."

"My dear children," said God, "it is wonderful to see you all. But you are disturbed by the happenings on Earth. It will take time for My children to absorb My Message, to sense who and what they really are, and finally come to terms with their higher consciousness. I am patient and will allow My children the opportunity to take the decision to better themselves, for I have granted them free will. However, Gabriel, after witnessing what Abraham, Moses, and Jesus have been through on Earth, I want you to particularly guide Mohamed during his lifetime. Intercede with him constantly. Help him to transmit not only the Fourth Part of My Message, but to promulgate the whole of My Message to Humanity, for Mohamed is the last that I will send to help My children. I will not send any more Signs, for with Mohamed's visit, My Message to Humanity will be complete. He is the last and final Sign."

"Yes, My Lord," said Gabriel.

"Abraham, Moses, Jesus," continued God, "I had earlier expressed My happiness to each of you for all that you established on Earth, and I want you to know how proud I am of your accomplishments. You have sown the seeds of wisdom and self-awareness, and in time, you will witness the blossoming of the consciousness that is within all My children."

"Yes, My Lord," they answered in unison.

"Mohamed, I will be with you during all your challenges on Earth. Seek My help during your times of difficulty."

"Yes, My Lord," said Mohamed.

"Now all of you return to your responsibilities, and convey these words to all My children: Do not fear the other, for each is a part of Me. Each of you is divine light, and is part of the sum that makes up the Whole. Whether you are in human form or in spirit, you are My children. My greatest joy is when you recognise your light within; because it is then that you will see Me and each other."

All seven bowed their heads and invoked, "Thy Will be done in and through me. Thy Will be done on Earth as it is in Heaven." They commenced their descent through the heavens until they reached the fourth dimension.

"Do you think we should gather all the angels and inform them of God's words?" asked Michael.

"That might not be a bad idea," said Gabriel, "We have not assembled together in a long time."

Michael and Raphael beckoned the angels and billions heeded the call. As they came forward, a rush of loving energy swept the atmosphere, just like a warm breeze on a summer's day. Their lights merged into a glowing form and illuminated the heavens.

In the hustle and bustle of settling themselves, Gabriel scanned the crowd and thought, "If only you could all remember that you are the same, and work together in harmony towards a unified purpose when you live earthly lives. You would be able to accomplish so much more than you realise. Your physical brains restrict your capacity to comprehend what could be. If only you had the confidence to resort to your consciousness – your spirit – then you would realise that you are limitless."

Once the angels quietened down, Gabriel conveyed God's words and concluded by saying, "Remember, we are all God's children. Each and every one of us. There is no difference amongst us, and God loves us all equally. It is crucial that in learning your lessons on Earth, and in repaying all the debts and obligations you have incurred, you do not forget to love one another and be kind, compassionate, and generous to each other. Violence should never be part of your character, for it destroys you from within."

All the billions of angels knelt down in a chorus of prayer to thank God for His blessings. It was a scene to behold, as billions sang in unison and shone their light and love on one another. As they began to disperse, Gabriel overheard their conversations.

"We will not let God down," said one, "and we will fulfil His Will on Earth."

"I will try my utmost to reach my higher consciousness and be a better being," said another.

"I must forgive all those who have hurt me," said yet another, "My anger and resentment are holding me back."

"We must make greater efforts to serve others and convey our love and affection for all beings," discussed a group who had moved off to one side.

Another angel said, "My ego has always got the best of me. I must overcome this barrier. Submission to the will of my higher consciousness: that is the key."

Gabriel was heartened by the discussions and felt a glimmer of hope rise within him. He turned to the other six. "This is our last chance to speak to humankind directly. Abraham, Moses, and Jesus, you have undertaken your tasks and fulfilled your respective commitments to God. It is now time for Mohamed to enter Earth and fulfil his commitment."

"We will continue to help wherever we can," said Abraham. The six gathered around Mohamed, shining their light and love in encouragement, and prayed for God to bless him. They embraced one another, and then watched as Gabriel and Mohamed made their way towards the world.

Mohamed was born on Earth and lived a fairly normal life. Having been orphaned at an early age, he was raised by his uncle and other relatives, and was much loved by his family. As a young boy, he tended the flock and generally helped wherever he could. As he grew older, Mohamed became a trader in goods like many of his tribe, relying on his life experience: literacy was rare for those who resided in his area of birth.

Gabriel kept a very close watch over him, for he knew this would be the last time that God would send a direct Sign and they had to get this right. The people of this region practiced idolatry, with a plurality of deities, and had still not embraced the principle of the One God. Gabriel waited until Mohamed's fortieth year to intercede, for he wanted to ensure that Mohamed was mature and experienced enough to be able to fully convey the Message.

As with those before him, there came a time when an unease began to stir within Mohamed. He began to contemplate the meaning of his life, realising that there was more to his existence than his daily routine. He found a special cave in which to rest, away from prying eyes, and began to reach deep within to still his mind. During his meditations, Gabriel would sit close by, waiting for the appropriate time to begin their work.

Then one day as Mohamed entered a meditative state, Gabriel knew the moment had finally arrived, and he moved in closer. As Mohamed withdrew deeper, Gabriel began whispering the missives, and so began the transmission of the Fourth Part of God's Message to Humanity.

Several years passed with Gabriel remaining close to Mohamed, guiding him through all his challenges. His was an eventful life, filled with violent battles and a myriad of obstacles – the people rebelled against his ideas and prevented him from establishing the Message. Aggression was not part of Mohamed's nature and did not suit him, yet he was constantly opposed and drawn into conflict: it began to destroy him from within. In the aftermath of a particularly fierce battle, Mohamed questioned whether his people would ever accept the One God or forever remain in ignorance.

Michael approached the scene to see what he could do to help.

"Mohamed must be struggling with all this fighting," said Michael, "How my heart goes out to him."

"I know what you mean," said Gabriel, "He has endured a lot. This constant warring with his family and with neighbouring tribes is wearing him down."

"I only went through one battle during my lifetime and I know what it did to me. This violence must stop," said Michael, "When will all this be over for him?"

"Not for a long while. He has not delivered the whole Message yet," said Gabriel, "But maybe we can give him a bit of respite. Will you ask God whether I can raise him to our dimension for a few minutes to revitalise his strength?"

"Of course," said Michael, and he withdrew into God. Gabriel remained by Mohamed's side, gently guiding him to begin his meditation.

After a few minutes, Michael returned and said, "God has given permission to raise Mohamed, but would like to see you both. So escort him straight to the seventh dimension."

"Very well," said Gabriel.

Once Mohamed fell into deep contemplation, Gabriel drew him up through the heavens.

"In the name of God, the most Beneficent, the most Merciful," invoked Gabriel and Mohamed.

"My dear children," said God, "I am very happy with the progress you have made so far. Continue to persevere, but you must find a way to end the violence and warmongering. Reiterate to My children that there is only one God, and that they must govern their behaviour towards one another according to the laws I set down through Moses. They must show compassion and love for each other, and forgive each other's mistakes, as I conveyed through Jesus; and they must embrace humility and diminish their ego, for only by submitting to their Divine Will, will they be able to reach

Me. This inner battle over their ego will be their greatest struggle; it is the struggle of the "jihad": the war within each individual to overcome his baser instincts and reach his highest consciousness."

"Yes, my Lord," replied Gabriel and Mohamed.

"Tell My children that they must refrain from violence towards one another. Every human being on Earth is My child, and the creatures I have created are of My Spirit. When My children hurt one another, they hurt Me. Violence is not a part of who they are. They must stop destroying humanity, for they are destroying Me; I am within each being. Now, go back to Earth and convey My final Message to Humanity. And know that I am with you at all times, guiding and watching over you. When you are in difficulty, turn to Me and seek My help, and I will carry you through your struggles."

"Thy Will be done in and through me. Thy Will be done on Earth as it is in Heaven," they invoked, as Gabriel ushered Mohamed down through the heavens all the way to Earth.

Mohamed resumed his mission and did everything he could to establish a truce and bring about peace. He continued to transmit God's Message and was guided by Gabriel throughout the remainder of his life. There were challenging times, when both wondered whether humankind would comprehend and embrace God's Message, nevertheless, Gabriel continued to encourage Mohamed.

After several more years, the moment finally arrived for Mohamed to return home. As soon as his spirit left his body, Gabriel reached out and pulled him close. Michael, Raphael, Abraham, Moses, and Jesus shone their light and love to help him recover and gain his full awareness.

"Mohamed, it is good to have you back with us," said Gabriel.

"Thank you for guiding me throughout my life," said Mohamed, "and it certainly is good to be home."

Abraham, Moses and Jesus rushed to embrace him. The

three Archangels stepped away and gave the Quartet the space to reconnect, for they had concluded their assignment – the Four Parts of God's Message to Humanity had been delivered.

Michael and Raphael took Gabriel off to the side; he was not as bright as usual, and they knew something was wrong.

"You need to rest, Gabriel," said Michael, "you have been working very hard for several hundred years now."

"I am a bit tired, but I am okay," said Gabriel.

"But you seem preoccupied," said Raphael, "is something troubling you?"

"I do not know whether humanity has understood the full breadth and scope of God's Message. As you know, God said Mohamed is the last direct Sign. I just hope that people embrace the whole Message, and that the missions undertaken by the Quartet were not in vain, not to mention the suffering each endured."

"We need to give it time, Gabriel," said Michael, "Let us wait and see. Whatever needs to be done next, we will be there right beside you."

Gabriel smiled affectionately and said, "We better join the others." They made their way towards the Quartet.

"It is good to be back fully amongst you," said Gabriel. They all embraced one another, grateful to have completed their task and conveyed God's Message to Humanity. Gabriel then escorted Mohamed to the seventh dimension to recover from his ordeal.

Once Gabriel returned to the fourth dimension, he took up his post to observe the happenings on Earth: would humankind absorb God's Message? As the years passed, he watched as some people embraced the teachings, while others rejected them outright. Many learnt their lessons in the Earth school, but some did not, and others still incurred new debts and obligations in their quest for wealth and power. This, of course, was nothing new to Gabriel. But what disturbed him the most were the divisions amongst the people who had chosen to follow the principles of God's Message to Humanity. The peoples of Moses, Jesus, and Mohamed had divided themselves into distinct groups, rather than embrace one another as various parts of God's Message. And with these distinctions, the hostility and aggression increased.

The seven angels watched from above as men and women fought amongst each other, spewing hatred and prejudice throughout, each unyielding in their righteousness. The Quartet were heavy with sorrow as they saw each of their parts of the Message manipulated by self-serving individuals. The seven angels continued to observe the evolution on Earth for many years, and then the corruption and brutality became too much to bear.

"What do we do, Gabriel?" asked Raphael, "Things are getting worse, not better."

"I do not know what to do. I must seek God's guidance," said Gabriel, as he withdrew into himself and ascended through the heavens.

"In the name of God, the most Beneficent, the most Merciful," invoked Gabriel.

"My dear child, I see that you and your siblings are concerned by the happenings on Earth. We must be patient and allow humanity to absorb and truly understand My Message. I will not intervene right now, for I am giving My children the opportunity to internalise its essence, and apply it not only to their individual lives, but also to their communities, their nations, and to humanity as a whole. I have, and continue to bestow more possibility and creativity on Earth so that My children may access the knowledge, innovations, and technologies that will allow them to better their own conditions, as well as those of their fellow beings around the world. I want to see whether My children will embrace their qualities of kindness, compassion, respect, generosity, and forgiveness, or whether they will sink into the depths of greed, jealousy, selfishness, prejudice, cruelty, and apathy. Whatever their choices in life, whether as individual human beings or as wider communities and nations, they will face the consequences of their decisions. My children on Earth must understand that they are tied together: they are all made of the same light, and their physical bodies are all made of the same clay and water on Earth. They will remain together, whether they are in spirit or physical form. Their individual decisions will decide their collective future on Earth. This is the last opportunity I am giving My children to right their course in the world. If they do not, I intend to purge the planet and begin again. One way or another, the era of truth and peace shall reign."

"Yes, my Lord," replied Gabriel, tearing up.

"Gabriel, do not be discouraged," said God, "This is a long process, riddled with many setbacks. Continue your work to help My children realise their true nature and reach their highest consciousness."

"Yes, my Lord," said Gabriel.

"Gabriel, the time for you to merge with My Light and remain permanently within Me is drawing near," said God, "Persevere with your work, and remember, I am constantly with you, guiding you along your path."

"Thy Will be done in and through me. Thy Will be done on Earth as it is in Heaven," said Gabriel, as he descended to the six waiting in the fourth dimension. He conveyed God's words to them.

"So we just have to be patient with everyone and persevere in our efforts," said Gabriel.

"We will do what is necessary," said Michael.

"What do you want each of us to do, Gabriel?" said Raphael. They all looked at Gabriel expectantly, waiting for direction.

"The four of you should help those in the fifth and sixth dimensions reach their highest consciousness," said Gabriel, "And Raphael, manage the angel schools and help transition those returning from Earth. Michael, monitor Earth and its evolution, and also supervise the guardian angels assigned to each human being. I will move between the dimensions to ensure everything is working smoothly, and provide extra help where necessary."

Time marched on, and the next few hundred years were occupied with reinforcing the training in the angel schools, and sending special missionary angels to Earth to help humankind comprehend their existence and learn their lessons. All worked hard to assist their siblings-in-light, with billions of angels moving about spreading love and light to strengthen the weak and bolster the strong. The workings of this multi-dimensional system was a sight to behold.

God continued His creativity on Earth and progressively graced humanity with the knowledge and technology to better themselves. Life on Earth became easier for a great many, although the majority of humankind still found life a hardship, living a hand-to-mouth existence. The divide between the rich and poor widened, and the rift between the spiritually advanced and the unenlightened deepened. Material wealth and spiritual prosperity matured inconsistently in various pockets all across the world: there were areas whose people were poor but who connected with their higher consciousness; others where the people were affluent but spiritually poor; and yet other areas whose people were both materially and spiritually advanced, or less developed in both. Gabriel just hoped that with each advancement in knowledge and technology, humanity would raise their spirit and embrace their higher consciousness, and that the ego's quest for material wealth and power would not overtake each individual's true purpose in life.

Gabriel watched the happenings on Earth very closely. He saw God's Message to Humanity grow further apart into distinct and separate religions, even though all three were based on the existence of the One God as begun by Abraham. And the disturbing hostility amongst them grew: the followers of each believed their path was the true one, the other being mired in ignorance. Egocentric interpretations and absurd rituals began to creep into the practices of all three, grounding their beliefs into bastions of power and control. These power bases were utilised for political gain in the misguided attempt for domination and to acquire wealth, fame, and fortune.

"This is preposterous!" said Gabriel, as he and Michael scanned the globe, "I cannot bear this."

Gabriel turned his attention to what was known as the East. He was gratified to learn that swathes of humanity had understood that human beings were on Earth for a purpose, many of whom were repaying their obligations and debts to one another: they called it "karma". It had its roots in the teachings of the special missionary angels who had been born in this part of the world millennia before. Many of these inhabitants embraced the principles of kindness, compassion, and forgiveness. However, as time evolved, some argued they were superior souls in relation to the weak and poor, who were supposed to endure their lot in life, for it was their karma. And again, a harshness, and sometimes cruelty, wound its way into acceptance within society.

Another group believed their existence in the world was to

achieve their highest consciousness, a state of "nirvana". It stemmed from the teachings of another special missionary angel sent to these parts. But here again, self-serving interpretations edged into the practices, losing sight of its essence.

"Life is so simple," said Gabriel, "It is just a matter of being kind, compassionate, and demonstrating our love for one another."

"Yet it is so difficult for humankind," said Michael, dejectedly.

Whether of the East, West, North or South, people on Earth were sidetracked on their journey towards the truth, the One, their egos mesmerised by the form of the physical world and basking in the materiality of their affluence.

Then a new phenomenon took hold: variations of the religions began to sprout all over the world, and humanity subdivided into sects and narrower paths. The foundations for some were based on the values of love, compassion, and kindness, but others were dogmatic and emphasised form over intelligent thought. Hostility and hatred amongst people increased, and the violence only grew stronger.

Raphael, worried by the developments, joined Gabriel and Michael.

"I fear matters are deteriorating very quickly," said Gabriel.

"Even the guardian angels have brought this to my attention," said Michael, "They are having a very difficult time taking care of their charges, trying to ignite the spark within each human being."

"But what I do not understand," said Raphael, "is why the followers of the Abrahamic religions are behaving like this? Even if they only embraced the one teaching of the Quartet, it would require them to be kind, compassionate, and generous towards all. What has happened to God's Message to Humanity? When a person completes their lifetime and returns home, their regret is heartbreaking. Every day I am faced with this situation as people transition back to this realm."

"I know how difficult it is to watch all this," said Gabriel, turning away from the world, "I am upset, too. However, God has repeatedly conveyed that He has granted free will to all His children, and it is up to each individual to decide for him and herself how each wishes to behave, and what steps each wishes to take, whether towards or away from their higher consciousness. We cannot force things in a certain direction. We can only guide."

"I am amazed at God's patience," said Michael. Gabriel noticed that the Quartet had appeared some distance away.

"My brothers!" exclaimed Gabriel, "Come and join us. It is wonderful to see you." The Quartet glided towards them in unity, illuminating the way as they moved forward, yet there was a discernible melancholy about them.

Abraham began, "We have come to speak with you, Archangel Gabriel. We are distraught by what humankind is doing in each of our names. We cannot bear it any longer. We must do something about it."

"We were just discussing how disappointed we are with the choices humanity is making," said Gabriel, "But do not be discouraged. God continues to remind us that He has granted free will to each of us, and that He is granting people on Earth the time and opportunity to absorb His Message to Humanity. We must be patient and allow for this to happen."

"But we do not understand how our people can turn on each other like this," said Abraham. Gabriel reached out to comfort him.

"I know how difficult it is to sit and watch the suffering inflicted in the name of faith, and how abhorrent it is when it is inflicted in the name of God – it cuts right through my soul – but we will have to be patient for the foreseeable future and help alleviate suffering wherever we can," said Gabriel, "I myself, will visit Earth as a human being again to see if I can influence humanity in the right direction." Michael and Raphael looked questioningly at Gabriel.

"In the meantime," said Michael, "the special missionary angels continue to be born into various parts of the world to help humanity along its path."

"Very well," said Abraham.

"Let us pray together for strength and courage to continue our work," said Raphael. All seven angels knelt in supplication. Their beings grew bright and illuminated the atmosphere as God enveloped them with love and grace. Once they all felt better, they embraced one another and returned to their work.

Gabriel, Michael, and Raphael watched the activities on Earth.

"When will you visit Earth, Gabriel?" asked Michael.

"I do not know, but not immediately," said Gabriel, "I want to monitor the world for the next few years. But we will continue to send special missionary angels to lead and guide humanity."

"On the bright side, more and more angels are advancing and entering the fifth and sixth dimensions," said Raphael, "The numbers we have residing there are unprecedented."

"That is good news, indeed," said Gabriel, "In the future, we will require their assistance to help enlighten humanity. At a certain time, they will need to be born on Earth in large numbers in order to affect a global shift."

"I will continue my efforts," said Raphael.

"Be resilient!" called out Gabriel, as Raphael hurried away.

Gabriel and Michael moved closer to Earth and watched its evolution in detail. They kept an eye on every corner, observing with expectant curiosity. By now, neither was surprised to see mischief, mayhem, and malevolence erupting in all parts of the world. However, one development stunned them – slavery – humanity had sunk to a new low. It was not only rampant, but was becoming an acceptable norm throughout the world. Such conduct was not limited to a certain part of the world, or to particular peoples or belief systems. In every area, humankind thought they could subjugate the other. Whether of the female gender, or distinctive race, or different shade of skin, the other seemed alien – no one saw themselves in each other.

"This is very tough to take," said Michael, welling up.

Gabriel strained with emotion: everywhere he looked, he saw men, women, and children suffering under its brutality. Some were worked to death, and others were beaten and subjected to sexual violence.

"I cannot stand this," said Gabriel, "and I do not know if they will ever learn." Both he and Michael turned away from Earth.

Suddenly, a wave of loving energy descended upon them as God tried to reassure them. The two angels managed to compose themselves.

"Gabriel, Michael," said Raphael, rushing towards them, "why don't you both take over my work? Let me monitor Earth for the time being. It will be good for all of us to changeover."

"Yes, thank you Raphael. I need a break from this," said Gabriel, "But remember to continue the visits of the special missionary angels on Earth. We must keep up the momentum and provide beacons of light for those who wish to embrace their higher consciousness."

"I will. Now the two of you get going," said Raphael.

Gabriel concentrated his efforts in the angel schools. He taught them about their light and how to reach deep into their spirit to experience how powerful they were. He instilled the need to remain connected to God when they donned physical bodies on Earth, and not be addicted to physical objects and desires. He emphasised that the love and compassion they had for each other in these dimensions must be carried over to life on Earth, for it was the only way that the world would be able to exist and flourish in its most authentic and pure form.

Many angels internalised the teachings and reached their higher consciousness, and as Raphael had previously reported, a great many graduated to the fifth and sixth dimensions. This boded well for the future, as Gabriel had every intention of sending as many missionary angels to Earth as he could at various times during Earth's evolution.

Many years passed with God continuing to grant humanity the knowledge, creativity, and technology to better their lives, even though warmongering and the quest for wealth and power carried on with a vengeance. Many religions and beliefs spread throughout the world, sometimes peacefully, sometimes through threats and violence. From his post in the higher dimensions, Gabriel still kept an eye on the happenings in the world.

Then one day, he felt the moment had arrived for him to visit Earth again as a human being, for he thought he should gain the experience of today's world. He decided to consult God.

"In the name of God, the most Beneficent, the most Merciful," invoked Gabriel, as he withdrew into himself.

"My dear Gabriel, I am happy to see you," said God.

"It is my happiness to be in Your Presence, My Lord," said Gabriel. It truly was bliss to be immersed in God's loving energy, away from the pandemonium in the lower dimensions. "My Lord, I believe it is time for me to visit Earth again, to obtain direct experience of where humanity is in its spiritual evolution, and try to influence it in the right direction. However, I want to obtain your permission."

"My dear child, it is a good idea, however, it is your choice, and you are not obliged to visit Earth in human form," said God, "I have only requested you to take on human form once, and I will ask you once again in the future, but it will still be your prerogative whether or not to accept."

"My Lord, I feel it is time for me to experience life on Earth as it is now," said Gabriel, "Many who have returned from Earth and whom I tutor in the angel schools convey to me that I do not comprehend what life on Earth is like today, and that I have an archaic, naive sense of human nature. They tell me that it is well and good for me to teach about love and forgiveness, but to practice it on Earth is extremely difficult. Therefore, I feel I must be born in the world and live an ordinary, normal life so that I am better able to help my siblings-in-light."

"Very well, My child," said God, "But remember to maintain your link with Me, and turn to Me when you are in difficulty. Even in your darkest moments, I will be with you carrying you through your suffering."

"Yes, my Lord. Thy Will be done in and through me. Thy Will be done on Earth as it is in Heaven," said Gabriel as he withdrew. When he reached the fourth dimension, he called out to Michael and Raphael to join him.

"I am returning to Earth as a human being again. It has been several thousand years since my last visit, and I must experience life on Earth as it is now," said Gabriel, "It is the only way that I will have the credibility to further the education of my siblings. While they have a great deal of love and respect for me, I can sense that they no longer feel that I am in touch with the latest experiences on Earth."

"Do you really need to take such a drastic step?" asked Raphael, "Whether it is in the past, present, or future, God's principles are still the same."

"You and I know that, Raphael, but I am afraid that our brothers and sisters do not understand this. In order to get through to them, I must demonstrate that I have the practical experience to back up my teachings," said Gabriel.

"Then allow me to be your guardian angel during your sojourn on Earth," said Raphael, "Perhaps Michael can monitor and take care of everything in the heavens during this time."

"Yes, of course," replied Michael, "I will request Kibwe and the Quartet to help. I am sure some angels who reside in the sixth dimension would also love to assist."

"I am fine with this, as long as everyone helps willingly," said Gabriel.

"I will go and request assistance now, so that the matter is decided before you go," said Michael, as he quickly ascended to the sixth dimension.

Raphael turned to Gabriel. "Have you decided where and in which gender you wish to be born?"

"I think I would prefer to be born female. I can observe the workings of humankind from within. I do not understand why the female continues to be subjugated to the male. Humanity must understand that the masculine and feminine needs to exist in balance. Neither should dominate the other."

"You are choosing a harsher life, Gabriel. Do you not want to be male so that your life experience is just a little easier? It does not mean that life will be straightforward and trouble-free, but at least you will not have to contend with the additional roles and burdens that are placed on women."

Just then Michael appeared and hurried towards them. "I have a team of ten helping me with all the work. So you can both relax, everything is in hand."

"Wonderful!" said Gabriel, "But Michael, please continue to send special missionary angels to all parts of the world. They must act as guideposts along humanity's journey."

"I will, Gabriel," said Michael, "Rest assured of that. There are many who are ready and willing."

"Excellent!" said Gabriel, looking towards Earth, "Now I need to make the necessary preparations for my visit."

"Michael, you should know that Gabriel intends to be born female," said Raphael.

"Why do you always choose the more difficult path?" said Michael exasperatingly. He was very concerned about Gabriel taking on human form, knowing that wars and battles raged everywhere, and there was no value to human life. Besides, women were always part of the spoils of war and they endured great suffering.

"I will choose a family that respects women," said Gabriel, "It is only by being born female that I will experience the full breadth of life and understand the pressures on both genders. I will comprehend life from a female's point of view, and will also be able to observe the male and internalise those experiences."

"If you must, Gabriel, but please be careful. You know you will not have any memory of who you are, but please maintain your link with God," said Michael, embracing Gabriel.

"Do not worry, Michael," said Raphael, comforting him, "I will be with Gabriel every moment of his life."

Gabriel and Raphael made their way towards Earth. As Michael watched them, he could not help the feeling of dread that rose within him: he looked upwards and said a special prayer for Gabriel.

23 LAYLA

Gabriel searched the world for suitable parents, and finally came across a family whom he believed would provide him with the experience he desired, given the parents already had several children of both genders. He began his inner preparations, with Raphael firmly at his side.

"Remember your link with God, Gabriel. I will be with you throughout," whispered Raphael, who was relieved to see the family was overjoyed to have another child. When the appointed time arrived, Gabriel invoked, "In the name of God, the most Beneficent, the most Merciful!" and slipped into the body of the baby.

The mother was surprised that the birthing process was not as difficult as she had expected: within minutes, a lovely girl was born. They named her Layla, for she was born during the night, her head covered with dark, thick hair and her eyes sparkling midnight blue.

The family loved Layla and her elder siblings doted on her. She was very special to them, although none could quite explain why; there was just a serene purity about her. As a young child, Layla seemed to have a maturity and wisdom beyond her years and they truly believed that she was a gift from God.

Layla grew into an attractive young lady, although one would not have called her beautiful in the classic sense. She had a captivating personality that seemed to shine from within and many were drawn to her – they were taken in by her charm.

Layla was spiritually inclined, and remained grounded in her belief in a higher power. She set time aside every day for quiet contemplation, where she connected with the spirits she believed were around her, and especially her guardian angel, whom she considered her closest ally.

While her family was not well-to-do, they had enough to live a sufficient, dignified life. Civilisation advanced rapidly and most people were absorbed with new ways to acquire wealth and improve their lives: creativity, invention, and trade were at the forefront of human endeavour, but Layla's family were content in their circumstances, living a quiet, village-centred life.

One day, Layla's father fell ill. This was a blow to the family financially, as they did not have any surplus to spare. They borrowed funds from a money-lender to afford the necessary treatment. Soon enough, they fell behind in their payments and the money-lender began to harass them. The situation continued for many months as they fell further into debt with no end in sight. This put tremendous stress on the family and her father's health deteriorated. Layla knew she had to do something; she approached them with a solution.

"I have sewing skills. I can obtain work as a seamstress and supplement our family's income," said Layla, "Whatever I earn can be paid towards the debt. It would give us the best chance of paying it off as quickly as possible."

"You're still a child, Layla," said her father, "You're much too young to take on such a responsibility."

"But I'm nearly sixteen!" said Layla, "I'm not a child, and in any case, there's nothing wrong with hard work. It'll also give me the experience I need." After much to-ing and fro-ing and Layla's persistence, her father finally relented and let her take in some work. Layla began by approaching her neighbours to do some mending, and as her experience and reputation grew, she moved into dressmaking and tailoring. Very quickly, she made a name for herself, and took on more lucrative work. She was able to earn enough to make large payments to the money-lender and contribute to the household. Their debt finally began to decrease, and with the burden lifted, her father's health improved.

Layla continued her business and called on the more affluent customers in their homes; it was easier to do the necessary fittings in private. During one such visit as she busily took the measurements of the lady of the house, her husband barged into the room.

"Why are you spending so much money? We can't afford such extravagance!" said the husband.

The wife jumped down from the stool. "I'm sticking to the budget!"

Layla shrank into the corner of the room and tried to make herself invisible – she wanted no part of this.

"Stop defying me," said the husband, narrowing his eyes.

"I will speak my mind!" shouted the wife, "In any case, you're the one who wants me to be well-dressed and presentable. I'm only doing what you asked!"

The husband lunged forward and struck his wife across her face. "Stop with these expenses! Money doesn't grow on trees! I have to work for it!"

Layla was shocked by the anger and violence; this was not something she was accustomed to, having been brought up in a loving, genteel family.

"You there!" said the husband, pointing to Layla, "Don't come here anymore, unless you want to work without pay! My wife has no money to spend on clothes." Layla looked down at the floor and quietly nodded. The husband stomped out of the room.

"I'm very sorry you had to experience that," said the wife, as she turned to Layla.

"It's not for you to apologise," said Layla. She hesitated for a moment, then added, "Why did your husband hit you? I've never seen such aggression."

"That's just his way," said the wife.

Layla's eyes widened in surprise. She picked up the dress. "I know you can't pay me the balance, but I will finish this anyway and deliver it to you."

"You're so kind! I wish I could pay you more." The wife scanned the room and her jewellery caught her eye as it glinted in the sunlight. "Here, take this," she said, selecting a bangle from her dressing table.

"No, you don't have to," protested Layla. The wife placed the bangle in Layla's hand.

"Please keep it. It has some value and may prove helpful someday," said the wife.

Layla left the house and returned a few days later to deliver the dress. The husband happened to be home and noticed Layla at the door.

"What's she doing here?" said the husband, furrowing his brow.

"She's only delivering my dress. There's no additional payment, so don't worry."

"I do worry. You better control your spending, otherwise we'll be out on the street. Do you know how much I owe the money-lender? If business doesn't improve, we're in trouble."

"I'm sure you'll think of a way out," said the wife, "You always do."

"Yes...I do," said the husband. He stared into the fireplace, straining to come up with a solution. After a few minutes, he said, "I'm going out."

"Where are you going? When will you be back?" said the wife.

"I don't know. Don't wait for me," said the husband, as he reached for his coat.

The husband walked along the streets, pre-occupied with his problems, wondering how to resolve his debt. He found himself on the road to the neighbouring town and walked to its centre. He bumped into some old acquaintances whom he had not seen in years; they invited him to spend the evening with them. They talked, ate, and drank until late. He hadn't felt so carefree in years.

He returned home late that night, and the very next day he went to see the money-lender.

"Will you take payment in-kind?" he asked the money-lender.

"It depends. What do you have in mind?"

"There are many businessmen in far-off lands who trade in various commodities. There's a lucrative market for young girls. What if I could provide you with one to sell off? It would pay off my entire debt."

"I've heard of this. They make a lot of money," said the money-lender, tapping his chin, "Whom do you have in mind? I can't just grab anyone. I'm well-known in these parts."

"Do you know Layla, the young seamstress? I'm sure you'd get an enormous amount for her!"

"Layla?! But I know her family so well! I'd be found out immediately!" said the money-lender. He shook his head from side-to-side, "No, no... I can't get involved in this. I have my reputation to consider. And in any case, how would I even arrange such a transaction? I don't know anyone in the business."

"Okay, calm down. I know a few people. I'll arrange everything. You won't be implicated, but you'll receive full payment – as long as you acknowledge that my debt to you is over," said the husband.

"Look, all I want is the money you owe me," said the money-lender, "How you obtain it is of no concern to me. Leave me out of it."

"Fine. You'll get your money," said the husband, and he quickly turned and began walking down the road. As soon as he reached home, he sought out his wife.

"The festival is coming up. Why don't you call your seamstress and have a new dress made for yourself?" said the husband.

"Really?" said the wife.

"Yes, really," he said, putting his arms around her.

"Wonderful! I'll send for her now. I already have a design in mind." She kissed his cheek and dashed off to collect her sketches.

Layla visited the house several times, and each time the husband happened to be home. He took great interest in the fittings and Layla's workmanship, and was generally kind and pleasant. He even apologised to her for his earlier behaviour.

On the day of the festival, the residents gathered in the square, and welcomed all the visitors from nearby villages. This was a chance to sell their wares, and there was much food and drink to enjoy.

Layla wore a new dress she had especially sewn for the occasion, and also slipped on the bangle the wife had given her; it glistened on her forearm as it caught the sun. Layla celebrated the festival with her family and friends. As she strolled around meeting and greeting the townspeople, they pampered her with foods and little gifts of all sorts.

In the middle of the day, at the height of the noise and reverie, the husband approached Layla.

"Are you enjoying yourself, Layla?" he asked.

"Yes, isn't it wonderful to meet so many people? And so many things I've never seen before!" said Layla.

"Have you seen the new textiles in that stall?" he said, pointing down a side street.

"No, I haven't," said Layla, straining to look through the people blocking her view.

"You should. The material would make lovely clothes. Here, let me show you." He firmly gripped her elbow and drove her through the crowd. Before she knew it, Layla was led down a lonely alley, an uneasy feeling rising from the pit of her stomach. Suddenly, a strange man rushed forward and grabbed her hands – he tied them together.

"What are you doing?" yelled Layla, "Who are you?" The stranger handed a sack to the husband, who turned quickly and rushed back to the main square.

"Help me! What's happening?!" said Layla.

She was thrown into a waiting cart pulled by a team of horses that galloped down the country road. Layla screamed at the top of her lungs, but to no avail. No one heard her amid the music and merriment.

The husband melted into the crowd and eventually made his way to the money-lender in the central square.

"Here's your payment in full," said the husband, pushing the sack into his hands.

"But, how did you —"

"Don't ask," interrupted the husband. He quickly left to find his wife. He saw her in the distance showing off her new dress to her friends.

Layla travelled for many hours into the night, unable to cut herself loose; she was tied down hand and foot, and carefully watched by the strange man. A calm descended upon her as she prayed to God to help her.

"Strength and courage," she repeated to herself. She appealed to her guardian angel to remain with her and protect her. Layla realised that whatever happened next, she would be forever changed.

Up in the heavens, Raphael was shocked by the events. Michael rushed over and they both prayed for Layla's strength to endure this ordeal. Many thousands of angels joined them, and they all beseeched God to save her. A loving energy descended upon them.

"Michael, come and see Me," said God.

"In the name of God, the most Beneficent, the most Merciful," invoked Michael, as he withdrew.

"My dear Michael," said God, "All of you must calm yourselves and be at peace. I am watching over Gabriel. Remember, it is Gabriel's choice to take on human form and experience life as it is now, and I will not interfere with Gabriel's fate. I have granted free will to all My children, including to those who choose treachery and an unconscionable path. It is now up to Gabriel to decide how he will handle the challenges with which he is faced. I am with him. He will turn to Me for strength and courage, and I will provide him with the solace he requires."

"Yes, My Lord," said Michael.

"Now, My child, carry on with your work, and be at peace," said God.

"Thy Will be done in and through me. Thy Will be done on Earth as it is in Heaven," said Michael, and he returned to Raphael and conveyed God's words.

"We will have to be strong and just help wherever we can," said Raphael, as he watched over Layla.

What followed does not bear description. Layla was subjected to great physical suffering, having been sold onwards to new owners. She slaved away until they reached the land far up north. These people had not been exposed to the civilisation of Layla's birth and she looked exotic against the women of the area. This proved to be her downfall: her value increased as a sexual slave. She was severely beaten when she resisted. Her owner kept her locked up, for Layla had a propensity to try to escape whenever the opportunity presented itself.

Raphael remained close to her, constantly whispering into her soul during her greatest suffering: "Keep courage and forbearance; look within to find your light."

Layla never gave up hope and held strong to God. Through the small window of her cell, she would hear the singing and rhythmic chants of the ascetic who lived down the road. It provided her with much peace and tranquillity. Many believed him to be of unsound mind, but the music he played would send Layla into a blissful trance, and she looked forward to his daily melodies.

Many years passed in this manner. When Layla was considered too old to continue, she was forced to work as a cleaner and washer woman, which she gratefully accepted.

By this time, most of her family members had died wondering what had happened to Layla – she had disappeared on the day of the festival never to be seen or heard from again. Racked with guilt, the money-lender had forgiven the balance of their debt, the family mistakenly believing that he had felt sorry for their loss. His secret, however, ate away at his soul, and he fell ill with disease and died a few years after Layla's abduction. The husband and wife whose argument had set Layla's destiny in motion became even wealthier and they moved to a big town where they prospered for many years.

Layla realised that at her advanced age, most of her own family would have passed on, or if not, were probably too old to deal with her return. So once her usefulness had completely worn out and she was tossed from the brothel, Layla remained in the land up north. She sold her bangle, which she had hidden from her captors, and it gave her just enough to put a roof over her head; she took in mending to earn her meagre living.

She continued to believe in God and always prayed for His grace; and she knew that her guardian angel was watching over her. When the time finally arrived for her life to end, Michael and many angels waited with Raphael, ready to receive Layla and help her with her transition to the fourth dimension. At the precise moment, Raphael reached for Layla and raised her into his arms. All the angels shone their love and light on her.

"Layla, I am your guardian angel," said Raphael, "Remain still and calm until you are fully acquainted with this realm." Slowly, the realisation set in and Gabriel became fully aware.

"Raphael, it is you! And Michael, too! How wonderful to see you!" They both embraced Gabriel and clung onto him affectionately.

"I am so sorry for all that you had to endure, Gabriel," said Raphael, "Are you okay?"

"Yes, I am fine," said Gabriel, "I am just glad you were constantly with me. Knowing my guardian angel was watching over me gave me a lot of comfort."

"I wish I could have done more to help you through your troubles," said Raphael, tearfully, "It was very difficult for me to watch you live through all that torment." Raphael looked away.

Gabriel held him. "I am fine, Raphael. Look at me. I survived and have returned home. Those who harmed me will have to account for their behaviour. Even though I did not expect to undergo such difficulty, I experienced and learnt a great deal. No angel can now accuse me of not understanding the unfairness of life on Earth! And I know I shall have to forgive a great many souls."

"All in good time," said Michael, "Now, you should rest. You have been through a harrowing experience."

"Yes, I admit I need time to recover," said Gabriel, "I also want to review and contemplate all that I have been through in this lifetime."

"Of course, Gabriel," said Raphael, "Carry on, and take all the time you need."

"Raphael, I am grateful to you for being my guardian angel," said Gabriel, embracing him again.

"Oh Gabriel, I still wish I could have done more!" said Raphael, "I do not know how you continue to live human lives on Earth. It is so difficult!"

"There is also a lot of joy, Raphael," said Gabriel, "It is how you choose to view life, no matter what your circumstances. I am not saying it is easy. As you know, there were times that I sank into the depths of despair. And my anger got the better of me on many occasions. But that is when I tried to find that inner peace and joy. I searched for the divine within." Gabriel comforted Raphael. "And life can be filled with fun and laughter."

"I suppose so. As long as you are okay," said Raphael.

"I am fine. Now let us move on," said Gabriel.

"Gabriel, go and rest," said Michael, "and Raphael, come with me and let us spend some time together before you get some rest as well."

Gabriel thanked all the angels for receiving him and withdrew into the seventh dimension. He laid his head down to recover from the brutality he had experienced. It had been his toughest sojourn on Earth to date.

Gabriel remained in recovery for a significant amount of time. His female body had been brutalised on Earth but he had left it behind. What greatly disturbed Gabriel was the inhumanity shown by people around Layla – what they were capable of. Whether it was her captors, those who visited the brothel, or passers-by who scorned her and her fellow prisoners – they exhibited a cruelty that Gabriel had never known before – they did not see her as human. None showed empathy and compassion for her plight, never mind rescue her. Nobody cared to listen to her story, understand her circumstances, or help her out of her misery. This troubled Gabriel, for it meant that many human beings were not maintaining their link with God and did not see their connection with one another – their humanity. Human beings were self-absorbed, judgmental, and succumbing *en masse* to their baser instincts.

Once Gabriel felt better, he raised his head and invoked, "In the name of God, the most Beneficent, the most Merciful."

"My dear child, are you well-recovered?" said God.

"Yes, My Lord," said Gabriel.

"I know how exhausted you are from your life as Layla," said God, "I was disheartened by what your siblings inflicted upon you. They acted with such callousness, and it pained Me to witness your suffering. But I am proud of how you handled the difficulties that came your way. You maintained your link with Me and never blamed Me for your predicament."

"My Lord, how could I blame You for the actions of my fellow humans? They chose their behaviour," said Gabriel.

"Yes, My child," said God, "But as you are well aware, many human beings hold Me responsible for the troubles they encounter. And they expect Me to rescue them from their problems. But I will not intervene and prevent My children from making their choices, even if they are bad ones, for it would take away their free will. Each person must choose how he and she will act, and react, to the set of circumstances with which each is faced."

"Yes, My Lord," said Gabriel.

"Gabriel, what you experienced was cruel, and clearly no fault of your own," said God, "You were swept up in a situation that was controlled by others for their own selfish ends. You did your best to escape your torment, but when you could not, you still faced life with as much strength and dignity as you could muster, and you turned to Me, the divine within."

"Yes, My Lord," said Gabriel.

"During your darkest moments, I held you in My grace and wept," said God, "I suffered with you and experienced your anguish, for I am deep within you. My children have forgotten: what you do unto the least of you, you do unto Me."

"Yes, My Lord," said Gabriel, recalling what God had conveyed to him many millennia ago: whatever we experienced in our individual existence, so did God; and to whatever we subjected ourselves or others, we also subjected Him. Gabriel recoiled as he remembered what was visited on him as Layla: the thought that God had undergone such spiteful, inhumane treatment repulsed him to his core.

"Gabriel, you have undergone a gruelling experience, all with the intention of helping your siblings," said God, "But I want you to remember that you do not have to take on human form unless you genuinely wish to. I am perfectly happy with you remaining in the upper dimensions and continuing your work."

"Yes, My Lord, I understand," said Gabriel.

"I will continue to bless My children with progress and advancement on Earth," said God, "I am providing them with the opportunity to learn; I am granting them great innovation and technology in order to improve the quality of their lives. Will they share this blessing or will they become possessive and greedy? What manner of civilisation will they establish on Earth? Will it be a selfless, noble society or will it be mired in self-interest and greed, disturbing the equilibrium of all that I have created? I will wait and see, and give My children even more opportunity to understand and apply My Message to their lives. I will be patient for now, and continue to give My children the time and space to learn. In the meantime, Gabriel, if you wish to resume your work, then I would like you to augment the lessons in the angel schools and ask those in the sixth dimension to help. This is their opportunity to contribute."

"Yes, My Lord," said Gabriel.

"And continue your efforts to turn the dark angels around," said God, "I am confident that they will eventually awaken to their true selves, but you must be constant in your efforts. Ask Michael and Raphael to help you with this group. Combine your forces to resolve this situation."

"Yes, My Lord," said Gabriel.

"Now go with My blessings, Gabriel, and I look forward to the day when you merge permanently with My Light."

"Thy Will be done in and through me. Thy Will be done on Earth as it is in Heaven," invoked Gabriel. He remained in God's presence for a few more seconds, soaking in the pure love and energy.

"It truly is bliss to remain within the Great Spirit," thought Gabriel. He slowly withdrew and descended through the heavens. Michael and Raphael received him, noticing that he did not seem as rejuvenated as the times before.

"Gabriel, are you sure you have rested enough?" said Michael.

"Yes, I have. It is just that I am disappointed that we are not making the progress that we should be. Many of our siblings have accessed their higher consciousness and are making great leaps forward. But for those who have not, they are acting as a counterweight, stunting our overall development, and even reversing many of our achievements. Success is eluding us," said Gabriel, as he looked towards Earth, "Whatever the case, God is being patient and will continue to advance the world."

Michael moved towards him. "Do not be despondent, Gabriel. We will persevere even if it means we have to work that much harder. There are many angels who now reside in the sixth dimension. We can call on them to swell our ranks and make a concerted effort to succeed."

"God has instructed to do just that," said Gabriel, "And we also have to do our best to enlighten the dark angels. God asked me to involve you both in this task."

"You know we are ready," said Raphael.

"Good. Let us plan our strategy together," said Gabriel. As they moved towards a quiet corner, a group of about fifty angels approached them, lowering their heads in deference.

"Archangel Gabriel," spoke one, "You will recognise me as your father during your life as Layla. I was distraught when you went missing, and now that I have found you well, my prayers have been answered." His face contorted with emotion. "I am so grateful that you chose to be my daughter on Earth. I knew you were a gift from God. I am just sorry that I could not protect you. I failed you."

Gabriel comforted him. "You did not fail me. You were a wonderful father, and I was proud to be your daughter."

A few angels came forward and Gabriel recognised them as Layla's family. They were delighted to be reunited and they embraced Gabriel lovingly.

Michael and Raphael decided to leave them to catch up. As they glided away, some rustling behind Gabriel caught their attention.

"Do you see that group of angels?" said Michael, indicating to his right.

"Yes. Why are they bent in prostration like that?" said Raphael.

Michael suddenly stopped. "Oh God! Those are the culprit angels who were instrumental in Layla's suffering. I am not sure whether Gabriel is ready for this."

Raphael looked closely and saw the money-lender, the husband, his wife, the slave traders, Layla's eventual owner, the men who visited their physical desires upon her, and the women who were revolted by her presence in their midst. Not one of them had showed any kindness, compassion, or mercy for the lady called Layla.

"How will Gabriel deal with this? They treated Layla so vilely," said Raphael.

"We better get back to him," said Michael. They moved towards Gabriel and flanked him on either side.

"Gabriel, take a look at the group behind you. Are you ready for this?" said Raphael.

Gabriel turned and his eyes widened as he realised who had arrived. "It looks like I will have to confront my nemeses sooner rather than later."

Many angels had witnessed the events of Gabriel's recent incarnation on Earth and gathered round to see what would happen. The crowd grew from hundreds to thousands, and within minutes swelled into millions of angels surrounding them. Gabriel was surprised to see that so many were aware of his recent life experience.

"Well, I have to practice what I preach," said Gabriel to Michael and Raphael, "Will you both help me?"

"Of course," said Michael and Raphael.

Gabriel faced the group who were now kneeling before him, their heads bowed in remorse. He reached deep within himself and drew on his strength.

"My dear siblings, stand up and look at me," said Gabriel. They slowly arose but kept their heads bowed.

"Look at me," said Gabriel.

"We cannot. We are so ashamed of our behaviour," said one.

"Please look at me, for it is equally important for me, as it is for you, that we see each other as we truly are. We must look into each other's light and confront our mistakes. It is the only way that we will all be able to move past our encounter on Earth." The angels struggled to raise their eyes, and when they looked straight at Gabriel, he could see the great pain and suffering within them. The money-lender stepped forward.

"Please forgive me, Archangel Gabriel!" he wailed, "I was so greedy! I was obsessed with material wealth and could not see how damaging this was to me and those around me. Please, please forgive me, Archangel Gabriel! I did not know it was you within the persona of Layla! Why did God not stop me?! I do not know how I will exist without your forgiveness! Have mercy on my soul!" The money-lender fell down at Gabriel's feet and continued to appeal for absolution.

Gabriel bent down and raised him by his shoulders. "I now have a choice. I can forgive you, and you accept your mistakes, learn from them, and never repeat them. Or I can refuse to forgive you and hold on to my resentment, angry at the injustices I suffered. The former would allow us to put this behind us and go our separate ways. The latter would force you onto a path to either face a similar experience as I had on Earth or spend an eternity here paying back your debt to me. So do I follow the road of compassion and mercy, or should I follow the path of resentment and vengeance? Archangel Michael, what do you advise?"

Michael turned to Gabriel. "If you choose revenge, then you are tying yourself to this soul for a multitude of years, until he is able to pay back every iota of the suffering he caused you. Is it not better to show compassion and forgive his actions? It does not mean that you condone his behaviour, for you recognise it to be wrong. However, by forgiving, it would not only pardon him, but more importantly in this case, it would free you from his hold on you. Archangel Gabriel, he bound you to your fate on Earth; do not let him bind you in the heavens."

Gabriel looked straight at the money-lender and smiled. The tenderness in Gabriel's eyes touched the money-lender; his tears flowed as he realised that Gabriel was forgiving him. Continuing to hold him by the shoulders, Gabriel said, "I forgive you for everything you did to me and my family. It does not mean that what you did was right, for I condemn it in the strongest terms. Each being comes from God, and must be treated with respect and dignity. Whether it is me or another, each person is an angel in human form."

"I am so sorry," said the money-lender.

"I forgive you for your misdeeds," said Gabriel, "but please learn from this. Do not become mesmerised by the physicality of Earth and repeat your mistakes."

"Oh, I never will again! Thank you, Archangel Gabriel!" said the money-lender.

"And one more thing. You asked why God did not stop you. You have free will, and with free will comes responsibility. It was you who took the decision to charge usurious fees, not God. It was you who was implicit in my abduction, not God. It was you who chose to accept the money and look the other way, not God. You are the one who chose to remain quiet on my whereabouts and let my family suffer, not God."

The money-lender nodded, acknowledging his actions.

Gabriel continued, "Finally, it was you who took the decision to forgive my family's loan. That was generous on your part, yet you did not give credit to God for "making" you do that! You consoled yourself for the rest of your life by saying that at least you did one good thing."

Gabriel looked squarely at the money-lender. "So you

see, you know right from wrong. You know how to govern your behaviour and you took decisions to suit you – everything was done in your self-interest. So why implicate God and blame Him when your decisions go wrong?"

"I am truly sorry," said the money-lender.

"It is important that you learn about yourself – who you actually are, your origins. I recommend you attend the angel schools," said Gabriel.

"I will, Archangel Gabriel. And thank you, again." They embraced each other and the money-lender retreated into the group.

Then the husband came forward. "I do not even know where to begin, Archangel Gabriel. How could I have done this to a fellow human being? My need to be rich and powerful blinded me. Please forgive me."

The husband's light was dull with despair. Gabriel held him by the shoulders. "Do you realise your mistakes? Do you understand where you went wrong?"

"Yes, I do," whispered the husband, "I was so caught up with my own life and my own needs, that I disregarded the consequences of my decisions. I ignored the suffering of others." He hung his head in shame.

"Look at me," said Gabriel. The husband slowly raised his head. His eyes were welling with tears.

"I forgive you," continued Gabriel, "Even though it was all your idea and your actions set me up for a life filled with pain and misery, I forgive you. Now stand tall, and do not hang on to your guilt. It will eat away at you for nothing. Forgive yourself. Remember, that is just as important as my forgiveness. Forgive yourself so that you are released. And again, I recommend you attend the angel schools to learn about who you actually are."

"Thank you, Archangel Gabriel. I assure you I will do my best to learn," said the husband. They embraced each other and he retreated into the group.

"Forgive me, Archangel Gabriel. My arrogance and vanity got the better of me," said the wife as she stepped forward, "and I never cared to inquire what happened to my dressmaker."

Gabriel smiled. "Thank you for the bangle. It proved useful at the precise moment that I needed it."

"I am embarrassed by my behaviour," said the wife.

"Do not be. And I do forgive you for whatever part you played in my misery," said Gabriel, "I said a prayer for you when I sold the bangle – it really did help me. So, thank you."

As the day progressed, one by one, each of the angels came forward. On learning that the lovely lady called Layla was really Gabriel, some were so repulsed by their actions, they cried openly and threw themselves at Gabriel's feet.

"How could I have done what I did to you?!" wept one angel.

Gabriel replied, "Whether it was me or another, you cannot force yourself on someone. Just because it was me does not mean it is worse. It is not okay to do that to anyone! Do you see how what you did has come around to confront you? Your actions are like a boomerang: what you put out there will turn around and come back to you. Every time you do something to another, you are doing it to yourself. And you are doing it to God, for He is within each being."

Gabriel forgave each one of them for their actions. Once all had been absolved, the millions of angels watching closed in around them to pray for God's blessings. Gradually, a great love and grace descended upon them. It was as if the skies had opened up revealing a tranquil, powerful energy. It prevailed upon them, enlivening each soul – each felt a lightness of being. The angels felt exhilarated with such Presence. It was the first time many of them had experienced this bliss.

"What is this feeling?" asked one angel.

"It is godliness," said Gabriel, "it is what we encounter as we move closer to God. The higher the dimension in which we exist, the stronger the sensation. It is the joy and lightness of being in our purest form."

This glimpse into what awaited them in the higher dimensions was enough to send everyone rushing to the angel schools, determined to learn how to reach their highest consciousness.

As everyone dispersed, Raphael turned to Gabriel. "That was beautifully done, Gabriel. It is amazing how God's discernible Presence can impact us. When we cannot sense Him, we forget He exists. It is our own lack of consciousness. One thing, though…I am surprised that God showed Himself so boldly."

"I believe it was for Gabriel," said Michael, "I think God wanted something more to come of his life as Layla."

Gabriel chuckled. "You give me too much credit. There were others who suffered just like me. Maybe God just wished to bless us in response to our prayers."

"Yes," said Michael, "but I do think it is more than that."

"Well, whatever the reasons, it has made an impact. Millions have made their way to the angel schools," said Gabriel.

"Which means we better get on with the lessons," said Michael.

"I just want a few moments to myself, if you do not mind," said Gabriel.

"Take your time, Gabriel. There is no hurry," said Michael, as he and Raphael began moving away, giving Gabriel the privacy he required.

Gabriel knelt down and thanked God. Whatever the reasons for His Presence, this final act solidified Gabriel's credibility, for now none could question whether he understood what life on Earth was like today.

The three Archangels combined their forces in the angel schools. Never before had the schools benefited from such attention, and many progressed by leaps and bounds. With teams assisting with Earth-related responsibilities, the heavens vibrated with the hustle and bustle of growth.

Knowledge and technology continued to advance on Earth igniting the curiosity of humankind. People began to explore the world, moving from one part to the other, initiating a massive trade in goods and in the exchange of ideas. These were perfect circumstances to demonstrate kindness, compassion, and generosity towards one another, and Gabriel hoped that those living on Earth would take advantage of this opportunity.

Gabriel turned his attention to the angels in the dark bubble. He discussed the plan with Michael and Raphael.

"Our strategy seems to have worked well in the angel schools, with all three of us concentrating our efforts. God directed us to apply the same tactics to awaken the dark angels," said Gabriel.

"Perhaps we should consider asking some of our siblings in the sixth dimension to help us," said Raphael, "I suspect this assignment will be difficult."

"Good idea, but they must be the strongest and most experienced," said Gabriel, "The last thing I would want is for a few to fall and get lost along the way."

"Shall I select some who would like to help with this particular task?" said Raphael.

"Yes, advise them to be prepared. But keep them on standby for now. We will only call upon them when it is necessary," said Gabriel.

"Very well," said Raphael, and he ascended to the sixth dimension.

Michael took the opportunity to press Gabriel on something that had been on his mind. "Gabriel, how are you feeling? I do not believe you are completely recovered from your last lifetime on Earth."

Gabriel looked up in surprise. "I feel fine, Michael. Why are you asking again?"

"Ever since you returned, your light does not burn as brightly as it normally does," said Michael, "And I think there is more to it than you are letting on."

Gabriel looked towards Earth and watched all the activities. "I suppose my last life affected me more than I realised. It is not that I am holding on to any resentment. I have forgiven those who hurt me and that part is all over. I think what still haunts me is the depth of human depravity. I never knew how dark our siblings could become."

"I can understand," said Michael, "I watched everything you went through. My experience on Earth was horrible but paled in comparison to what happened to you. Yet I still cannot get over humankind's propensity for violence. I never want to return as a human being again."

Gabriel turned away and struggled to maintain his emotions. "I am afraid I feel the same way. I do not think I ever want to spend another lifetime on Earth. God conveyed to me that it is always my choice whether or not to take on human form. I just hope that I am able to manage the work effectively from here. If I cannot, I am afraid I will have to enter the world again. My promise to God was to do my best to help my siblings, and that may mean another lifetime on Earth."

Michael reached out and comforted Gabriel. "You know that both Raphael and I are with you, and are here to assist you in every way, so do not take it all on yourself. We also made a promise to God. If it is necessary for one of us to live a physical life again, I will do it."

"I could never ask you to do that, Michael," said Gabriel.

"But I would volunteer," said Michael, "It would be my free will."

"We will see. It is my responsibility, and I must see it through," said Gabriel, "We will decide this issue in the future, if and when it arises."

"Very well," said Michael.

Gabriel looked towards Earth again. "You know, now that you have mentioned it, Raphael is also not shining as brightly. I wonder whether he has been affected by my experience on Earth. He was beside me, going through everything with me."

Just then, Raphael appeared and came towards them. "It looks like we have a strong team. They are ready for the assignment, whenever we call them."

"Great. Now come and sit here. I want to ask you something," said Michael, patting the seat next to him. "Have you come to terms with what you witnessed as Gabriel's guardian angel?"

Raphael turned away. "Ah, so you have noticed." Raphael slumped further into his seat. "The wickedness and immorality of our siblings was shocking. I felt so powerless to help you, Gabriel!"

"It is okay, Raphael! You did everything that you were supposed to!" said Gabriel, "Anymore, and you would have interfered with everyone's free will."

Michael held them and said, "I really believe you both need time to deal with what you experienced. And now is as good a time as any."

"We cannot delay our work, Michael. We must deal with the dark angels," replied Gabriel.

"A few more moments will not make a difference, Gabriel. I think we should visit the seventh dimension. Let us rejuvenate ourselves." Without waiting for a reply, Michael tightened his hold and drew them up through the heavens.

Once they reached the seventh dimension, each lay his head down and rested within God. The stillness within was exactly what they needed: it calmed them and allowed them to recalibrate each of their energies into a perfect balance. After a few minutes, as they were about to descend, God called out to them.

"Gabriel, Michael, Raphael. Come and see Me before you go." The Archangels reconnected with the Light, and invoked, "In the name of God, the most Beneficent, the most Merciful."

"My dear children, were you going to leave without seeing Me?" said God.

"We did not want to disturb you, My Lord," replied Gabriel.

"You can never disturb Me," said God, "I am always delighted to see you. I hope all three of you are feeling brighter and stronger than when you first arrived? I want your lights to dazzle the heavens, and not fade under the pressure of your responsibilities."

"Yes, My Lord," they said in unison.

"I do understand how difficult your task is," said God, "Some of My children have given in to temptation and gone far astray, and it is excruciating to witness their behaviour. But do not fret and worry about their inhumanity, and do not be discouraged. You are helping Me to guide your siblings, but the ultimate responsibility is Mine. It is I who will take the final decision as to what to do with those who refuse to heed My words and continue on their destructive path."

"Yes, My Lord," they replied.

"My dear children," said God, "If you ever wish to decrease your workload, or remove it entirely, just tell me. It pains me to see you unhappy. The work should not become a burden to you. Only carry on with it if you wish to. And whenever you need to rest and recover, do not hesitate to withdraw into Me."

"Yes, My Lord," said the Archangels.

"I reiterate: I want you three to be content in your work, and not feel pressured to put yourselves in any kind of peril in order to help your siblings," continued God, "And remember, I will finally take the necessary decisions when the time comes, and each individual will be answerable to Me, their highest consciousness. Now return to the lower heavens unburdened and light-hearted. Shine brightly and illuminate the heavens, for all is well."

"Thy Will be done in and through us. Thy Will be done

on Earth as it is in Heaven," invoked the Archangels as they began their descent. Billions of angels looked on in awe, for the Archangels lit up the heavens with a fiery blaze.

Gabriel turned to Michael and Raphael. "Do you both still want to continue with the work?"

"Of course, Gabriel!" they replied.

"Then prepare yourselves, for now we deal with the dark angels."

24 BRAVE

The Archangels made their way towards the area where the dark angels usually congregated. Once there, they found a whole host of angels, significantly more than when Gabriel last visited. They looked at one another in astonishment.

"What happened?!" said Gabriel, "How can so many get it so wrong? Everyone has been working so hard to raise the overall consciousness, yet look at the number residing here."

A crowd began to gather round them as some became aware of their presence.

"Archangel Gabriel, why are you here?" asked one of the angels.

"We have come to visit you," said Gabriel, "But can I ask, why are so many of you assembled here?"

"Most of us have just arrived after a lifetime on Earth," said the angel, "We want to return to Earth as soon as possible so that we can enjoy its many creations."

"You do realise that life on Earth is not just for enjoyment, but to learn the lessons you require to raise your awareness?" said Michael.

"Yes, but I cannot learn," said the angel, "I am not like you, Archangel Michael. I am ordinary. I do not possess your capability or power." The three Archangels looked at one another in disbelief.

Michael moved closer to the angel. "What do you call yourself?" he asked.

"I am Jyoti," said the angel. The Archangels smiled at the irony of the situation, and Gabriel signalled to Michael to carry on.

"Do you know the meaning of your name?" asked Michael.

"It means light," said Jyoti, "like the light in a lamp, or sunlight. It is a name that my parents had given me in an earlier lifetime, and I kept it."

"Ah, but do you understand its real meaning and significance?" asked Michael.

"Its real meaning? What other meaning could it have other than light?" said Jyoti.

"When you look at us, do you see light?" said Michael.

"I see brightness," replied Jyoti, "The three of you are radiant! You burn very brightly yet it does not hurt my eyes to look upon you. What you radiate is different from the light found on Earth."

Michael explained, "This brilliance that you see is the light found within us. It is not light from an external source that either warms you or illuminates your way as you live your physical lives on Earth. It is an inner light, what many call the light of God, and this light is who you actually are. Light of God. This is the meaning of Jyoti."

Jyoti looked quizzically at the three Archangels, not quite believing Michael. "But I am not like you, Archangel Michael. How can I be the Light of God?" said Jyoti.

"You are exactly like me," said Michael, "We all burst forth at the same time from the same light, whom we refer to as God, the Universal Force, the Great Energy. The only reason that my light seems to burn brighter is because I have raised my consciousness to a certain level. The higher your consciousness, the more luminous you become." Jyoti contemplated Michael's words and her discomfort began to show.

Gabriel realised that this was probably overwhelming for Jyoti, especially with the three of them staring at her. "Michael, why don't you and Jyoti find a quiet place and converse in private? Raphael and I will carry on." Michael nodded in agreement.

"Jyoti, will you accompany me so that we may continue our discussion?" asked Michael.

"Yes, of course, Archangel Michael," said Jyoti, and they stepped over to one side. Gabriel and Raphael turned towards the other angels, some of whom had been listening to the conversation.

"Are you all here so that you can return to Earth quickly?" asked Gabriel.

"Yes," they replied.

"But why are you trying to live a physical life on Earth when you have just come back? What is compelling you to return so quickly?" asked Raphael.

"We love the creation on Earth. We truly enjoy the beauty and bounty God has bestowed, and we want to be closer to God, nearer His creation," replied one angel.

"But God has created much more," said Raphael, "The splendour in the upper dimensions is even more beautiful than on Earth."

The angels glanced at one another, and then looked behind Gabriel and Raphael. They were puzzled. "But we do not see anything."

"It is not because it is not there," replied Raphael, "You are just unable to see it at the moment. You need to raise your consciousness in order to see and experience such beauty."

"But how do we do that? We are not like you, Archangel Raphael. We are just plain, ordinary individuals who enjoy life on Earth as human beings. We would not dare attempt to be closer to God in the higher heavens. We are not worthy."

"Oh, yes you are," replied Raphael. He looked at Gabriel, who gestured to carry on.

"Why don't you all come aside with me so we can continue our conversation?" said Raphael, "I want to explain a bit more, if you will allow me." They all moved to sit in a circle around Raphael.

While they settled themselves, Gabriel whispered, "Continue with your discussion, Raphael. I am going to probe deeper into the darkness to see what I can find." Raphael looked up worriedly.

"Do not be concerned," continued Gabriel, "I am just going to check out the situation. I will not do anything drastic without you and Michael at my side."

Gabriel inched his way into the darkness. As he moved forward, he felt a great pressure bearing down on him. It got heavier the deeper he went. He recognised some of the angels with whom he had conversed many thousands of years earlier: he had tried to convince them to not turn their backs on the higher dimensions. They seemed bleaker than he remembered. As Gabriel moved further in, he felt the sadness and gloom penetrating the atmosphere.

"This is indeed a joyless place," thought Gabriel, "I would not want to remain here for long. No wonder everyone is in a hurry to return to Earth!"

Gabriel continued scanning the far reaches of the dark bubble. With each step, he felt more sombre and dismal, and he realised that he had to help these angels out of their misery. Gabriel now comprehended why God had emphasised this matter had to be dealt with: it was not only an issue of the havoc some of these angels caused on Earth, it was also a question of compassion – they needed help. It was imperative for these siblings to be raised from their sad, joyless existence. It was unfair to leave them here, caught in this unending loop of physical birth and death.

Gabriel saw Michael signalling him. "Wait for me, Gabriel," said Michael, as he caught up to him, "Jyoti has agreed to try and learn how to raise her consciousness. I took her to the angel schools."

"At least we managed to influence one individual to move in the right direction," said Gabriel, as he looked around, "Now for the others…"

They both surveyed the area and absorbed all they could about the state of their siblings. While each of these angels exuded a different shade of darkness, there was no mistaking that they had all embraced a murkier existence, and some more sinister than others. It was going to take all the strength and courage the Archangels could muster to turn this situation around.

Raphael appeared from the distance and approached them.

"I think I managed to make some headway. The group have gone to the angel schools," said Raphael.

The Archangels heard a voice behind them. "What are you doing here?" said an angel, and they quickly turned around. He was so dim with darkness, the Archangels could barely see his light.

"I am called Gabriel."

"I know who you are," said the angel, "I want to know what you are doing here."

"We have come to visit you," said Gabriel, "You are our siblings-in-light and we miss you."

"Why would you miss us?" said the angel, "There are billions of angels and we are such a small, insignificant group. You are the Archangels and you sit with God. You are strong and powerful. Why would you want to associate with us? We are not like you."

"You are just as strong and powerful as we are," said Gabriel, "Give us a chance to show you. Come with us and let us give you a glimpse of the bliss and splendour you are missing."

"I do not know if I believe you," said the angel.

"Why don't you gather a few of your group and accompany the three of us? Let us show you," insisted Gabriel. The angel hesitated and seemed unsure of what to do.

"What do you call yourself?" asked Gabriel.

"I am Lucas," said the angel. The Archangels looked at one another and smiled.

"What a beautiful name, Lucas," said Michael, "You know that it means Luminous."

"I did not know that," said Lucas.

"Gather some of your friends and come with us. There is no need to be concerned. We will not force you to do anything you do not want to do. All is within your control," said Gabriel.

"Very well." Lucas marshalled some of his friends, and when he introduced them to the Archangels, they again looked at one another in amusement, for these angels called themselves: Qadir (the powerful), Shideh (the radiant), Joyce (of the Lord), Bertha (brilliant and bright), Adriel (follower of God), Hikaru (shining brilliance), Isabella (God is my oath), Themba (trust, hope, faith), Trygg (true, faithful), Setia (truth), Orenda (great spirit), and Dusan (divine spirit).

Gabriel turned to them and said, "You are our first group of explorers. We will take you to the upper dimensions to get a glimpse of what could be yours. You are the pioneers, and in this sense, you are the Brave Angels. If you are ready, let our quest begin!"

The Brave Angels accompanied Gabriel, Michael and Raphael, who drew them deeper into the fourth dimension to support their beings. Many angels came to receive them: they shone their light and love onto these explorers to uplift them and provide some relief from their gloom. A spark began to appear within each.

A host of angels crowded around to observe the proceedings, whispering amongst themselves.

"How could the Archangels bring this group here?" questioned one.

"I know one of them from my last lifetime on Earth. He is not as innocent as he looks!" said another.

"Do not even mention the vice that one got up to," said another, pointing in their direction.

"They are so unenlightened. I find it unpleasant to be near them," said another angel.

The gossip and condemnation continued, reverberating throughout the heavens and finally reaching the ears of the Brave Angels. Gradually, the group began to deflate, and the little spark that had begun to appear started to degrade, until finally they hung their heads in humiliation. As their confidence broke, a fear settled in, and anger began to rise from within. Some of them looked to the periphery of the fourth dimension, searching for the dark bubble. The Archangels knew they had to salvage the situation quickly, and Gabriel began to address the crowd.

"I want to introduce you all to the bravest angels I have met in many thousands of years. These Brave Angels agreed to accompany us so that we may show them all of God's creation. They are here to glimpse what awaits them in the higher dimensions. If they choose to take this path, we are here to help them. I am very proud of our siblings' courage and bravery, and most importantly, I am touched by their open-mindedness and willingness to trust us in this quest." The Brave Angels began to look more confident.

Gabriel continued, "I am very happy that many of you recognise your true selves and realise that we are all linked and in this together. Love, kindness, and compassion are what we are about, not righteousness, criticism, and condemnation. To be judgmental is not part of our light. We must all come together in harmony and help raise those of us who require our assistance and wish to be helped. At the very least, we must not condemn one another, for by doing so, we are only hurting ourselves." Some of the gossiping angels looked down in embarrassment, mortified that Gabriel had heard them.

He continued, "Let us all come closer and shine our light and love on each other, and recite a prayer in humility and gratitude." The vast majority of angels closed in. From the corner of his eye, Gabriel saw a few move away in disgust, with one muttering, "I certainly do not want to be associated with that group; they will only taint my light with darkness. I am moving closer to God's pure light."

Michael signalled Gabriel, asking whether he should go after them. Gabriel nodded from side to side, whispering "They will have to face their arrogance in their own time, when they recognise it for what it is."

The rest of the angels formed a chorus of prayer, and singing songs of joy and happiness, willed the Brave Angels to release their fear and shame. The atmosphere began to permeate with positivity. The Brave Angels started to feel lighter and clearer, and gradually, their lights began to sparkle.

The Archangels were relieved at this development and concluded the proceedings. Slowly, everyone began to disperse.

"Raphael," said Gabriel, "This is your domain. Shall we give the Brave Angels a tour of the angel schools? This way they can see the sorts of lessons that are taught."

"Of course," said Raphael, "Would you all please follow me?"

They visited all the classes: those on how to reach your light within, another which spoke to the qualities of compassion and kindness, one that taught their students how to remain linked to their higher consciousness when on Earth, another on what the ego was all about, and a myriad of other lessons and tutorials.

"I did not know there were actual lessons on this," said Joyce.

"But, of course. How else would you learn?" said Raphael.

"I thought you just have to have it in you. You just have to know," said Joyce.

"But that denies growth," said Raphael, "And you have to be challenged to grow. Something must stimulate the evolution. There is always something or someone along the way, no matter how insignificant it may seem at the time, that helps shape who you are. You never do it alone."

"What is important is that you never stop trying to reach for your best self. It is your highest consciousness," said Michael, "And one of the ways to do this is to learn from others and accept help when you need it."

Once they had visited the classes, the Archangels then readied the group for their trip to the fifth dimension.

"This may be difficult for you at first," said Michael, "given your energies do not vibrate fast enough to enter this dimension. But we will help to elevate you so that you can experience it, even if it is only for a few seconds."

The Archangels joined their forces and raised the Brave Angels. The group could not believe what they were experiencing. There was beauty, love and light all around and the sensation was nothing like they had ever encountered on Earth. The colours were much more vivid: they saw tints and hues they never knew existed. The atmosphere infused them with energy; they were invigorated.

Qadir, in particular, felt stronger and more powerful than ever, and Lucas could not fathom the luminosity that radiated from his being. Both Adriel and Dusan felt content and at peace, as if they were finally home.

And then the Archangels dropped and released them into the fourth dimension. The Brave Angels needed time to stabilise themselves.

"Now, if you are ready for the sixth dimension, we will open a portal so you can take a peek," said Gabriel.

"We cannot go there to see what it is like?" asked Hikaru.

"Your vibrations are not strong enough to enter that domain. The three of us barely managed to elevate you to the fifth dimension," said Gabriel. He pointed to a corner. "Let us go there."

The group followed him and moved in close. Gabriel unsealed a section, and Michael and Raphael raised each angel to glance into the void. The sight was different from what they had just experienced: it was calm, still and beautiful. White light illuminated the space, filling it with pure love and contentment; there was an absence of fear.

"Can you tell the difference between the fifth and sixth dimensions?" asked Gabriel.

"The fifth was revitalising, a burst of positive energy; you feel elated, where nothing is impossible," said Bertha, "whereas the sixth seems to be much calmer, yet more empowering – there is a quiet strength and serenity about it."

"Very good. You have seen what most have not," said Gabriel, "If you wish to exist more permanently in such states, you must raise your consciousness so that your spirit vibrates at the required level. It is the only way to remain there for any length of time."

"What is the first step to raising our consciousness?" asked Isabella.

"First, you have to want to. Then, go to the angel schools and learn how," replied Michael.

"I have been so blind and stupid," said Joyce, as she began to weep, "I do not deserve such happiness."

"Of course you do," said Michael gently, "Just because you lost your way for a moment does not mean you cannot, or should not, achieve the ultimate happiness. If you wish it, then all you have to be is willing." Michael comforted her.

"Those of you who wish to raise your consciousness, come with me and I will take you to the angel schools," said Raphael.

"Before we do that," said Qadir, "we must inform the others who are still existing in the dark bubble. I want to help them understand that there is much more to experience here, and that the existence on Earth is just a temporary illusion."

Gabriel intervened, "You must first strengthen yourselves by learning how to maintain your own vibratory levels before you try and help others. Go to the angel schools, and when you are ready, you can come and assist us with those who remain in darkness. In the meantime, we will go back and help them."

"Very well," responded Qadir.

The Brave Angels left with Raphael. Gabriel and Michael entered the dark bubble and relayed the story of the Brave Angels. The news of this opportunity began to spread within, and many came forward to explore the upper dimensions.

"We had better call on those angels in the sixth dimension who are on stand-by. We will need their help to escort everyone," said Gabriel.

Gabriel and Michael supervised the operation, with so many dark angels curious to take a glimpse of what lay beyond. Gabriel felt they were finally gaining ground, as all but a few had turned towards their lighter selves. While these few were just a handful, Gabriel knew the mischief they could get up to and hoped they would not cause too much trouble on Earth.

25 DESPAIR

Time marched forward on Earth, and with trade continuing to expose populations to new things and ideas, the world prospered. A variety of arts flourished within many societies: fields such as architecture, literature, and poetry contributed to the culture and understanding of that period. Thought, ideology, and philosophy also evolved in numerous areas and spread throughout the world. However, the progress was accompanied by an increase in conflict and war. In particular, the several parts of God's Message to Humanity took on lives of their own, battling it out for supremacy. Whether religious, political, or both, fighting and discord pockmarked the globe, rooted in peoples' fear of the other and the unknown, and in the unrelenting quest for power and dominance.

As the centuries passed, many parts of the world experienced famine, while others were struck by disease. A particularly bad episode plagued the northern part of the world, wiping out nearly a third of its population. Religious doctrine continued to exert political power and influence over the societies they dominated, unyielding in their authority.

"How can God's Message to Humanity be misused like this?" said Gabriel out loud, as he became increasingly concerned at this turn of events.

Michael and Raphael heard Gabriel from afar. As they approached him, he seemed visibly distressed; his light had lost some of its lustre.

"Gabriel, are you okay?" asked Michael.

"I am fine," said Gabriel, not taking his eyes off the world.

Michael glanced worriedly at Raphael.

"Gabriel, you should take a break," said Raphael, "Maybe do something else for a while. Shall we exchange places?"

"I want to continue monitoring Earth," said Gabriel, "Things are advancing so rapidly."

"Do you want some company?" said Michael, "It will be interesting to observe the evolution on Earth."

Gabriel turned towards them. "Really, I am fine. But if you wish, Michael, it will be nice to have you around."

"I will get back to my work, but you know where I am if you need me," said Raphael.

Time evolved to a period where science, invention, and philosophy blossomed. A rapid rebirth also occurred in the arts and the humanities, notably in specialties such as painting, sculpture, literature, and music.

"God continues to bless the world with so much creativity," said Gabriel, "Look at how the quality of life is improving. It is beyond my imagination."

"There are so many opportunities for individuals, communities, and societies to share their wealth and knowledge," said Michael, looking on in disbelief.

"I just hope that people grasp that they are all connected," said Gabriel, "The opportunity to establish a prosperous, peaceful equilibrium is well within reach."

Gabriel and Michael continued to scrutinise the advancements with a great deal of interest. They saw the expansion of trading empires as great centres of commerce established themselves the world-over. Explorers travelled from one culture to another, discovering and learning along the way. And then Gabriel saw something that sickened him, for it rekindled memories of his own recent experience: certain groups traded in a very specific commodity – human beings.

Slavery had existed in many parts of the world throughout

Earth's history, but this was the first time that men and women were traded collectively as merchandise, with entire populations shifted across the globe.

"I cannot stand to watch this," cried Gabriel, turning away, "Have they not learnt anything?"

Michael held Gabriel, trying to comfort him. "It will be okay, Gabriel. Maybe it is a good time to call Raphael."

"No, I want to see what is happening on Earth," said Gabriel, as he turned to face the world again.

Gabriel and Michael watched as great schisms and splits occurred within each part of God's Message to Humanity against a backdrop of continuous aggression and conflict. They looked to the East, hoping to find some consolation in its development. But exploitation had even seeped into the customs and traditions of peoples who had embraced the principle of karma: it became a self-serving tool, utilised to oppress sections of society for personal gain. Dominion over others, especially those who were judged to be of inferior mind, body, or soul, was considered acceptable behaviour. Whether of the East, West, North, or South, divisions into class, caste, status, and social groups became the norm: whole populations were made to serve the interests of the few.

Gabriel seemed to shrink under Michael's hold.

"Are you alright?" asked Michael.

"Yes," said Gabriel.

Gabriel's attention darted around the world watching cruelty and injustice strangle societies. Not only had the parts of God's Message to Humanity been hijacked by those with ulterior motives, but most of humankind had resorted to some form of selfishness.

"The ego and the physical world have triumphed," said Gabriel, as he fell down in despair; the thud of his despondency reverberated throughout the heavens.

Michael stared in shock as Raphael rushed towards them.

"Gabriel! What's wrong?!" said Michael, trying to lift him.

A flurry of angels gathered round and shone their light on Gabriel, trying to raise him.

"I do not think I can carry on with this work," whispered Gabriel, his tears flowing freely.

"Do not worry, Gabriel. Take a break," said Michael, "Just do not lose hope."

"There are so many of us helping," said Raphael, shining the full force of his light and love on Gabriel, "You are not alone."

"It is not that. I just cannot tolerate the cruelty anymore," said Gabriel, "Honestly, our work is an exercise in futility."

He was inconsolable.

"Gabriel, spend some time with God in the seventh dimension," said Michael, "You need to centre yourself and get a hold of your grief."

"Yes, I need God," said Gabriel, as he tried to get up.

"I will take you," said Michael, as he glanced at Raphael.

"I have the work covered here. There are many helping. You two go ahead," said Raphael.

Michael drew Gabriel into the seventh dimension, where he found God waiting for them. God surged forward and enveloped the Archangels in His Light.

Before either could speak, God said, "Michael, I am very pleased that you have brought Gabriel to Me. Now let him be. Take My blessings and return to your work. I will call you when Gabriel is ready."

"Thy Will be done in and through me. Thy Will be done on Earth as it is in Heaven," invoked Michael as he bowed his head and began his descent.

"My Lord, I am sorry I am so weak. I cannot seem to raise myself from this sorrow," said Gabriel.

"Do not speak, Gabriel. Just rest within Me until you are well-recovered. Draw your strength from Me." And with those words, Gabriel laid down his head and let go.

Gabriel rested within God for quite a long time although he knew he could not remain permanently. He had not been granted permission nor had he raised his consciousness to the required level, clearly demonstrated by his melancholy. This despair was not part of God's light – it was the ego asserting itself. Gabriel's light was not pure enough to eternally merge with God.

"In the name of God, the most Beneficent, the most Merciful," invoked Gabriel.

"My dear child, are you feeling better?" said God.

"Yes, My Lord," said Gabriel, "I have come over the worst of it."

"Very good," said God, "Now I want you to sit back and listen to Me very carefully, Gabriel."

"Yes, My Lord," said Gabriel.

"My child, each individual is responsible for his and her own actions and reactions, and you must not take this burden on yourself," said God, "Do not take to heart the cruelty and depravity that your siblings are capable of inflicting. Your love and compassion for them pleases Me, but I do not want you to be consumed by it all. Do what you can to help them Gabriel, but you must also protect your soul. Turn to Me for strength and courage."

"Yes, My Lord," said Gabriel, "I think I have been doing this for too long. I am tired and no longer have the constitution to witness humanity's self-destruction."

"I understand, Gabriel," said God, "You know that I have granted My children free reign over Earth, but I will change the parameters if they continue to abuse this privilege. And I will do what is necessary to maintain the balance amongst all life forms. But for now, I will remain patient and give My children the opportunity to learn their lessons and maintain the equilibrium on Earth."

"Yes, My Lord," said Gabriel, casting his eyes down.

"Now tell Me what is in your heart, Gabriel," said God.

"My Lord, I need a reprieve," said Gabriel, "I think it is

best for me to step down from all my responsibilities. I am not at my strongest."

"If that is your wish, Gabriel," said God, "I have always conveyed to you that you should undertake this work only if you are willing, and that you may stop whenever you wish. I am very happy with the service you have rendered to your siblings over many, many millennia, and I could not be prouder of all that you have achieved. You have helped millions of My children raise their consciousness and draw closer to Me. If you want to slow down or cease your involvement, then I accept your decision."

"Thank you, My Lord," said Gabriel, bowing his head, "I need time to recover and reflect upon matters."

"Very well," said God, "There are others who can take over your responsibilities. To whom would you like to handover your work?"

"I believe Michael would be the logical and reasonable choice, although Raphael would be equally worthy," said Gabriel.

"Very well, My child," said God, "Let us call Michael to see whether he wishes to undertake this work."

Michael heard God summoning him and he ascended to the seventh heaven. He was happy to see Gabriel upright and recovered.

"My dear Michael," said God, "Gabriel is feeling much better and as you can see, he is sparkling again. However, Gabriel has taken a decision. He would like to relinquish his responsibilities and he has recommended that you take over. Are you willing to accept this work?"

Michael was aghast. As the realisation set in, he looked at Gabriel questioningly. "My Lord, is this really necessary? Gabriel can take time off and return to this work when ready. In the meantime, Raphael and I can manage together with the others. There is no need for him to step down."

"I have made up my mind, Michael," said Gabriel, "I have thought long and hard about this. I can no longer watch my siblings debase themselves; I do not think my soul can take anymore, and I need to step away."

"But Gabriel, we are all with you!" said Michael, "We are here to support you with anything and everything. I cannot conceive of doing this work without you at the helm!"

God intervened. "My dear Michael, it is Gabriel's choice whether he wishes to undertake this work. He cannot be forced or pressured in any way. Remember, Michael, I have granted free will to all of you."

"Yes, My Lord, I understand," said Michael, tearing up.

"Dearest Michael," said Gabriel, "I am not leaving you or abandoning the work entirely. I am just stepping down from my responsibilities. I have recommended you to take up the leadership role, if you are willing. I am still around and will continue to help where I can."

Michael looked at God and then at Gabriel. He saw the desperation in Gabriel's demeanour. Michael finally relented. "I accept this assignment, My Lord. However, if Gabriel ever wishes to return to his responsibilities, I will gladly relinquish this role."

Gabriel visibly relaxed.

"My dear Michael, I am especially proud of the compassion and generosity of spirit you have demonstrated today," said God, "Not only have you agreed to continue My work, but you have relieved Gabriel of his responsibilities, which has given him a great deal of peace of mind. However, if at any time you choose not to continue with this assignment, then just say so."

"Yes, My Lord," said Michael.

"Michael and Gabriel," said God, "remember as you move along your chosen paths that I am with you always. Turn to me during your difficulties, and know that I never leave you alone to fend for yourselves. I am there to guide you and carry you through all the challenges with which you are confronted. You merely have to ask."

"Yes, My Lord," they replied in unison.

"My dear Gabriel, before you leave, I want to reiterate to you that you are my closest angel and are the most like Me. Your light burns brightly and deeply, and is nearly purified to merge with My Light. Take the time you need and strengthen yourself further. Come and visit Me whenever you wish and remain within Me for as long as you wish. If you ever want to return more fully to this work, then tell Me."

"My Lord," said Gabriel, "It is still my greatest desire to merge permanently with Your Light. I will return to my quest when I am ready."

"I am waiting for you," said God.

"Thy Will be done in and through us. Thy Will be done on Earth as it is in Heaven," they invoked and began their descent. Raphael came forward to receive them.

"Gabriel, how wonderful to see you!" exclaimed Raphael, "How I have missed you!"

"It is lovely to see you, too, Raphael," said Gabriel. They all embraced each other and found a private spot to continue their conversation, as numerous angels had begun to gather around them – many had witnessed how badly Gabriel had been affected by humankind's behaviour.

"Raphael, I need to tell you something," said Gabriel.

"What is it, Gabriel? Are you alright?" said Raphael.

"I am fine. You need to know that I have withdrawn from my responsibilities, and Michael will take over. He will now lead the efforts to help our siblings." Raphael was taken aback.

"Is this true, Michael? How will we do this work without Gabriel?" said Raphael.

"I am afraid it is true," said Michael, signalling to Raphael to prevent him from further protest. "God cautioned me not to pressure Gabriel into continuing with his responsibilities. It must be his choice. So I have agreed to take on this role, with the caveat that if Gabriel ever wishes to resume his work, I will immediately step aside."

"But I cannot believe this," said Raphael, looking at Michael questioningly.

Gabriel smiled at them, and said, "I will still be around to assist. I just need some time away from the full responsibility."

"Very well," said Raphael, "I am accepting this with a heavy heart, Gabriel. Although I do have every confidence in your leadership, Michael, and will do my utmost to help you."

"Thank you, Raphael," said Michael, "Now, Gabriel, what would you like to do? You have the choice."

"I would like to visit all the dimensions and observe what is happening," said Gabriel, "I will first spend time in the sixth dimension to meditate and strengthen myself. And when I am able, I will return and help where I can."

"Very well," said Michael, "But you do know that we will keep an eye on you. Whenever you wish to be with us or join us for any activities, then just do so. In the meantime, we will get on with the work. Raphael, let us discuss how we wish to organise ourselves from this point forward." They both embraced Gabriel, then watched as he made his way to the sixth dimension, wondering whether he would ever be the same again.

26 REFLECTION

Gabriel spent some time reflecting on all that had transpired since he had begun this work. There were great successes and numerous failures, and significant progress had indeed been made since the beginning of time when they first burst forth from God. Many of his siblings had raised their awareness, including those in the dark bubble.

"Then what is it that has affected me so?" thought Gabriel, "Why do I feel so low?"

Gabriel settled himself in a quiet spot and readied himself to begin his meditation.

"Gabriel, how nice to see you," came a voice from behind. Gabriel spun around.

"Seth! What a nice surprise!" said Gabriel.

"It has been a long time. Are you feeling better?" said Seth.

"Ah...so you saw what happened to me," said Gabriel, looking embarrassed.

"Yes, I did," said Seth, comforting Gabriel, "I was going to come and help, but Michael managed to draw you into the seventh dimension."

"Thank God for that," said Gabriel, looking upward.

"You know, Gabriel, this is very much like your experience as Noah," said Seth. Gabriel looked at him quizzically.

"My life as Noah? How so?" said Gabriel.

"You went through a lot of soul-searching in that lifetime," said Seth.

Gabriel chuckled. "I never thought of it like that. I suppose I am trying to find out what is disturbing me deep within."

"You know, I would love to reconnect with you, if you have the time," said Seth.

"I was just about to begin my meditation, but spending time with you is a better offer," said Gabriel, smiling at his old friend as he stood up, "Do you remember our walks along the river?"

"How can I forget those?" said Seth, laughing.

"Shall we go down to the fourth dimension?" said Gabriel, "We can catch up on everything and I also want to watch the activities on Earth."

"Yes, absolutely," said Seth, putting his arm around Gabriel. They made their way to the lower heaven and found a good vantage point from where they could observe the world.

Michael and Raphael looked up from their work, delighted to see Seth with Gabriel. The Archangels waived to them, leaving the friends undisturbed.

God continued to bestow prosperity on Earth. Great strides were made in science and technology, and disciplines such as physics, mathematics, and astronomy advanced quickly. Enlightened ideas and philosophies also took root, pushing the boundaries of human thought. Many people resisted their ruling masters and forged ahead to change human society. The individual exercised his free will to take control of his life and destiny.

"It is almost as if people are waking up to their true potential," said Seth.

"They are self-aware. Their consciousness is rising," said Gabriel. He looked towards Michael and Raphael. "I must say, they are doing a fantastic job."

"They have really helped bring about change. So many have raised their consciousness, both on Earth and in the heavens," said Seth.

"Yes, they have," said Gabriel.

"You do know that all this has happened under your

leadership," said Seth, "It has taken millennia to get to this point."

Gabriel laughed out loud. "I suppose you are right."

Michael and Raphael were delighted to see Gabriel in better spirits.

"Seth is good for Gabriel. Hopefully, he will be able to steady Gabriel and open his eyes to see what he has accomplished," said Michael.

"Seth seems to be providing him with perspective," said Raphael.

Time on Earth marched on and society continued to develop. Industrial innovation advanced many nations by leaps and bounds. Machines and new sources of power enhanced the efficiency of daily life and living standards improved dramatically in some quarters. Trade and commerce expanded exponentially and populations experienced sustained growth: the seeds of global interdependence were sewn.

"Shall we walk around for a bit?" asked Seth.

"Yes, that would be nice," said Gabriel, with a twinkle in his eye, "but we do not have a river to follow."

Seth chuckled. "Those were some of my happiest times on Earth. And that tree!"

Gabriel hooted with laughter. "I cannot believe I chopped the whole thing and built the ark!"

"You worked very hard," said Seth, "It is incredible what we can do when we put our minds to it." He pointed to the world. "Can you see the fruits of your labour? Look at all the people on Earth. Look how many have embraced God. Look at the number who reach for their higher consciousness. There really is good in the world."

Gabriel smiled, nodding affirmatively.

The two friends walked around, observing all the happenings in the world and in the heavens. Gabriel noticed the marked attachments many angels still formed with either their masculine or feminine side. This three-dimensional Earth concept was being carried over to the fourth dimension.

"It seems that our fellow beings are allowing their gender identity to penetrate their spirit," said Gabriel, "they cannot see themselves as the opposite gender."

"But gender is a physical concept, not a spiritual one," said Seth.

"And they must not lose the ability to balance their spirit. It is crucial to the development of each one's consciousness to deal with the whole of one's being, not just half," said Gabriel. He stopped and looked in the direction of Michael and Raphael. "I must let them know to augment their lessons on balancing the spirit."

Seth and Gabriel resumed their walk and surveyed the happenings on Earth. As more societies encountered each other, hostility and aggression increased in the pursuit for dominance. In some parts of the world this escalated into conflict and warmongering. But then something caught Gabriel's attention: people were beginning to rise against slavery, with some abolishing this practice altogether. This greatly pleased him and it soothed his soul. Gabriel glanced at Michael and smiled; his eyes sparkled for the first time in many years. Michael made his way towards them.

"How are you, Gabriel?" enquired Michael, "and you, Seth?"

Seth nodded in acknowledgement.

"I am doing well," said Gabriel, "You and Raphael are really doing a stellar job. I see that special missionary angels continue to visit Earth, and some of them have provided great leadership."

"We are only following your lead and continuing the work you started, Gabriel," said Michael.

Raphael suddenly appeared and embraced Gabriel tightly. "We miss you, Gabriel. Even though you are present and we can see you, we still miss you."

"I understand, Raphael. But I still need time," said Gabriel.

Raphael turned to Seth. "And how are you?"

"I am fine. And enjoying Gabriel's company. It reminds me of our lifetime together," said Seth.

"We are just glad that you are around, Seth," said Raphael.

"By the way," said Gabriel, "you need to augment the lessons on keeping the spirit in balance. Angels should not favour a particular gender. This preference is gripping their spirit. They must be confident, balanced beings."

"We will follow through," said Michael.

"Also, continue sending the special missionary angels to Earth," said Gabriel, looking at the world, "I can see they are a positive influence. In these times of great struggles and wars all over the planet, it is crucial they serve as beacons of light for their fellow beings."

"We will increase the numbers who are taking on human form," said Michael, as he grinned at Raphael. The two of them embraced Gabriel and Seth and went on their way.

"It looks like Gabriel is slowly making his way back to us," said Raphael, "I am looking forward to that day. I miss him. I feel as if we are a tripod with one leg missing."

"With the way he is scrutinising the activities on Earth, I believe he is fully engaged," said Michael, "He just needs this time to reflect upon matters without any pressure, and without being interrupted by day-to-day activities. I suspect this is why God accommodated Gabriel so quickly in his desire to relinquish his overall responsibilities. There seems to be some greater purpose of which we are unaware."

Raphael turned to look at Gabriel, who was far in the distance. He seemed completely absorbed by activities on Earth.

"I never thought of it like that," said Raphael.

"Whatever the case," said Michael, "we better follow through on Gabriel's instructions!" They both laughed as they made their way to the angel schools.

With Seth at his side, Gabriel continued surveying the world. Many societies progressed at an accelerated rate, with commerce and technology driving them forward. Others still grappled with basic needs. As the world grew smaller, the hostility between communities and nations increased in the never-ending pursuit for dominance, wealth, and power. Technology was skewed in one direction to serve the motives of the powerful: they produced bigger, stronger, and faster machines and implements of war. And then another significant event occurred that had never been seen on Earth before: large nations began battling each other on a global scale. A world war.

"This is absurd!" exclaimed Gabriel, "what are they fighting for?! What a waste of human life!" Seth held Gabriel and comforted him. Many angels wept at the cruelty humankind was inflicting on itself, and a deep morose began to permeate the atmosphere in the heavens.

They watched as Michael instructed many angels to rush towards Earth to influence their charges and help prevent such destruction. Those who lost their lives fighting in the war began to cross over, and Michael and Raphael organised other angels to receive them.

Raphael called out to Gabriel. "This is a similar scenario to when you were Noah. Swathes crossed back during the flood. We are implementing the same strategy to deal with the volume of people returning to our realm. We have to help them reacquaint with this side." Gabriel nodded in acknowledgment.

"Who knew all this was happening when we floated in the ark?" remarked Seth, "We thought we were alone and still, with only the one God observing us. Yet look at the flurry of activity here."

Gabriel watched as millions died during the war. The angels worked hard to receive these souls and soothe their suffering. Others gathered into a choir and performed beautiful music to help ease the transition. Michael sent angels to provide comfort to the soldiers and families left behind, and many formed circles of prayer and protection around those individuals who were most afflicted by the horrors of war. Gabriel was pleased by the good will and effort being made by angels in all the dimensions to help their siblings.

"You are right, Seth. So many have raised their consciousness," said Gabriel.

The war finally ended, and with death and destruction all around them, Gabriel hoped that at least a portion of humankind had learnt a valuable lesson and would not repeat this dreadful mistake.

Michael and Raphael were finally able to slow down and take stock. Gabriel and Seth went to see them.

"Are you both coping?" asked Gabriel.

"We are fine, although we would not have managed without the millions of angels helping us," said Michael.

"I agree," said Raphael, "we have come a long way from where we first started."

"We certainly have," said Gabriel, "I am delighted by the progress."

"If you do not mind me saying, I am so impressed with the systems you both put in place," said Seth, "I had no idea of the complexity."

"It is all Gabriel's vision. We are just following through," said Michael. He hesitatingly added, "Would you like to help, Gabriel, or do you still need more time to reflect? What about you, Seth?"

"I want to continue watching society progress on Earth. When I am ready, I will jump right in," said Gabriel. He turned to Seth. "What would you like to do?"

"To spend more time with you," said Seth.

"Very well," said Michael, "you know where to find us."

They all embraced one another and Michael and Raphael left to resume their work.

Gabriel and Seth found a comfortable corner and settled in to monitor Earth. There were advances in all areas of human endeavour: science, technology, the arts, the humanities. Societies built the foundation for civil liberty and the respect for human rights – even the female gender was being recognised as equal, although this did not happen everywhere. Against this backdrop, political posturing and warmongering continued the world-over. Seth noticed Gabriel slowly scanning the globe, murmuring softly.

"Gabriel, is everything alright?" asked Seth.

"I am just praying over humanity, willing them to embrace their higher, spiritual self," said Gabriel.

"They will. So many show kindness and compassion to others," said Seth, "and especially after the great war."

"I have seen this before. And if there is one thing I have learnt, it is that we cannot be complacent," said Gabriel, "Human beings have short memories."

Time pressed on as Gabriel and Seth monitored Earth, and Michael and Raphael continued their work.

Then one day, as the heavens hummed along as usual, Gabriel suddenly hoisted himself up. The movement knocked Seth over. Many angels stopped in their tracks and stared up at Gabriel: his presence was so enigmatic, that his slightest repositioning changed the atmosphere. Many angels rushed towards Gabriel to see what was happening. Michael knew something was wrong. He tore through the crowd to reach Gabriel, whose tears flowed freely.

"What's the matter, Gabriel?!" asked Michael, as he helped Seth up. Both were alarmed by Gabriel's reaction.

They followed the trajectory of Gabriel's gaze to Earth. They were shocked by what they saw: groups of humans were being extinguished *en masse*. One particular individual led this atrocity, but many followed his instructions. Others still, turned a blind eye to the cruelty. Men, women, and children were rounded up and led to slaughter. Michael recognised the perpetrators as some of the dark angels he had seen in the dark bubble. Gabriel had warned that these dark angels could wreak havoc on Earth, but this was the epitome of evil.

"Michael! Raphael!" shouted Gabriel, as he jolted everyone into action, "Activate all the angels again! Send them to protect and comfort the victims, and to help them with the transition when they cross over."

Michael and Raphael sprang into action and billions of angels rushed to help the victims. Gabriel was beside himself when he realised that most of these atrocities were perpetrated against the group who had embraced the Second Part of God's Message to Humanity. In a matter of seconds, the Quartet appeared.

"Archangel Gabriel," said Moses, "all four of us wish to assist. Please tell us what we can do to stop this."

"I am afraid we will not be able to stop it," said Gabriel, "This is between God and His children on Earth. The only thing we can do is try to guide the perpetrators away from their actions. We must soothe and comfort all those who are impacted by this horror. Go to Michael and receive your assignments," said Gabriel.

He turned to Seth. "I am sorry I knocked you over."

"Do not concern yourself, I am fine," said Seth, "What can I do to help?"

"Let us head over to Michael. He will give us our assignments," said Gabriel.

They all worked tirelessly. Angels were assigned to help the victims and their families on Earth, while some eased the transition when they crossed over. Many worked with the perpetrators to try to influence them to stop their ghastly behaviour, while others still formed prayer circles around the affected parts of the world.

Gabriel flitted back and forth from the heavens to the worl , receiving and escorting victims by the thousands as they heir untimely deaths. And then the battles commenced. The l entered another war on a global scale: a second world war.

The death and destruction accelerated as whole nations fought each other. Michael and Raphael increased the response to deal with the devastation.

On one occasion as Gabriel received and escorted those who crossed over, he heard God calling out to him.

"Yes, My Lord," replied Gabriel.

"As they cross back, I want you to escort those who have committed these heinous acts to a separate place within the lower heaven that I have marked out," said God, "I will identify the perpetrators to you. I will deal with them directly, and I do not want you nor any other angel to get involved. They will not be permitted to enter their dark bubble in the fourth dimension, nor will they be allowed to join all of you, regardless of the dimensions in which you reside. And certainly, they will not be able to take on human form on Earth, for I am removing this privilege. Remember, Gabriel, it is I who will deal with these children of Mine, not any of you."

"Yes, My Lord," said Gabriel, "Thy Will be done in and through me. Thy Will be done on Earth as it is in Heaven."

Gabriel obeyed God and personally accompanied the identified souls to the place God indicated. This was a difficult task, for Gabriel had to contain his anger, maintain his composure, and indeed treat these culprits with compassion and kindness, for in the end they, too, were God's children and his own siblings.

"What will happen to me, Archangel Gabriel?" asked one of the perpetrators.

"That is between you and God," replied Gabriel.

"I am frightened, Archangel Gabriel. Please help me," pleaded another. Gabriel had to reach deep within him to not lash out, for all he wanted to do was holler "how do you think your victims felt?!" But Gabriel managed to cling to his godliness and control his reaction.

"You must deal with God directly," said Gabriel, "Just remember that God is Love itself, and you are His child."

Suddenly, a group of angels came rushing forward in an angry mob, shouting at the dark angels.

"You are pure evil!" yelled one.

"You should be shunned and left to fester on your own!" said another, "You do not deserve any compassion. Archangel Gabriel, why are you escorting them? You should not allow their darkness to taint your light. I am surprised at you!"

Gabriel stood in front of the dark angels and protected them from the onslaught. "It is not for you to judge! Look within yourselves and tell me that your hearts are pure and that not even one spot of darkness taints your light! Just because your siblings have lost their way, does not mean you have the right to ridicule and pass judgment. Do not stoop to their level and emulate them: you are doing yourself a disservice."

Gabriel continued in a calmer voice. "You must understand that these perpetrators are weak in spirit – they have a lot to learn. But every being deserves love; mercy and forgiveness are the highest manifestations of love. It does not mean that you condone their behaviour, it only means that you are reaching for your highest consciousness. Instead of spouting anger and hatred, shower your light and love on these dark angels. They are the ones who require the most help." Gabriel then covered the perpetrators with a veil of protection and ushered them to the place God had indicated.

Michael and Raphael watched Gabriel, and their hearts went out to him.

"How difficult it must be for him to show such compassion!" exclaimed Michael.

"I cannot fathom Gabriel's strength," said Raphael, "Deep within him, he is actually forgiving these dark angels. He is certainly a better soul than I am. I do not think I would be able to look at them with kindness, never mind protect them from others. How much I still have to learn!"

Gabriel continued with the tasks assigned by God as well as those given by Michael. After several years of unspeakable horrors, humankind finally put an end to the war, but not without annihilating many tens of thousands with a single bomb, the magnitude of which the world had never seen before – the survivors continued to experience its after-effects long past that dreadful day.

After the chaos, the angels finally had a moment to collect their thoughts.

"Seth, are you alright?" asked Gabriel.

"I am fine, but a bit tired," said Seth.

"Return to the sixth dimension to recuperate," said Gabriel.

"But I do not want to leave you alone," said Seth.

"We are with Gabriel," said Michael, as he and Raphael approached them, "Please rejuvenate yourself. We will likely require your assistance in the future, if you wish to help."

"Very well then," said Seth, as he embraced them all.

"Thank you for your company, Seth," said Gabriel, "It was lovely to spend time with you. It gave me perspective." Seth smiled at Gabriel, then withdrew into the sixth dimension.

The Archangels found a quiet spot and sat down together. Each had been struck by the appalling events on Earth and took some time to settle himself.

"Are you both okay?" asked Gabriel.

"As well as can be expected. It has been a particularly difficult period," said Raphael, nodding in disbelief, "Two world wars?!"

"I could never have conceived that we could sink so low. Such wickedness! I thought I had seen everything, but this scale of irrationality is beyond my comprehension," said Michael.

"I want both of you to withdraw into God and rest. Michael, if you allow me, I will manage your responsibilities while you are away," said Gabriel.

"But you need to rest, too, Gabriel," said Michael.

"Do not protest. Don't you remember your word?" said

Gabriel, "You said you would relinquish your responsibilities as soon as I wished to step back in."

Michael smiled. "And are you stepping back in? Or is it just a ruse to get me to take a break?" Gabriel cackled with laughter.

"I thought so," said Michael, nodding his head from side-to-side.

"Gabriel, I will remain here with you. Michael, you go ahead," said Raphael.

"No, you will not," responded Gabriel, "I am absolutely fine and I want both of you to rest. There are plenty who will help me."

"Very well then," said Michael, as he reached out to embrace Gabriel.

Each went his separate way: Michael and Raphael were particularly affected and welcomed this respite.

The first thing Gabriel did was to send a host of special missionary angels to be born on Earth to try and wrest humanity from their hostile ways: they had to learn to resolve their conflicts through dialogue rather than resorting to aggression and violence. Gabriel urged the special missionary angels to advocate for these ideals in a non-violent manner and to establish stability, confidence, and hope in the areas in which they were born.

Gabriel scrutinised Earth very carefully and was relieved to see humankind establishing the necessary mechanisms and institutions to promote diplomacy. Pockets of conflict and violence erupted from time to time, and these were contained through multilateral discussion. Humanity still had a long and bumpy road ahead, but at least they were headed in the right direction.

Gabriel noticed the struggles beginning between the people who followed the Second Part of God's Message and those who kept to the Fourth Part, all in a bid to inhabit the same piece of land and raise separate flags.

"That is disappointing," thought Gabriel, "why fight over

the right to live on that particular stretch? There is enough space for them all. There is no need for one to dominate." Gabriel moved closer to scrutinise the area.

The Quartet appeared just behind him.

"Archangel Gabriel, what is happening? Why is there such hostility?" asked Abraham.

Gabriel turned to face them. He could see the anguish in their demeanour.

"I do not understand why they are fighting amongst themselves. Do they not realise that we are siblings? We must share God's abundance," said Moses.

"Why are they so bent on physical possession? Do they not realise that true belief and devotion is centred in the heart?" said Mohamed.

"To be a true believer means to show love, compassion, and generosity to the other," said Jesus.

"How can people get God's Message to Humanity so wrong? We need to sort this out," said Abraham.

Gabriel took them aside. "I know how hurtful it is to watch God's Message hijacked by pedestrian, worldly matters and not intervene. I, too, have questioned this, and God has repeatedly conveyed to me that He is granting humankind many opportunities to raise their awareness and better themselves. It is each individual's choice as to how to behave and react to situations, and we cannot stop them. It is their free will granted by God Himself. It is up to God to decide if and when to remove this privilege and deal with the consequences of human choice. In the meantime, all we can do is help those who are open to receiving our help and try to influence those who are not."

"May we be assigned to this area?" asked Abraham, "After all, they are known as our people and we must try and reconcile them."

"Of course, Abraham," said Gabriel, "Gather all the angels you need, and go ahead and establish your presence there."

Just then, Michael and Raphael came towards them.

"We have seen what is happening," said Michael.

"The four of us are going to try and bring some resolution to this," said Abraham, "God's Message to Humanity must be internalised by the people." The Quartet recused themselves and withdrew to the sixth dimension to gather more angels to help with their work.

Michael and Raphael sat next to Gabriel.

"Are you both well-recovered?" asked Gabriel.

"Yes, we certainly needed this rest after reacting to one of the worst periods in Earth's history," said Raphael.

"And how are you, Gabriel?" asked Michael.

"I am fine. Humanity, on the other hand, is navigating its way to bring peace and stability to the world. Areas of conflict still dot the globe, but hopefully these will reduce over time," said Gabriel. He stood up and faced Michael. "And now I return your responsibilities to you, Michael. Just let me know what my next assignment is."

Michael chuckled. "Gabriel, you must remain at the helm."

"But I only temporarily relieved you," said Gabriel, "You are at the helm. Just give me my assignment."

"Your assignment is to resume your full role and lead us," said Michael. They howled with laughter.

"Michael, in all seriousness, I am not ready for that," said Gabriel.

"Very well, I understand. In any case, it is time for you to rest. You need to rejuvenate yourself for your future work," said Michael.

Gabriel smiled, embraced them both, and slowly withdrew into God.

Gabriel was grateful for the break, for he was growing weary again. As soon as he arrived in the seventh dimension, he laid his head down and took a prolonged rest. Dealing with death, destruction, and pure evilness was gruelling, for it ate away at the spirit. And then to have to escort the dark angels while showing compassion and kindness – that was a truly strenuous exercise – Gabriel was exhausted by his experience.

"Humanity is now able to effect destruction on a global scale," thought Gabriel, "And some will not hesitate to go down this path." He finally relaxed into God's loving energy.

As he rested, Gabriel contemplated how he had begun his journey to help his siblings so many years ago. So much had happened – he had experienced a great deal of joy and anguish over the years. He remembered how bright-eyed and eager he was at the beginning. While the concept of ageing did not exist in the heavens, for God's light was not a material, physical element subject to decay, Gabriel did feel that his light did not sparkle the way it used to. If he was a human being on Earth, people would have commented that life had taken its toll and he looked old and tired.

Once he felt rested, Gabriel raised his head and invoked, "In the name of God, the most Beneficent, the most Merciful."

"My dear Gabriel," said God, "are you well-recovered?"

"Yes, My Lord," answered Gabriel.

"Very good. I am glad that you have taken this break and that you have had a chance to rejuvenate yourself. I want you to know how happy I am with all that you have accomplished recently, as well as with what you have achieved over the millions of years since you first began helping your brothers and sisters. You have served Me and your siblings with a generosity of spirit that is unprecedented. Now it is time to begin the last phase of your work, if you choose to accept this responsibility. But first, I want to relate something to you. I want you to sit back, and listen to My story and what I have experienced all these years with you."

Gabriel was taken aback and looked straight into God's eyes, something he rarely did. God smiled and said, "Yes, Gabriel, even I have a story to tell."

"Yes, My Lord," Gabriel said softly.

"A very, very long time ago, you all burst forth from Me into separate entities, a part of Me, but apart from Me, so that I could share My Love and Light with you. I created the universe and everything in it so that you could explore the many facets of yourselves. I created the Earth in order to provide a place for you to encounter the Creative Spirit. And I granted you free will so that you could experience all that you wished, and so that you could love one another, and Me, with your generous and compassionate light."

"As time progressed, I realised that not all of you were choosing to be your best; you were ignoring your whole self. I watched for a while, giving you all the space and freedom to make your choices, hoping that each of you would choose love and generosity over selfishness and indifference. Many of you chose to follow a lesser path, and I searched and waited for those of you who were willing to demonstrate the love and nobility of which you were all capable, and help your fellow beings embrace the entirety of the Love and Light of their whole selves."

"And then one day a bright, sparkling light twinkled towards Me, and I saw the distress in its energy, and I called out to it, "My child, My shimmering light of love, why are you in such a state?" And then Gabriel, you answered, "I am worried for my fellow beings, for they are sinking into darkness and they are a part of You and me. How do I help my fellow beings? It distresses me to see them inflicting such pain on one another, for each is only hurting himself." I then asked you whether you would be part of the signs, reminders, and guidance that I send to your siblings to steer them away from darkness. And you replied, "Yes, I will be part of Your work to help my siblings!" And that is when I twinkled and sparkled with joy, for the one I was waiting for had finally arrived."

Gabriel was stunned into silence.

God continued, "All I needed was for one of My children

to initiate the work and lead the way, and I knew that many would follow, and that the momentum would be established to carve a different path, to act as a counter to the lesser road that many of My children were travelling. For many years you toiled away at your work, throwing yourself into the effort with a great deal of enthusiasm, all in a bid to help raise the consciousness of your siblings so that they could recognise their light."

"Then one day, Gabriel, you conveyed to Me that which I had longed to hear: that you wished to share your love and light with Me, and merge permanently with My light. You wished to give love, rather than take and receive. And that is when I knew that the seeds of the new era of truth had been sown, for again, I needed just one of you to demonstrate true love and affection, and open up the possibility for others to travel this same route. And when you relinquished your responsibilities to Michael, I was very proud of your ability to detach yourself and make room for others in the best interest of your siblings. It was then that I knew that you were nearly ready to take the final step in preparation for your goal to merge with Me. But I tested your resolve to reach for your highest consciousness by asking you to escort the darkest angels, those of My children who had caused such pain on Earth, to their new place of existence. And not only did you succeed in this task, but you were a glowing example to all those who watched you. By your demonstration of compassion and kindness to those of your siblings who had so clearly embraced darkness, you provided an even higher goal towards which My children could strive. And, what is more, you provided a glimmer of hope to the darkest angels, for they, too are My children: you showed that atonement and redemption is possible for every single being."

"And now begins the final phase through which you must pass, Gabriel, if you choose to do so, to reside permanently within My Love."

Gabriel bowed his head and whispered, "My Lord."

"The wars, conflicts, and hostilities of the current time

on Earth demonstrate that humankind has now surpassed the threshold, and they have made their choice. The lack of compassion and empathy is truly disgraceful. Despite all the opportunities I have granted, humanity has chosen to go down the path of selfishness and material gratification. The poverty and suffering on Earth is unbearable to witness, when I have provided ample resources for all of My children to live in dignity. My children have lost their way, with their violence, their apathy, their corruption, and their unwillingness to share the abundance on Earth. And they continue to exploit Earth and bleed her dry of her life-force regardless of the consequences."

"Gabriel, you will recall what I said in the early days when you first began this journey. I had conveyed to you that I provide you with what you need, not what you want. I respond to your needs, not your desires. And sometimes what you need is silence from Me in order for you to learn that which you do not know, and to experience that which is incomprehensible to you. It is only in this way that you will mature, grow, and evolve closer to Me. But now what you need is My intervention."

"The time has now come for Me to take away that most powerful quality, even for a few moments, that I had bestowed upon all My children: Free Will. Humanity has forgotten Me, and has chosen to ignore that there are consequences to their actions on Earth. They have forgotten that I am Brahman, the Universal Force; that I am Allah, the All-Knowing and the Compassionate; that I am the Great Spirit, and Ever-Present; that I am the Beginning, and the End; that I am the Creator and the Destroyer; that I am God."

The heavens reverberated with God's voice, and Gabriel recognised that the moment had finally arrived when God Himself, the Father and the Mother, would directly intercede on Earth.

God continued, "I will completely cleanse the Earth, as each nook and cranny has been polluted by humanity's greed, and their insatiable appetite for self-indulgence and self-satisfaction, without accounting for their behaviour, and without regard to the condition of their fellow beings. I will shift the world into a new direction, and cleanse it of all its materialism and evil ways, in order to bring forth an era of spiritual awakening not seen on Earth before. My actions will herald in a new age where My children will finally realise and understand that it is the soul that is important, and that they are spiritual beings and not physical creatures; and that being born into human form on Earth is just a temporary occurrence in their existence in order to help them learn and move closer to Me."

Gabriel listened intently as God continued, "I am tired of all the fighting amongst the religions and beliefs on Earth. The divisions that humankind has created is anathema to My Message to Humanity. Each of the tenets taught by Abraham, Moses, Jesus, and Mohamed was to be followed by the whole of humankind, not just by a certain group of people which then formed their own religion based on one of the teachings. My Message in its entirety was to be embraced by humanity: it was My Message of oneness; to live within the parameters of principles and laws, for there is order to the Universe; to love one another and to show compassion and kindness, for each is a sibling to the other; and to suppress one's ego and submit to one's higher consciousness, for each is divine like Me. My children established separate paths based on just one of these principles, and no path is absolutely correct. The worst practice of all these religions and belief systems is for the followers to condemn the other, believing that each is entitled to righteousness over the other."

God continued in a booming voice, "And then to utilise a religion to justify harming and killing in My Name is absolutely abhorrent to Me! It is not acceptable and I will no longer tolerate such behaviour! Change is coming to Earth!"

Gabriel listened attentively to God's words. In all his years of communicating with God, Gabriel had never heard God speak so forcefully and with such fervour. It confirmed to him that God was now taking matters into His own hands.

God paused for a few seconds, and then continued, "My children are not only destroying each other, but are destroying Earth and all that I have created within it. This quest for material wealth and self-aggrandizement must be arrested. Gabriel, I would like you to visit Earth as a human being again, for I wish you to lead humanity in the right direction after I cleanse the world of all its malaise. This jolt must occur in order for My children to be given a chance to start again and tread the path towards their consciousness. It is not just a physical jolt, but a spiritual jolt to awaken humankind's higher consciousness to recognise that he and she are brilliant sparks and that each shall return to the ocean of light."

"Gabriel, I want you to be born a human being, but in such circumstances, that no one in society as it exists today would recognise you for who you actually are. You must lead an ordinary, uneventful life, and I will block all your memories and powers so that even you do not recognise yourself. You must go through life with the same choices, struggles, and decisions as every human being on Earth. And at the right time, I will rouse your spirit to begin the work that you must accomplish as your last responsibility before you merge with My Light. Gabriel, this is your final, and probably the toughest assignment I am asking you to undertake."

God paused and gave Gabriel time for His words to sink in.

"My dear child, I have specifically chosen you for this assignment not only because you are the most capable, but because most of humanity recognises your persona. They call you Gabriel. You are the one who transmitted My Words through Abraham, Moses, Jesus, and Mohamed. You are also the one who guided all the gurus, masters, prophets, and spiritual leaders. Whether of the North, South, East, or West, all these special missionary angels worked under your tutelage."

"You would be able to unite all My children and lead

them into a new age of spiritual development, where humanity has the opportunity to evolve into greater beings, just as you have. What My children do not realise is that each can achieve the same spiritual heights as you, and therefore, in that way, you are no more special than any other soul. Each human being is equal to the other and each has an equal opportunity to reach Me. What individuals choose to do determines their path towards eternal peace and contentment. I want you to teach this to your siblings. Teach them My values of balance, inner strength, and spirituality."

"My dear child, I would like you to reflect upon all that I have spoken, and take the time to comprehend it. But I will limit the time for your reflection, because I must have your decision quickly. Life on Earth is skewing further and further out of balance, and I am compelled to begin My work."

Gabriel withdrew deeper and allowed all of God's words to penetrate his being.

"My Lord," said Gabriel, "I am nearly ready to accept my assignment. However, if You allow me, I would like to confer with Michael and Raphael before conveying my answer. Would You permit me to speak with them?"

"Of course, Gabriel. I will await your return."

"Thy Will be done in and through me," invoked Gabriel as he withdrew.

He called out to Michael and Raphael.

"Gabriel, you are back! Are you well-rested?" said Michael.

"Yes, and I want to consult with you both on a very important matter," said Gabriel. He took them aside. "I have received a significant message from God that I want to share with you in confidence. I also want your views on what I should do."

"Of course, Gabriel, we are listening," said Raphael.

Gabriel conveyed everything, including what God had asked him to do. He spoke of the cleansing of the Earth, he spoke of taking on human form again, and he also told them that this would be his very last assignment. The two Archangels were astonished.

"What do you think?" asked Gabriel.

"This is what you have been working towards for a very long time, Gabriel," said Michael, "Are you ready for it?"

"I think I am," said Gabriel.

"You know that we will do whatever it takes to help you," said Raphael, "And you do realise that out of the billions of us who are willing to help God, you are the only one with the required strength to undertake such an assignment."

"Raphael, I certainly believe that either you or Michael could do this. I am not the only one," said Gabriel.

"Yes, you are," said Michael, "You are the only one who has reached the pinnacle of your highest consciousness. It will require great strength and resolve to accomplish God's wishes."

"Would you both help me, if God permits it?" asked Gabriel, "I will not be able to do this alone."

"Of course, Gabriel. You know that we would do anything for you and God," replied Michael.

"Then accompany me to the seventh heaven. I want to convey my decision in your presence," said Gabriel. The three began their ascent, and as they soared, they illuminated the heavens with their brilliance.

"In the name of God, the most Beneficent, the most Merciful," they invoked.

"My dear children," said God, "How nice to see you all together. Are you well?"

"Yes, we are, my Lord," answered Michael.

"Very good. Gabriel, have you made a decision?" said God.

"Yes, My Lord. I agree to undertake this last assignment, but I would like Michael and Raphael to personally help me in all the tasks that lay ahead," said Gabriel.

"Of course! As long as you both willingly wish to help Gabriel," said God.

"Yes, My Lord," said Michael and Raphael in unison.

"Then you have an extremely strong team, Gabriel! I am glad of this, for you must succeed in your work. And yours is not an easy assignment," said God, "Gabriel, time is ticking away on Earth and I would like you to begin sooner rather than later. The three of you may decide how you wish to organise and implement this assignment. But know that I am with you always and will guide you through your work. Turn to Me for help during your difficulties. And Gabriel, remember to maintain your link with Me, for I will be with you through your joys, and through your trials and tribulations."

The Archangels bowed their heads in reverence and invoked, "Thy Will be done in and through us. Thy Will be done on Earth as it is in Heaven," and descended to the fourth dimension.

They found a quiet spot and began making their plans. They discussed when, where, and in which gender Gabriel would be born on Earth. They decided that not only would Michael and Raphael be part of a team of guardian angels for Gabriel, but that they would recruit others from the highest heavens to help protect him as he progressed through life. The three Archangels worked through all the details of what Gabriel needed to experience in his last lifetime on Earth: he needed to be prepared to lead humanity through the great awakening and into the new spiritual age.

And then the time came to implement their plans.

"How I will miss you both," said Gabriel tearfully, for he knew that his life would be long, and that he would be witnessing first-hand the great atrocities that human beings inflicted on one another in the current period on Earth. "I hope my heart and soul will be able to bear it. Please help me to turn to my higher, spiritual self and not debase my soul."

"We will both be with you, Gabriel," said Michael, "and we will not let you go astray. We will constantly send you signs and reminders, so that you make the right choices."

"And remember," said Raphael, "God will be guiding you

in the right direction, and will carry you through your difficulties. Let these be your last thoughts before you embark on your quest."

The three Archangels embraced each other, with all the billions of angels looking on and shining their light and love on them. And before they knew it, Gabriel invoked, "In the name of God, the most Beneficent, the most Merciful!" and entered the body of the infant baby to be born in the world.

In the beginning there was light, but now there is darkness. Its shadow penetrates everywhere — in humankind's hearts, in their thoughts, and in their actions. Darkness begets darkness, and its shadow is forming a sombre mist around the world. Only a little thought is being given to the light, for humankind is about the body — the vessel that encapsulates the light — about how to display it, clothe it, satisfy its urges, and re-create it in man's image. Humankind is very much about the life of privilege they can live, accumulating wealth, and finding ways to spend that wealth, all in the misguided attempt to distinguish each from the other. Materialism is the new god. The sun illuminates the world, but there is darkness everywhere: poverty, prejudice, greed; jealousy, selfishness, apathy; corruption, exploitation, violence.

God has sent me yet again to bring a message to humanity to move towards light, and this is the last time.

They call me Gabriel, and I have arrived on Earth.

73310444R00163

Made in the USA
Middletown, DE
13 May 2018